THERAPISTS AT WORK

THERAPISTS AT WORK

A Demonstration of
Theory and Technique

Edited by

Donald S. Milman, Ph.D.

Co-director, Postdoctoral Program in
Psychotherapy, Institute of Advanced
Psychological Studies, Adelphi University

George D. Goldman, Ph.D.

Director of Clinical Services,
Postdoctoral Psychotherapy Center,
Institute of Advanced Psychological
Studies, Adelphi University

KENDALL/HUNT PUBLISHING COMPANY

2460 Kerper Boulevard,
Dubuque, Iowa 52001

B   401995   01

We dedicate this book to all
the therapists connected with
the Postdoctoral Program in Psychotherapy.

CONTENTS

Acknowledgments, ix
Introduction, xi

Chapter

1   **Freudian Psychoanalysis**   1
    Reuben Fine
    Theoretical Presentation
    Freudian psychoanalysis attempts to effect a total reconstruction
    of the individual person. Its ultimate goal is mature love. The
    essential aspect of its technique is making the unconscious con-
    scious. Technique and goal should be sharply separated.

2   **Patient Interview**   15
    Reuben Fine

3   **Existential Psychoanalysis**   31
    Sabert Basescu
    Theoretical Presentation
    Existential psychotherapy does not refer to a body of special
    technique or procedures. It refers to an attitude toward, and the
    context of, psychotherapy. This paper discusses the attributes that
    are descriptive of the existential attitude.

4   **Patient Interview**   43
    Sabert Basescu

5   **Modern Psychoanalysis: An Operational Theory**   59
    Hyman Spotnitz
    Theoretical Presentation
    The theoretical essay by Dr. Spotnitz describes the ongoing
    development of a broad psychotherapeutic science for the treat-
    ment of all psychologically reversible disorders. Modern
    psychoanalysis, in this specific sense, is viewed as an extension of
    Freudian psychoanalysis.

6   **Patient Interview**   71
    Hyman Spotnitz

7   **Gestalt Therapy: Therapy Without Resistance**   95
    Erving and Miriam Polster
    Theoretical Presentation
    Therapy Without Resistance proposes the abandonment of the
    concept of resistance and accordingly the acceptance of behavior
    at face value. We describe the power of the momentum developed
    by a carefully focused sequence of actual events and the culmina-
    tion of this sequence in closure and new meanings.

8   **Patient Interview**...................................... 109
     Erving Polster

9   **Transactional Analysis: Some Developments in the
     Relationship Between Transactional Analysis and Psychoanalysis**   129
     Harris B. Peck
     Theoretical Presentation

     In founding transactional analysis, Eric Berne carried with him
     much of his psychoanalytic background. Initially he saw T.A. as
     complementary to, and a preparation for, psychoanalysis. With
     his later contributions and those of his disciples in such areas as
     script analysis and redecision therapy, the scope and level of
     T.A. in psychoanalysis have become increasingly comparable.

10   **Patient Interview**...................................... 141
     Harris B. Peck

11   **An Introduction to Multimodal Behavior Therapy**............. 161
     Arnold A. Lazarus
     Theoretical Presentation

     The multimodal orientation stresses that seven distinct yet inter-
     related areas of "personality" must be assessed in every case.
     These are: Behavior, Affect, Sensation, Imagery, Cognition, In-
     terpersonal relationships, and various Biochemical/Neuro-
     physiological processes. A "Modality Profile" is then con-
     structed, and therapy becomes a systematic and problem-focused
     attempt to remedy each and every excess and/or deficit that
     emerges.

12   **Patient Interview**...................................... 173
     Arnold A. Lazarus

Index, 191

ACKNOWLEDGMENTS

This book, and the conference on which it was based, could never have come about without the help of certain people here at Adelphi and at Kendall/Hunt Publishing Company.

For their work on the conference which was tireless, innovative, and conscientious, we wish to thank our secretaries, Mrs. Marge Burgard and Mrs. Sally Jones. They certainly made our lives at Adelphi much simpler and more pleasant by their efficiency, effectiveness, graciousness, and charm in doing their jobs. For their being there when we needed them and for their help in organizing many things, we wish to thank Ms. Bernadette Clark, Ms. Mary E. Gentile, and Ms. Barbara Wilckens.

The working relationship with members of the Kendall/Hunt staff made a hard job easier by their pleasant and effective cooperation.

And, of course, we thank the Milman family, Marilyn, Douglas, and Lise, and the Goldman family, Belle, Ira, Carol, and Debbie, for their patience and tolerance when we were so busy with so many things.

D.S.M.
G.D.G.

INTRODUCTION

In the development of psychotherapy as we presently know it, the name of Sigmund Freud is by far the most prominent. Although there are some antecedents to his conceptualizations and continual additions, the area of psychoanalysis is inexorably allied with his name. Philosophers and writers over the years have directly and indirectly dealt with some of the issues of personal motivation which are parallel to Freud's eventual position. More directly connected to psychological work was Charcot in France who dealt primarily with hypnosis and suggestion. Breuer and Freud both moved from hypnosis to a talking technique. Although Breuer began this work, he soon dropped from the scene, and Freud became the major innovator in the area of psychoanalysis.

All the technical evaluations from within the Freudian sphere, and from without as well, could be subsumed under a simple description that their aim is to make the person more aware of his behavior. The definition of psychotherapy would be very clear if this was the major and only characteristic. However, it is not simple and direct. For example, there are techniques of supportive psychotherapy, behavior modification, biofeed-back, etc., that may have little to do in a real sense with expanding the patient's awareness.

The matter of therapeutic evolution is further complicated by the fact that what is done in therapy is frequently inextricably interrelated with notions of what causes human beings to function in the ways they do. Ideas of personality structure and the complexities of what makes human beings behave in the ways they do, as well as complex descriptions of the manner of their functioning, have usually been directly connected with how one goes about effecting change. However, since technique of psychotherapy and theory of personality are not necessarily connected in one-to-one relationships, or even at all, one wonders why they are so often interrelated.

The most obvious reason that theory of personality and theory of technique are so intimately connected is that historically this is the way it all began. Freud used his psychoanalytic approach as both a technique of treatment and as an investigative tool. The material from his work with patients ultimately was the cornerstone on which his complex theory of personality was constructed. As material emerged from his work in therapy, he revised and reconstructed the edifice of psychoanalytic theory. To many, the two different aspects of psychoanalytic psychology, psychoanalysis and Freudian personality theory, were one and the same.

Not only did and does the general public hold this belief, but it was part and parcel of the psychoanalytic social club as well. Psychoanalysts within the original group who deviated too far from the original model were sent to a psychoanalytic Siberia. However, Freud seemed less fervently committed to his followers' adherence to the treatment party line than to their adherence to the personality theory—and particularly to the issue of libidinal theory. Thus, Ferenczi introduced major modifications in technique without being ostracized, because he still "believed" in the notion of the id. In contrast, Jung and Adler were bitterly rejected when they dared to disagree with some of the basic tenets of psychoanalytic theory. In more recent years, Franz Alexander still considered his major reconstruction of psychoanalytic technique as psychoanalysis, because he still believed in, and utilized a model of personality theory that was Freudian.

A striking parallel is evident in all the major theories of psychotherapeutic technique. Most frequently, technical innovations have gone hand in hand with theoretical innovations concerned with the how and why of personality development and structure. There are instances where technical changes have been introduced without concomitant personality theory building, and the obverse is also true. However, most frequently, major shifts in technique of change have had concomitant development of personality theories. The early Freudian deviationists, Jung and Adler, developed schools of thought that had considerably different approaches to psychotherapy. Later theoreticians, such as Sullivan, Horney, Klein, Berne, Rogers, Fromm, May, etc., included both theoretical and technical material which varied in major ways from that of other theoreticians.

Are these developments similar in form and content to that of the foremost (and some consider the original) pioneer of human behavior, Freud, or are there differences? If they are similar, then theory and technique change, because they are drawn from different experiences with different material from different patients. This can and may be a viable explanation. As viable is the possibility that, in order to have the necessary status, one must develop both a school of personality and a technique which are unique. It may not be only that one can see so far because he stands on the shoulders of a giant, Freud; it may also be that one cannot be a giant unless he sees things from a different perspective than that of the giant. One cannot easily obtain converts if he is selling the very goods which are obtainable someplace else as well. Unfortunately, this may be as true with psychotherapy as it is with religion.

Another valid explanation for therapeutic and theoretical diversity is that we are dealing with additional material as a function of different sampling techniques. Patients may be different because of culture, time, and place. It is also possible, since the therapist is the mediator of the observed data, that he can and does see and even obtain material for his judgments which is filtered through his unique perspective. Thus, he may be adding a new dimension because he is misled or because of his bias. In either case we have a newer perspective that may be accurate or inaccurate.

The new feature in this overall perspective, and one which must be an important factor in these developments, is the personality of the theoretician. The therapist's personality is the unique addition that makes it difficult to clearly demarcate therapy as a scientific procedure, replicable and valid. It adds that unknown quantity that causes some people to refer to the therapist as an artist and to the product of therapy as a unique outcome.

This disagreement and diversity would indeed be very frightening to the uninitiated if it was the entire picture. It is not. There is a great deal of overlap between personality theorists and technical theorists. There is more similarity than dissimilarity. There is more agreement than disagreement. And this is not solely a matter of semantic disagreements and nuances of expression. It is felt by many, and supported by research, that there is more similarity of procedure among experienced therapists of different persuasions than there is within inexperienced therapists with similar theoretical beliefs. Thus, there is a great deal of evidence to support the notion that theoretical diversity and disagreement has led to an expansion of our understanding of the ways people function, and that it ultimately adds to our armamentarium that enables us to effect change in people.

With the differing therapeutic approaches, with or without theoretical underpinnings, the question remains for both the lay public and the professional: Does therapy work? Initially there was some question about whether the results of research indicated that therapy did work. At this time there is a considerable amount of information pointing in the direction of therapy's effectiveness. However, the difficulties of outcome research are so complicated that the results are not always unequivocal. Just looking at a few of the variables which might be involved shows what a difficult task confronts us. Consider different approaches by different therapists with different amounts of experience with different types of patients. The addition of just one variable, for instance, the type of problem of the patient, raises so many new issues that the hope of ever approaching a partial answer seems insurmountable. The question of what is mental illness is one that has been debated thoroughly and extensively by very knowledgeable professionals without any definitive resolution. If we cannot be certain of defining what it is we are out to change, how can we be certain of what is changed?

These issues raise the issue of protection of the public not only from possibly unskilled and poorly trained professionals, but even from well-trained and well-intentioned mental health workers. This has brought the question of psychological treatment into the area of consumer protection, and consumer advocates are beginning to enter the fray.

This book is directed at amplifying some of the questions which relate to these issues. It is, however, not directly concerned with the issue of providing the lay public with answers to their moot questions, although it certainly could be of some assistance to them. It is more directly concerned with providing some concrete information to give practicing psychotherapists a window on the world of practicing therapists. The frame of reference from which this book derives is that therapists need an opportunity to view the work of other therapists, not only from the perspective of theory, but with the additional information garnered from having an opportunity to view different therapists with different persuasions in action.

In essence, what we have constructed for this book is an experimental paradigm of therapy. First, we have asked therapists to provide us with descriptions of their theoretical and practical orientations to therapy. We have selected practicing psychotherapists with differing theoretical orientations toward therapy who would, therefore, demonstrate a fairly broad spectrum of therapeutic approaches. We have then asked them to deal with a patient presently in treatment with a specific problem. Thus, we had an opportunity to hear what they usually do and then to see how it was implemented. We then have an opportunity to hear how this unusual situation was handled and why and how it differed from their usual model. Obviously, although we have called this an experiment, it has many limitations as a research model. As an opportunity to compare theory and practice *in vivo*, it is a unique contribution to the literature of psychotherapeutic practice.

In thinking about how we might best set this "experiment" into motion, we considered characteristics which would be desirable in our participating therapists. The most obvious variable we wanted to obtain in our therapists was that of ability. We wanted people who had considerable experience as therapists and who were recognized professionally as being outstanding practitioners. We also wished them to be spokesmen for particular points of view. Thus, we wanted professionals who were not only practitioners but also active contributors to the form of the art they espoused. We felt that this ability to articulate in writing the philosophical and practical aspects of their trade would provide the clearest and fullest presentation of ideas to the reader.

In considering potential participants we were, of course, interested in their theoretical persuasions. It was obvious that we could not include all possible orientations within one volume; nor did we feel such diversity was necessarily desirable.

In ultimately selecting the particular individuals as participants, the reasoning behind the choices of the persons is included in the preceding paragraphs. The choice of particular orientations was slightly more arbitrary, particularly when one could argue specifically for the inclusion of other orientations which have been omitted. The easiest orientation to justify as part of the book is that of Freudian psychoanalysis (Reuben Fine). Not only is there historical ground, both present and past, but it seems to be fundamental for professionals within the field and as a counterpoint for differing positions to have that position represented. Existential psychoanalysis (Sabert Basescu) is represented not only because it has been a major force in effecting psychotherapeutic change, but because it represents an interesting combination replicating historical roots of psychology. It reintroduces the older marriage of philosophy and psychology. However, this one is obviously not new wine in old bottles but is the fermentation of a well-aged product with a body and flavor which whets our psychotherapeutic taste buds. Modern psychoanalysis (Hyman Spotnitz) is part of the continual development of psychoanalytic theory. However, it enters waters that were, until recently, hardly charted, because they are the Bermuda Triangle of psychotherapy—treatment of the more disturbed patients. To Freud, the narcissistic neuroses or psychoses were considered untreatable. In more recent years, this group of patients has been the focus of much positive therapeutic attention, and the "Modern Psychoanalyst" is among the group of pioneering therapists. Gestalt therapy (Erving and Miriam Polster) has been a major therapeutic school for years. It has been somewhat unique in its focus on the here and now in treatment and in its inventiveness and innovation both in technique and theory. Transactional analysis (Harris Peck) follows gestalt therapy in the sequence primarily because it includes gestalt techniques in its format. It has many roots, timber, and branches as well. Founded in psychoanalytic procedures, it includes many aspects of Sullivanian and Horney approaches as well. It also encompasses a great deal of information and strategies which interface with group procedures. Last, but certainly not least, we wished someone who represented the broad spectrum which might be subsumed under that broad rubric eclecticism. However, since an eclectic approach might even be less definable than the inherent uniqueness of Existentialism, we looked for a person who presented the flexibility of an eclectic with theoretical consistency and scientific rigor that provided a clear-cut frame of reference. Multimodal behavior therapy (Arnold A. Lazarus) was our starting and stopping point here. This approach met all the criteria we had set for this approach and more. Thus, we believe this book represents the advantages of diversity and specificity at the same time. We are pleased with its breadth and surprised by its uniqueness and spontaneity.

Chapter 1

FREUDIAN PSYCHOANALYSIS

Reuben Fine, Ph.D.

Reuben Fine, Ph.D

Reuben Fine is clinical Professor of Psychology and supervisor of psychotherapy at the Postdoctoral Program in Psychotherapy, Institute of Advanced Psychological Studies at Adelphi University. He is Director of the New York Center for Psychoanalytic Training, and Director of The Center for Creative Living.

I

Psychoanalysis (the qualifying adjective "Freudian" is redundant and will be omitted) represents a combination of philosophical resolutions and psychological understanding. Ordinarily this is phrased as the close union of theory and technique; proper technique flows out of a proper theory.

The theory of psychoanalysis is the general system of psychology. It is necessary to stress that with the advances of psychoanalysis from Freud on, every aspect of human functioning can be included within its purview (Fine, 1975). Behaviorism and behavior therapy, to the extent that they are valid (which may not be as far as some think), can be included within the framework of psychoanalysis. The reverse is not true.

Psychoanalysis can be cast in scientifically adequate form (Canning, 1966). That it needs refinement in many areas cannot be denied; such refinement is going on all the time. Nevertheless, most of the strictures against the "unscientific" character of psychoanalysis derive from misunderstanding, whether deliberate or otherwise (Fine, 1969). Inasmuch as the primary focus of this symposium is on technique, questions of theory, important as they are, will have to be omitted. There is such a copious literature on the subject available, from Freud on, that no specific references are called for.

II

Naively, psychotherapy would appear to be the treatment, with intent to cure, of emotional disturbance. The history of the twentieth century has profoundly shaken this naive view. Unfortunately, the major part of the profession has not caught up with the essential discoveries; as a result what is seen on the present scene presents extraordinary confusion. It is necessary to restate the doctrines of psychoanalysis in light of what has come out since Freud. Regrettably there is no way of avoiding a certain amount of dogmatic assertion; for the mass of evidence available, reference will for the most part have to be made to other sources. However, it is well to bear in mind that evidence *is* available, and that psychoanalytic psychology is a science built up on an empirical basis, not a series of airy speculations.

The first point to be noted is that the concept of "psychiatric illness" is misleading. Ever since the mid-Manhattan study of the 1950's there has been ample proof, if more were needed, that the vast majority of persons in our culture suffer from emotional conflicts of varying degrees of severity (Rennie, 1962). Nor is our culture worse off than others in this respect; it is, in fact, highly likely that it is better off. A search for bliss in the past also discloses nothing but a long series of myths which have been fed to people for centuries. As a result, history is being rewritten; eventually it will encompass what is now called psychohistory (cf. de Mause, 1974).

The discovery of the widespread incidence of "neurosis," or more correctly, unhappiness, has several profound implications. First of all, ours should be considered the age of awareness (Fine, 1972), not the age of anxiety. There has never been a period in human history, especially in Western history, when near-universal unhappiness did not prevail. In fact, a case might even be made for the thesis that, in spite of everything, the current world situation offers more happiness than any earlier historical epoch, although what it does offer is pitifully small compared to what might be.

One of the major philosophical hypotheses or positions of psychoanalysis is that human beings can attain happiness through the pursuit of the analytic ideal: i.e., if they love, have pleasure, enjoy sex, have a rich feeling life yet one guided by reason, play a role in the social order, have a sense of identity or self, can communicate, live creatively, play a role in a family, are able to work, and are free from psychiatric symptomatology.

Since the analytic ideal is rarely found, people can be divided into two broad categories: adjusted and madadjusted. Since neither of these offers any protection against inner conflict of varying degrees of severity, it would be more appropriate to divide people into those with an adjustment neurosis and those with a maladjustment neurosis. The nature of culture is such that the largest percentage of members of any society learn to adjust to it. The connecting link between the individual and society is the superego, which is transmitted by the family. In any given culture the majority of the population perforce has a superego which teaches it to conform to societal precepts; these people who conform suffer from an adjustment neurosis, since the superego is ordinarily at a considerable distance from the analytic ideal. A much smaller percentage deviates from the majority, and suffers from a maladjustment neurosis.

Historically, and currently, the adjustment neurosis has been confused with "normal" behavior. It is rather one test of a culture's degree of health to see how closely "normal" (i.e., statistically average) behavior comes to the analytic ideal. In our culture the distance is still considerable. Nevertheless, the growing awareness of this distance through popular books and even newspaper articles has impelled an increasing percentage of the population to seek salvation through psychotherapy.

For the maladjustment neurosis the psychotherapist could consider that he had secured a reasonable result if the patient could be returned to society. E.g., if a hospitalized schizophrenic can be brought to the point where he can function in some kind of average way, the therapist could be satisfied.

But since the adjustment neurosis by definition means that the individual is functioning in society, this criterion of a return to "normality" becomes meaningless. Accordingly, a whole new philosophy of "illness" and of "treatment" becomes necessary in order to handle the problems of these individuals. Although the conceptual framework of psychoanalysis is available to provide this philosophy which has been summarized in the analytic ideal, the mental health professions on the whole have not yet caught up with this changed state of affairs. They treat the adjustment neurotic as if he were a maladjustment neurotic, often tragically with total failures and disastrous results.

It is here that the medical model breaks down in its entirety. The diagnostic system most often used, that of the American Psychiatric Association, DSM II, dating from 1968, is of little value in the practical situation; sometimes it is worse than useless. The strange pyrotechnics involved in the APA's change of the classification of homosexuality several years ago (Socarides, 1974) show once again, if more proof were needed, that these psychiatric categories are almost meaningless, and that their maintenance serves political rather than scientific considerations. Similarly the diagnosis of "borderline," which has become so popular in the last ten years, seems to serve the political purpose of emphasizing the primacy of psychiatry, rather than the scientific purpose of enlightenment and adequate treatment (Mahrer, 1969). It is a well-known sociological observation that organizations involve a struggle for power, and a struggle has been pursued with intensity in the mental health professions, where psychiatry has attempted to maintain its supremacy by stressing organic factors and the medical illness model. The power struggle should not serve to obscure the real scientific issues (Szasz, 1973).

III

The communication of the analytic ideal by ordinary hortatory devices serves some useful purpose, but its value cannot be over-estimated. As a judge once said in a pornography case, no one was ever seduced by a book; with equal justice, it can be said that nobody was ever cured by a book.

As a result of the failure of rational therapy, Freud developed a number of technical devices, which still form the core of all dynamic therapy. Often these are put forth in the form of slogans: first came "make the unconscious conscious"; next the working through of transferences and resistances; then "Where the id was the ego shall be"; and finally, in 1937, came the formula—the object of analysis is to create the most suitable conditions for the ego functions. Insofar as anyone tries to do systematic or dynamic psychotherapy today, one or more of these formulas is applied.

Psychoanalysis is no longer a novel procedure. It has been tried on thousands of persons, in all countries of the world, even under primitive conditions (cf. Roheim, 1932, Sachs, 1937, and others). If Breuer's first case, of Anna O., is taken as the starting point, psychoanalysis is approaching its hundredth birthday; if Freud's cases in the 1890's are taken instead, it is only an octogenarian, again not a youngster. Far more experience has been accumulated with psychoanalysis and psychoanalytic therapy than with any other form of psychotherapy. This experience must by systematized, codified, and evaluated.

On the whole, experience with psychoanalysis has been far more favorable than is commonly believed. Analysts have generally dealt with difficult patients, many of them given up as hopeless by the conventional psychiatry of the day. Most of them have improved, as the early studies of Fenichel (1932), Jones (1936), and Alexander (1937) showed, even before World War II. From a theoretical point of view, the broad structure of psychoanalysis, as laid down by Freud, has been accepted by an increasing number of mental health professionals and social scientists, though considerable argument centers around a multitude of details. The dynamic image of man is here to stay.

From the very beginning several stock arguments have been adduced against the effectiveness of psychoanalysis. Most prominent today is Eysenck's (1965) well-known thesis that there is no objective evidence that psychotherapy works better than no treatment at all. It is astounding how often Eysenck's conclusions have been quoted without careful perusal of his data. As long ago as 1970 Meltzoff and Kornreich did examine Eysenck's data carefully, and they concluded that he had omitted most of the relevant studies in the literature. If these studies are included, the results of psychotherapy compare much more favorably with those of untreated control groups. Thus Eysenck's study is essentially a fraudulent one, unacceptable as a term paper in a good clinical psychology course, such as those taught at Adelphi U. Yet this pious fraud has been quoted and requoted innumerable times as "proof" that psychoanalysis does not work. (A similar comment may be made about the well-known paper by Evelyn Hooker (1958) which purports to show that homosexual men are just as well adjusted as heterosexual men. Careful examination of her data also reveals it to be a scientific absurdity (Fine, 1957). Compare also Stone and Schneider (1975) who show that even Hooker's Rorschach data are grossly incorrect, and have been contradicted by a number of subsequent studies which have demonstrated the presence of clear-cut signs of male homosexuality in the Rorschach.)

A second stock argument is that psychoanalysis is no more effective than psychoanalytic therapy, or for that matter any other type of therapy (Bergen and Garfield, 1971; Spitzer and Klein, 1976). The problem here lies in the nature of the evaluations of psychotherapy. The gross statistical approach seems to be sufficient to show that psychotherapy is superior to lack of treatment, but not sufficient to discriminate between analytic therapy and non-analytic; here very careful clinical evaluations are necessary (cf. Kernberg, 1975; Pfeffer, 1963; Fine, 1976).

Further, there are two serious problems connected with the comparison between analytic and non-analytic therapies. First, the differences are often more apparent than real; e.g., Bergen and Suinn (1975, p. 512) state that "the supposed major differences between the behavioral and traditional insight therapies are not as great as was once believed, either in outcome or process." Thus the mere *naming* of the type of therapy gives no real clue to what the therapist has been doing. Second, and allied to this, is the fact that the process of psychoanalysis is often misrepresented, many times grossly so, even by its practitioners (Hamburg et al., 1967). Again, only a presentation of all the data is essential to provide some kind of meaningful answer.

Worthy of mention is the recent study by Lazarus (1971, p. 349), one of the deans of behavior therapy. Lazarus surveyed 20 behavior therapists to find out where they took their troubles. Of these, 10 were in psychoanalytic therapy, 5 in gestalt therapy, 3 in bioenergetics, 4 in existential therapy, 1 in group dynamics, and not one in behavior therapy! In explaining their choices, different therapists made the following remarks: "I have decided to give the opposition a fair try"; "My therapist is a beautiful human being and that means more to me than his theoretical orientation"; "Let's face it, if you can afford it in terms of time and money, psychoanalysis is still the treatment of choice." In contrast, it can be noted that since about 1930 all psychoanalysts have been required to undergo a personal psychoanalysis, usually far more rigorous than that undertaken by most of their patients. Further, the distinction between a "didactic" and a "therapeutic" analysis was dropped many decades ago; it is frankly recognized that all human beings brought up in our culture have psychological problems, and must undergo a personal psychoanalysis to reach their optimal psychic potential (Lewin and Ross, 1960).

While the Freudian formulas are quite clear as guidelines, they remain quite vague in their implementation. What unconscious drives should be interpreted first? What aspects of the transference should be stressed? Which ego functions should be favored over others, assuming, as is almost always the case, that conflicts may arise? All these and a host of similar questions allow for a wide latitude of response, which accounts for the wide variations in practice among psychoanalysts. It is generally held, and with good reason, that these variations are intimately related to the personal maturity and lifestyle of the analyst. In statistical studies, this accounts for the wide divergencies demonstrated even by analysts with similar backgrounds as in Glover's well-known study of the practices of British psychoanalysts published in 1938. These divergencies would also help to account for the famous fiasco of the American Psychoanalytic Association (Hamburg et al., 1967).

My own point of view, which has been elaborated in a number of books and papers (Fine, 1971; Fine, 1975), is that the choices made by the analysts create philosophical problems which have to be dealt with as seriously and in as much detail as any other problem encountered in therapy. Thus, psychoanalysis moves to the position of a philosophy (Fine, 1977).

A third stock argument is that, while psychoanalysis may be applicable to milder forms of emotional disturbance such as the neuroses, it fails with more severe forms such as the psychoses which require organic treatment because they rest essentially on some organic impairment. At best this is a dubious argument buttressed by questionable statistical manipulations, such as the drop in the population of the mental hospitals. It may be noted that as long ago as 1930 Harry Stack Sullivan reported a discharge rate of 60% of first admissions of acute schizophrenics in his own work in the 1920's; this figure has not even been equalled by the drug treatments. Bleuler (1974), in a recent review of some 250 cases of schizophrenia over a period of more than thirty years, finds that they stabilize themselves after a certain period, and that treatment results seem to be independent of the drugs used. Achte and Niskanen (1972), two Finnish psychiatrists, have studied the discharged schizophrenic patients in a Helsinki hospital for the years 1950, 1960, and 1965. In 1950 none of the drugs were available, in contrast to the later years. On the whole they found little difference, again indicating that the long-term social recovery of the schizophrenic is not affected by the tranquillizers. Further, disturbing reports are now reaching the community and the profession of the long-term side effects of many tranquillizers, such as tardive dyskinesia (Crane, 1972).

The conclusion seems inescapable: the significance of the "drug revolution" has been grossly overestimated for reasons of pride and politics, i.e., buttressing the claim of psychiatry that organic treatment is necessary for the psychotic (May, 1968). It would seem rather that the paucity of available facilities condemns the schizophrenic to a miserable life, unless early psychosocial remediation is undertaken, perhaps for the lifetime of the individual.

A fourth stock argument is that virtually nothing is known about mental illness, and that psychotherapy is a procedure in which the therapist stumbles around in the dark dealing with mysterious conditions which occasionally respond in some unknown way. This nihilistic argument rejects all of modern psychodynamics, because it has not yet reached the alleged stage of theoretical physics in which the science can be pinned down in demonstrable mathematical formulae. This argument, favored by many behaviorists, is based on the exclusion of common sense and introspective processes from psychology. It is often accompanied by references to Kuhn's theory of scientific revolutions (Kuhn, 1962), a plausible series of fantasies which ignores the actual history of science. This attitude has led to a long series of useless experiments which have advanced the science of psychology very little. By rejecting psychodynamics, the experimental psychologists introduce a fundamental flaw into their scientific enterprise, a flaw which Wittgenstein once described with the remark that in experimental psychology problem and method pass one another by.

IV

This is a position paper. Extensive evidence for the points of view presented is available in a widu body of literature, to which only reference can be made (Fine, 1975; Fine, 1969).

In the light of these theoretical remarks, a number of other questions, many of a practical nature, can be approached.

1. *Who should undergo psychotherapy?* Theoretically the answer would be: anyone who deviates sufficiently from the analytic ideal. Research indicates that such significant deviation occurs among the vast majority of the world. Psychotherapy thus becomes both a form of universal education and a variety of social reform. It should, in fact, be regarded as an essential kind of social reform for the present world dilemma. The refusal of official American psychiatry to take a stand on the prostitution of psychiatry to political purposes in the Soviet Union is one of the many grave weaknesses in that body (Fine, 1974).

2. *Who should do psychotherapy?* What should the background of the psychotherapist be? Here psychoanalysis introduces an insistent, novel, and highly significant element: only those who have been through a satisfactory personal analysis are permitted to do psychoanalysis.

Generalizing, it can be said that only those who have been through a satisfactory experience of personal therapy should be permitted to do psychotherapy. Such a position stands in marked contrast to the present state of affairs, where first a person acquires a degree in one of the three major mental health professions, then moves on to some form of postdoctoral training to acquire true psychotherapeutic competence. This postdoctoral training almost invariably involves personal psychotherapy of one kind of another; as the study by Lazarus cited above indicates, half the behavior therapists choose personal psychoanalysis.

Acceptance of this position would lead to a large-scale reorganization of the whole training process, a reorganization which is long overdue. Ideally the entire entering body in every college should have some psychotherapy (the more intelligent ones do so anyhow nowadays). Some of these will benefit enormously from the process, others relatively little. Further study in psychology and the social sciences should then be limited to those who have benefited from their personal psychotherapy. By the time they have reached professional status, they will have attained such profound insights into themselves and others around them that they will be fully competent to practice intelligently, and be able to work further toward a meaningful science of man, which will get the theoretical structure away from the present-day confusion and scientific ignorance demonstrated in psychology and the social sciences. No doubt, this proposal will be regarded, and rejected, as too Utopian, to which two replies can be made: first that "theory" derives from the Greek word for vision, and we need a good vision; second that "Utopia" means, no place, and can be replaced by "Topia," meaning there is such a place right here and now.

3. *When should psychotherapy begin?* An answer to this question has already been suggested above. The contemporary practice of waiting until serious ego-dystonic and culture-dystonic symptoms appear is extremely unsatisfactory. As a start some therapy can be undertaken at each stage in the life cycle which involves extensive change, i.e., at the rites de passage. Such "preventive counseling" has already been undertaken by some forward looking psychiatrists (Weininger, 1976).

It will no doubt be objected that such large-scale psychotherapy would require an enormous and impossible expansion of training facilities. To begin with, this is not quite correct; what is needed at the outset is *proper* training, not more training. Currently there are perhaps 150,000 mental health professionals in the country; of these not more than 10% are adequately trained (cf. Henry, 1971). Further, if large-scale reorganization of the training system is called for, as I believe it is, it would make most sense to do it along theoretically meaningful lines. It scarcely needs emphasis that the educational system of the country (and all countries as well) is once again in a state of acute crisis; to come out of this crisis properly will require intelligent planning.

4. *How successful can psychotherapy be?* If the analytic ideal is taken as a long-range goal, then psychotherapy on the whole is a reasonably successful enterprise, but its results will necessarily vary. Necessarily therapy and education will go together in increasing measure; where one leaves off and the other begins is often hard to say. Certainly as the emotional-intellectual climate becomes more favorable to the analytic ideal, as has been happening in this century, the results of psychotherapy can only be expected to improve.

5. *Of what value are the non-analytic therapies and non-analytic devices?* This is a complex and difficult question. To begin with, proponents of these techniques should be asked to present the doctrines and results of psychoanalysis correctly. Instead, on the current scene there is usually a propagandistic barrage against psychoanalysis which bears little relation to the truth.

Viewed in the light of ideal therapy, further generalizations about these non-analytic techniques are difficult to make. Some of them, like the Reichian bioenergetics, need not be taken seriously by any well-trained professional; even at their best, as in Reich himself, they represent a kind of medical malpractice, even though they are often practiced by physicians. Others, like Gestalt therapy, are so vague and amorphous that each suggestion has to be discussed individually.

By and large, psychoanalysis places central emphasis on the working through of transference and resistance; the goal is a fully satisfactory love life, with full erotic gratification. Other therapies, usually because of opposition to psychoanalysis, tend to ignore or downplay reorganization of the personality. They may have some good therapeutic suggestions, which can be incorporated into psychoanalytic therapy. In fact, I feel that psychoanalysis does too often err in avoiding adjunctive devices which may get the patient past some temporary impasse. But unless the whole technique is very carefully managed, the avoidance of transference-resistance would necessarily lead to a partial result, or no result. Thus the essential difference is that psychoanalysis provides a total therapeutic framework, and the best chance for a fully successful therapeutic experience; the non-analytic therapies represent, on the whole, partial solutions. Aphoristically, one might say that psychoanalysis aims at full orgasm, while the non-analytic therapies provide one or more variations of foreplay.

6. *What can be done with the maladjustment neuroses?* Many of the maladjustment neuroses (psychoses, in more ordinary parlance) present formidable obstacles to treatment, both practical and theoretical. By and large, treatment can be expected to be less successful with them than with the adjustment neuroses, though there are many exceptions. The policy, in force for the last twenty years, of dismantling the mental hospitals in favor of community care, can only be applauded; however, proper care must be exercised to provide adequate community care, which on the current scene is all too often not the case.

7. *What are the limitations of psychotherapy?* It should by no means be thought that psychotherapy is being offered as a universal panacea. We are all well aware of the innumerable obstacles in its path.

From a theoretical point of view the major limitations lie in low intelligence and miserable socio-economic conditions. Persons below a certain intellectual level do not seem to respond to insight therapy as it is practiced (Myers and Roberts, 1959). Sometimes they do seem to respond to manipulative schemes of various kinds. Primarily, however, they seem to require an altered social climate, in which their handicaps will not get them into trouble.

The culture of poverty is a real phenomenon; it seems to be extraordinarily difficult or impossible for human beings to overcome terribly oppressive socio-economic conditions, although there are always exceptions. For these, the poverty-stricken, again what is needed is an altered social climate, direct social reform rather than indirect. Once the worst of the poverty is eliminated, internal difficulties become more prominent, and ordinary psychotherapy can then assume its proper place.

There is every reason to believe that the scope of psychotherapy, in spite of these limitations, is far greater than commonly assumed (Stone, 1954). And indeed it would appear that despite the most intensive antipsychotherapeutic broadsides imaginable, increasing numbers of persons are turning to therapy, and benefiting from it. The educational possibilities seem to be even greater than the direct therapeutic possibilities.

8. *Where do we go from here?* Psychotherapy must be viewed in long-term historical perspective to get an adequate picture of where we have come from, where we are, and where we are going. If we look back a century, to 1876, it is clear that Freud and his followers have created a whole new profession, that of psychotherapy, based on what is essentially a new science, dynamic or psychoanalytic psychology, with extensive applications to all the sciences which deal with man and with a vision of creating a unified science of man. The analytic ideal is in many respects similar to the humanistic ideals which have represented the best in Western civilization for 2000 years (cf. Shorter, 1975).

It is one of the ironies of history that mankind has discovered a scientific means of salvation almost simultaneously with a scientific means of destroying the world. Which of these will prevail is not for me to say. I would urge, however, that as psychotherapists we should maintain a sense of guarded optimism, conscious of the enormous potential for good that psychoanalysis has placed in our hands.

References

Achte, K.A., and Niskanen, P. (1972). *The Course and Prognosis of Schizophrenic Psychoses in Helsinki.* Monographs from the Psychiatric Clinic of the Helsinki University Central Hospital, No. 4.

Alexander, F. (1937). *Five-year Report of the Chicago Institute for Psychoanalysis, 1932-1937.* Chicago: Chicago Institute for Psychoanalysis.

Bergen, A.E., and Garfield, S.L. (1971). *Handbook of Psychotherapy and Behavior Change.* New York: John Wiley.

Bergen, A.E., and Suinn, R.M. (1975). Individual Psychotherapy and Behavior Therapy. *Annual Review of Psychology,* Palo Alto, California: Annual Reviews, Inc. 509-556.

Bleuler, M. (1974). The Long-term Course of the Schizophrenic Psychoses. *Psychological Medicine,* 4, 244-254.

Canning, J.W. (1966). *A Logical Analysis of Criticisms Directed at Freudian Psychoanalytic Theory.* Ph.D. Dissertation, U. of Maryland.

Crane, G.E. (1972). Prevention and Management of Tardive Dyskinesia. *Amer. J. of Psychiatry,* 129, 466-467.

de Mause, L. (1974). *The History of Childhood.* New York: The Psychohistory Press.

Eysenck, H. (1965). The Effects of Psychotherapy. *Int. J. of Psychiatry,* 1.

Fenichel, O. (1930). *Zehn Jahre Berliner Psychoanalytisches Institut.* Veinna: Int. Psychoanalytischer Verlag.

Fine, R. (1969). On the Nature of Scientific Method in Psychology. *Psychological Reports,* 24, 519-540.

——— (1971). *The Healing of the Mind.* New York: David McKay.

——— (1972). The age of Awareness. *Psychoanalytic Review,* 59, 55-71.

——— (1973). *The Development of Freud's Thought.* New York: Jason Aronson.

——— (1974). Psychotherapy and the Social Structure. *Book Forun,* Vol. 1, No. 2 Rhinecliff, N.Y.: Hudson River Press.

——— (1975). *Psychoanalytic Psychology.* New York: Jason Aronson.

——— (1975). *Die Psychoanalyse als Philosophisches System.* Unpublished lectures at U. of Heidelberg.

——— (1976). *A Research Methodology for Evaluating Psychotherapy.* Unpublished manuscript.

Freud, S. *Standard Edition of the Works of Sigmund Freud.* 24 vols. London: Hogarth Press and the Institute of Psychoanalysis.

Hamburg, D., et al. (1967). Report of ad Hoc Committee on Central Fact-gathering Data of the American Psychoanalytic Association. *J. Amer. Psychoanalytic Association,* 15, S41-861.

Hooker, E. (1958). Male Homosexuality in the Rorschach. *J. of Proj. Techniques,* 22, 33-54.

Jones, E. (1936). *Decennial Report of the London Clinic of Psychoanalysis.* London: The Institute of Psychoanalysis.

Kernberg, O., et al. (1972). *Psychotherapy and Psychoanalysis. Final Report.* Topeka, Kansas: Bulletin of the Menninger Clinic.

Kuhn, T.L. (1962). *The Structure of Scientific Revolutions.* Chicago: U. of Chicago Press.

Lazarus, A. (1971). Where Do Behavior Therapists Take Their Troubles? *Psychological Reports,* 28, 349-350.

Lewin, B., and Ross, H. (1960). *Psychoanalytic Education in the U.S.* New York: W.W. Norton.

Mahrer, A. (1969). *New Approaches to Diagnosis.* New York: Columbia U. Press.

May, P.R. (1968). *The Treatment of Schizophrenia.* New York: Science House.

Meltzoff, J., and Kornreich, M. (1970). *Research in Psychotherapy.* New York: Atherton.

Myers, J.K., and Roberts, B.H. (1959). *Family and Class Dynamics in Mental Illness.* New York: John Wiley.

Pfeffer, A. (1959). A Procedure for Evaluating the Results of Psychoanalysis. *J. Amer. Psychoanalytic Association,* 4, 418-444.

Rennie, T., et al. (1962). *Mental Health in the Metropolis.* New York: McGraw-Hill.

Roheim, G. (1932). Psychoanalysis of Primitive Cultural Types. *Int. J. of Psychoanalysis,* 13, 1-224.

Sachs, W. (1937). *Black Hamlet.* London: Geoffrey Bles.

Shorter, E. (1975). *The Making of the Modern Family.* New York: Basic Books.

Socarides, C. (1974). The Sexual Unreason. *Book Forum,* Vol. 1, No. 2, 172-185. Rhinecliff, N.Y.: Hudson River Press.

Spitzer, R.L., and Klein, D.F. (1976). *Evaluation of Psychological Therapies.* Baltimore: Johns Hopkins U. Press.

Stone, L. (1954). The Widening Scope of Indications for Psychoanalysis. *J. Amer. Psychoanalytic Association,* 2, 567–594.

Stone, N.M., and Schneider, R.E. (1975). Concurrent Validity of the Wheeler Signs of Homosexuality in the Rorschach. *J. of Personality Assessment,* 30, 573–579.

Sullivan, H.S. (1962). *Schizophrenia as a Human Process.* New York: W.W. Norton.

Szasz, T. (1973). *The Age of Madness.* New York: Doubleday.

Weininger, B. (1976). Personal Communication.

Chapter 2

PATIENT INTERVIEW

Case History: "Jim"

This patient has been in treatment on a once-a-week basis for a little over a year and, though he has made significant progress, he is still preoccupied to the point of being obsessed with his estranged wife Ann, his children, and what's becoming of them and how mentally ill they are or will become. This preoccupation so pervades his consciousness that he can do little to grow to socialize with other women in an enjoyable fashion, and that he does not think about the future in terms of marriage and family or anything except the routines of living and working.

A. The presenting problem, when the patient entered treatment, was that he was preoccupied with "latent homosexual" thoughts. He constantly felt he was regressing and about to go crazy. He was obsessed with the word "loco" as well as with a knife and seeing it all the time in front of him. He would explain that it was a fantasy knife and that he knew it was a fantasy knife, but that he felt he actually could see it, and that he was going to take a knife and kill his wife. He had seen two other therapists before coming to the present therapist and expressed as goals: "I want to get all my anger and hostility out of me. I want to be less fearful, and I want to become a good husband and father."

B. The patient is a 38-year-old high school teacher and coach, separated from his wife since September of 1974. His wife is a West Indian and passes for white, although the patient, especially now in his anger, considers her to be black. The patient was raised in a small town in Pennsylvania where his father worked all the time, rarely having any contact with the patient, and his mother was an angry, yelling "always working around the kitchen" type of mother. She was characterized as always having a lot of anger, no love, no sex, no communication with anyone. The patient withdrew and became threatened by her yelling, screaming, and throwing things. A sister was born and was considered to be "emotionally retarded." Life became too difficult for the parents to take care of the patient and he was sent away to a school near Great Barrington, Massachusetts at age six. At this school he met his first black people, and his roommate was a black boy who was his friend and was kind to him, contrary to the rejection with which the other children treated him. When he went back to the local school at home after a year, he was advanced to the third grade but failed this and needed tutoring. At age 15 he was sent off to a military school where he gained some acceptance by playing on the basketball team. College was difficult and "people said he

15

wouldn't make it,'' but he did, going first to one college and then finishing at another. After getting his M.A. he worked as a busboy at Grossinger's because, to quote him, "there were just so many history teachers around." For the last 12 years, though, he has been working in one of the L.I. school districts as a history teacher and coach. He is, in addition, matriculated for a Ph.D. in history. The patient and his wife taught in the same school district but had different shifts, and it was the patient who would stay home with the two sons, now ages five and eight, and take care of them and the home. The wife was unpopular with the patient's mother, although she gave lip service to accepting her. After the separation, the patient's mother initially didn't want to have anything to do with her grandchildren whom she considered to be "niggers." Despite the patient's ambivalence toward his mother, he appeared to be quite attached to her and his family, and the patient's wife would often complain about his preoccupation. The patient became preoccupied with his wife's distance from him and re his explanation, withdrew from her because of it. The wife's perspective was that it was the patient who was withdrawn and depressed so that she became more and more discontent with him and the marriage, finally asking him to leave for a trial separation which eventually became permanent. He started treatment after the separation, although he had had one consultation while he was still married. He would not continue at that time because the therapist had told him that his marriage was bad and would break-up, which he didn't want to believe and couldn't accept.

C. and D. The patient came to therapy with an almost idealized positive transference, since this therapist had magically foreseen the future and, in addition, had been recommended by two psychologists whom he had seen. The first area worked on was his hostility and the resultant guilt and depression. After this his preoccupation seemed to go in terms of both his latent homosexuality and his fear of a psychotic break. We have worked on his relationship with his parents (his father died recently), and he was able to integrate his feelings about this. His sister has been referred for psychotherapy, but this is an area he has seldom been able to work on even though it is, perhaps, more than a coincidence that his sister and his wife have the same first names and some transference might have taken place. The transference has mainly been a positive one where the therapist is the good father who is there for him and available in time of emergency. In times of crisis the patient telephones and asks for direct advice on any and all areas of his life. In his idealization little if any of the negative transference comes through, and most of his negative feelings are toward his estranged wife, where he has little or no perspective as to his part in the break-up of the marriage.

E. In nurturing him from the incipient psychosis to his present borderline functioning, therapy has perhaps been too supportive and not allowed for a build-up of a negative transference. This has resulted in very little analysis of his negative feelings lately in any context other than his relationship to his wife. This anger he, of course, considers to be legitimate, and it is very difficult to analyze.

This case history prepared by George D. Goldman, Ph.D.

Patient Interview

Reuben Fine, Ph.D.

Doctor: Well it's very nice of you to come. You volunteered for this interview?

Patient: No, Dr. G asked me if I would be interested, and I said yes. Then I thought about it a couple of hours later, and I thought no, but then I decided to come.

Doctor: You've been in treatment for about a year?

Patient: I've been to six different people before you.

Doctor: To six different therapists?

Patient: Over a period of ten years.

Doctor: You must be a little discouraged by now.

Patient: No, not now.

Doctor: Now you feel optimistic.

Patient: Now I feel less . . . I just feel better, after being through one marriage . . . and fourteen years of teaching tennis and history . . . plus two sons that I love very much.

Doctor: How old are your children?

Patient: Eight and five.

Doctor: Do you have something you'd like to get out of this interview?

Patient: Dr. G said it would be an experience.

Doctor: Okay, it's going to be an experience. I'd like to ask you a few questions, focus on a few points which may be a little sharp, but if you don't feel like discussing them, well, don't. But if you can, it would be helpful. How do you feel about your love life?

Patient: Well, I'll tell you briefly about it. I married a very sexy lady who became a sexy lady for an old love, and we've been separated for a year and a half and getting a divorce in two months. At twenty-eight I thought love was associated with orgasm, and at thirty-eight I think love is associated with trust. I'm really basically concerned with developing more as a human being and being able to help my two sons who I miss very much.

Doctor: Were you very much in love with your wife when you married her, before you married her?

Patient: Well, I married a woman out of my religion and out of my race, from the island of Jamaica. Everybody told me not to marry her, but I married her anyway. My mother called me up at 4:00 in the afternoon, started screaming and yelling like she usually did . . . I hung up and married Ann at 5:00.

Doctor: You were due to marry her at 5 anyway?

Patient: Well, 5:30. More than that I don't know. Then she married me again to consolidate our friendship. She became Jewish. I'm not too sure why, but I guess because she wanted to please my parents. They told me if I married her they would never talk to me again. Maybe that would have been okay.

Doctor: How old were you when you got married? Twenty-eight you say?

Patient: I was twenty-eight . . . September 30, '66.

Doctor: Had you been in love before then?

Patient: With her?

Doctor: No, with somebody else.

Patient: Different, different types of love.

Doctor: What happened? Do you remember the first love in your childhood around six or seven . . . first love affair?

Patient: Yeah, I remember a woman who worked for my mother, but that was. . . . It's very obscure. I remember one experience I had when I was very young. It was with my grandparents and this aunt of mine. She's like a step-grandparent, step-grandmother. She's really like my surrogate mother. I was with my grandfather and my grandmother, and my mother came into the room, and I bit her. I don't know why I remember that experience. The mind works very funny in that I remember certain things at different times, and I'm not too sure why. And I know how overwhelming words can be, because knives can kill you instantly, but words have a longer effect upon your very existence. But anyway, I don't want to deviate too far.

Doctor: You say you were in love with an older woman at that time?

Patient: Well, no, she was a woman who worked for my mother. I was in love with my mother, I guess. Every son is. My mother's very beautiful, attractive, intelligent. But very angry.

Doctor: (inaudible) You might have had your share of hatred for your mother too?

Patient: I have had a tremendous amount of animosity toward my mother and father.

Doctor: Do you remember any time it shifted from love to hate?

Patient: From love to hate, I don't know. All I know is that at the age of six they sent me to a private school in Massachusetts. I was there for a year and a half. There were a boy and a girl there who happened to be black, and this boy became my roommate. We lived different. He used to go to church on Sunday and the people used to censor our mail and conversations. Like this place was in Great Barrington, Massachusetts, and when my father and mother would call me, he would be there. Anyway, this boy wrote a letter that got back to my parents and afterwards they came up for me and I left. I have a sister who is mentally retarded, and I think more emotionally retarded. As a girl growing up she had a lot of high fevers. She fell on her head. I guess you'd call her emotionally retarded. I had a father who always criticized and a mother who always screamed and yelled and had a lot of death wishes. She had a tremendous hatred for my grandmother which is understandable. My sister was retarded, my father criticized, my mother screamed. I was away at the age of six.

Doctor: That's rather unusual. What did your father do?

Patient: My father died some time ago. He was a candy man. He was in the wholesale candy business, and he worked like sixteen, eighteen hours a day. He didn't have too much time for his son.

Doctor: It's rather unusual to send a boy in your social class away to school in Massachusetts. Did he have some special reason for that?

Patient: No, my sister was becoming a problem. My parents couldn't cope with the two of us, so they sent me away. Well, you know, I went away to the school. But my whole early life was so screwed up, like in first grade I went to second grade. But then when I went to this private school they put me back into first grade. I went through the whole year. This was during the war, World War II, 1944. I came back to Pennsylvania, and they put in into third grade. In other words, I never had second grade. Then I failed third grade. At the age of fifteen I went to a military school where I learned the importance of discipline. Of course, I hated it, and I wanted to come home. I had a grandfather who I admired very much. I knew that if I copped out there, he would never talk to me. That was the reason why I stayed. I stayed for a year and I learned a great deal about discipline and the importance of discipline, and to study. They wanted me to stay, because they knew it was better for me to be away from my family, but I didn't. I came back and went to a private school and played basketball. I went to college, worrying all the time that I wouldn't make it, because I took a test, an entrance examination test, and I did very poorly in it, and they projected that I wouldn't do well. So for a year and a half in college I had this thing that I wasn't going to make it. By then somehow or other, they call it confidence, I must have acquired a little now and then, and I managed to get through with a 2.4 average. I went to graduate school and took a master's degree. I went into teaching and got a job here on Long Island. I went to different schools, getting different credits. And then just recently, well in 1968, I taught a year at a college. I taught a full year of history. I used to memorize fifteen or twenty pages to give lectures to the students. The next year they started cutting back on the program. John was a year and a half old at that time. In 1970 I began teaching tennis . . . JV tennis team. In 1972 my problem began to develop. Should I talk about it?

Doctor: Sure.

Patient: I'd like to tell you what happened. Ann and I had a fairly good marriage, I would assume, because in six years we had two beautiful children. We had a home which is now worth sixty thousand dollars. We had stocks. We had an acre of land in New Mexico. For six years of marriage I really didn't think it was that bad. We went to Jamaica, and in Jamaica things began to happen. Ann is an artist, and she was fooling around with some sort of rock and contacted an infection. The majority of doctors didn't have the right type of medication, so we ended up the day of New Year's Eve with this particular doctor. A strange thing happened when we walked into the room. I don't know, I got a feeling that my wife and him would have liked for me not to be there. You know, it was just a feeling. I think a lot of gut reactions are sometimes more real than reality. Anyway, she was operated on that night and she was okay, but the doctor suggested she stay in Jamaica, so she did. Well a lot of things happened. She claimed that I was so concerned about her because I was a Jew. I don't know whether it's only Jewish people who are preoccupied and overly concerned about their wives. Maybe it's a poor overstatement, but when she was going through this problem I was extremely upset.

Doctor: You thought she was screwing around with this doctor?

Patient: No, no, I was upset not because of that. I was upset because of the fact that she was in such pain. Anyway, she was operated on, and she was allright. The doctor said she'd have to stay. She stayed, but because I was so upset about her situation and because I didn't want to come back to America without her, she began to feel that it was a sign of weakness on my part. In any case, I assumed this doctor and she had something, because he called her from Jamaica. The only reason why I feel this way, and I'm not sure because I wasn't there, is that when I came back from Martinique a couple months ago I had met a girl there, and I called her. . . . And the reason I called her was not to find out how the weather was. But in any case, between January when she came back and when my fantasy began in the middle of July, things had gone on that I apparently wasn't aware of. Her step-mother died for one thing, and her step-mother despised her. I never could understand why at that time. She died and in June a teacher of hers who had a very positive force on her life died also. She wanted to go back to Jamaica to the funeral. I said, like a funeral, what do you want to go to a funeral for? So I won the argument and lost the war. In July I began to develop a fantasy. I had the fantasy about from July until the middle of February. I have had tremendous obsessions in my life. I've had practically every one. My obsessions become so strong that reality . . . there's a funny balance. The obsession becomes so strong it becomes very real to me. I had this thing, and I didn't understand it at all. I went to a man I had previously gone to. I don't want to mention his name, because it's irrelevant. He's a nice guy and I went to him for two years. He was basically a social worker, but he helped me. The thing was, he was a civil rights advocate. My wife was Jamaican, and he must have influenced me to one extent to marry her, which I did. I married her in spite of every God damn color complex under the sun, including fear of having a dark-skinned child. I married her anyway, because I loved her very much. So I went back to this man, because he had helped me before. He was a Freudian, and he used to . . . it wasn't that he was good or bad. He was working on a three-year plan. The three-year plan was, I think, that he wanted to have me on his payroll. Now, I don't want you to have the opinion that I have anything against psychiatrists, because I had one who helped me. But I do know that there are some who like to keep patients on. But, anyway, I respected the man and admired him, so I went to him. I didn't know what the hell was happening to me. I thought I was going crazy. I'd never seen a fantasy before, but the fantasy was very strong. It was a knife fantasy. I imagined that I was killing my wife. I saw a knife, and I really saw it. It was extremely visual to me. It did go away. It was very interesting to me how it went away. I don't know if it was by osmosis or what. The guy said to me one time, "When it comes up, say so what!" I don't know if that was it, but it went away. The thing about understanding is that, once you've been through something and you've reached the end of the road, you can look back and see what has happened. Now I'm living with a woman who claims she is in love with me. She sees me going through these things. She said that she saw it in my face. You know, whatever it was, it must have been some expression, but I couldn't get her to go to the psychiatrist with me. Now I can look back and I really think, well, anyway. . . . She didn't come to the psychiatrist with me the first four, five months. Ultimately she did. It was interesting that when she started coming with me, my problem began to evolve, it started to leave. After six months of this fantasy, I developed a pattern of not sleeping. I could hardly sleep at all. This was compounding my problem, because the body was affecting the mind, and the mind was affecting the body. Anyway, no matter how bad the guy was, I was able to get over the fantasy, and there was a point where I didn't even bother to see him two or three times. I was beginning to think I could beat it without him. Then Ann started having an affair with a guy. You know when a woman is in love with you, you know when she's not in love with you, okay? Things began to develop, like one day she would say to me, I'm going to buy a horse with Bill. When she said that to me in May, I almost went through the ceiling. He was an old love that she had had a long time ago. This guy was the best man at my marriage with this woman. He wasn't what I considered attractive. . . . I mean, you look at a woman, you look at a guy, say a guy is attractive. Maybe that's my hangup. He was older, he was forty-five. He looked like he was sixty. He was the most boring person I ever met. He talked a lot, but apparently Ann had something for him, because they began an affair, and as they were having an affair my things began to develop. My problem was that I was going to this man, and he became the critical father. I would tell him I had developed all kinds of homosexual thoughts, and instead of not putting a value judgment on it, he did. One time he said "You have latent homosexual thoughts." That produced four months of obsession, because I'm very obsessional. After he said that, for the first time in my relationship with this woman, I couldn't make love to her. In other words, what I'm saying is that words have such tremendous effect upon whatever it is. She was having an affair, and I developed latent homosexual thoughts. But I was able to resolve all of that, and we went to Europe. Then all of a sudden this guy began to appear in my house for lunch. One time we went to a basketball game, and Bill was there; and I just let it hang, because I didn't think she could possibly get emotionally involved with him . . . because that was my problem. The next spring I stopped therapy with this man for the whole summer. I just didn't go. Then when I got back to school my obsessions came back, because part of my problem was being in school. I worked on a split session. I didn't work in the morning, and in the afternoon I worked from one to six. I had my kids in the morning. I had reached a point in my career where I was bored to hell with my work, because I didn't have to prepare. I used to go to school without any preparation whatsoever, because with all my knowledge I could do it. And I'd been obsessing so greatly that I was in an endless whirlpool of shit, to say the least. I couldn't understand, I couldn't get out of it. I would go from one obsession to another. Then the guy called me. I don't know why. He called me, and we started talking, and he said to me, "You sound much better." Well, great, you sound much better, I haven't seen him in three months. . . . But I sort of put my foot in the hole. I said, "What do you think my problem is?" Well, I was doing the stock market and I was talking to him. "Well," he said, "you're masochistic." Then I began to develop another fantasy. My fantasy was perpetuated by a basic nervousness of my whole emotional being. I was not sleeping. I was being with young kids and being with kids I love very much, but I shouldn't have been there, because I had a childhood which left much to be desired, but I stayed. I stayed because my father was never available for me, and I want my sons to have what I didn't have. I developed all kinds of crap, and I began then to go on my fourth thing. I thought I was losing my mind. For a year and a half I thought I was losing my mind, because my obsessions and my things became very strong. I stopped going to him and I tried somebody else. It's very interesting that during that time somehow I knew this man wasn't helping me. So I went to a man in Smithtown. We talked for an hour and then he said to me, "I can't take you." So he recommended Dr. G. He called up Dr. G. and I talked to Dr. G. on the phone and he told me to come. And I came to his office. It was very funny. I came into his office and I was flying high, because when you're obsessional and you're angry and you're the whole thing, it's there. Dr. G. took one look at me and said, "Calm down." Well, I didn't calm down. . . . I didn't calm down until about three years later, or two years, or one year. We had a talk and Dr. G. said to me, "You're having a problem with your wife." I said, "What do you mean, I'm having a problem with my wife?" I had this thing that my marriage was, I didn't know what the hell it was, but I didn't think that was it. . . . But he told me the truth, and I couldn't accept it. It also seemed a little expensive, and it was, but that's irrelevant. . . . But because he told me the truth, and because I couldn't accept it, I went back to this other man. That was my first association with Dr. G. When the new year came I went to another man out in Stony Brook. He did the same thing with me. I told him the story, and instead of taking me, he sent me to his colleague. I didn't want to go to his colleague, but, I went to him. He helped me. He was doing _____ . He told me what it was. He was fairly good, but the problem was he wasn't explaining to me what _____ theory is supposed to do for me. Now that I'm through all this I know what it is supposed to do. Anyway, I went to him for a while. I seemed to get better, and then the cycle reversed itself. Whenever I found myself being in a position of being confused, I would drop a guy. Then I went to my rabbi. He helped me until I saw a letter Ann had written to this guy, and that sort of blew my mind. It said, "I don't think you're going to leave your wife." That shattered the reality of the myth that my wife was faithful. Then I started going to another psychiatrist and he was a little critical. He was truthful. He said, "What kind of a marriage do you think you have?" Well, in September we broke up. She told me the second night, "I love you, I want to be with you," the whole shit. I said, "Oh, I'm getting the hell out of here," which, of course, is the mistake I made, because I should have asked her to leave. Well, I left. I signed a separation agreement. I really didn't know what the hell I was signing, but I wanted to placate her. I wanted to appease her, because I couldn't believe that she could possibly love this guy . . . but that was my problem. This man I was with was so annoyed that I signed a separation agreement, he asked me to leave. He didn't ask me to leave, he said, "Well, come once a month and I'll pat you on the back," and I left. When I was in graduate school I first heard of the doctor's program in Stony Brook. So I was with that. I left there for a while, went back to this other man who was doing _____ with me, but I realized that breathing exercise wasn't for me. I started talking with a man who was in my school who was like a social worker, and he mentioned Dr. G.'s name. When he mentioned his name, it was just a gut reaction. The whole thing was a gut reaction, and I said, "Well, that's the man I'm going to go to." I didn't have that much money, because my state form came back with just a small refund. So I took the refund and called up Dr. G., and I've been with him now for fifty-five sessions. He's helped me tremendously, because he's been honest with me and he's been very forceful. He's combined two of the characteristics of my parents. My father was very truthful, so truthful that he blew a million dollars during the war, and my mother was very demonstrative. With the _____ to calm my nerves, and Dr. G. to give me a new perspective on life, here I am.

Doctor: All these troubles with Ann, were you ever unfaithful to her?

Patient: No.

Doctor: Why not?

Patient: Well, that's our difference, the concept of loyalty. Her concept of loyalty and truth is what's happening at the moment, and that's why I had so much difficulty with her. She told me one thing, and yet she was spending most of the time with him, because they worked together in school. She would tell me that she was so happy I married her one day, and the next weekend she would be out with him. For a long time I knew they were doing their thing, and I wanted her back. But a couple months ago I was talking to a friend of mine. She's been through three marriages, but she's a very bright lady. I think the nice thing about getting older is that you can look at life a little more objectively and you can understand life a little better. We were talking one day. She had met Ann and she was very impressed, because Ann is very beautiful to look at, and delightful to know, but when it comes to character, she's got a lot of character with a small c but very little with a large c. . . . And she said to me, "Do you want to go back to Ann, do you want to go back to a bum?" I said no. . . . And that was it. That was it. I began thinking about the things she said to me, and I decided I'd rather spend the rest of my life alone than go back to Ann. Even though I have two sons that I. . . .

Doctor: Do you have a girlfriend now?

Patient: Let's say this, there's a girl. . . . She's not a girl, she's a woman . . . who likes me. We go out. If you want to come with me a few times a month, allright, otherwise I can't be bothered. I want to be alone. I went to Martinique and had an affair with a native and she was very nice. She has the prettiest smile I've ever seen. And she was very good for me. Then for four months I didn't have any dates for all the resaons, all excuses you can find. Then I had a blind date. Then I went out a few times with this woman. And that's basically it, you know.

Doctor: Do you masturbate?

Patient: No, I would say that I do and I don't. I don't make a habit of it. I just don't think about it, as preoccupied as I was, because I found that there are much more important things about life than one particular organ of the body.

Doctor: What happened with girls when you were younger? Did you hit puberty, did you have any girls?

Patient: Well, I had a crush on a girl for a long time, a very beautiful girl. Like most guys growing, I was into basketball. Really, I played a lot of basketball. I think the reason I didn't end up in a nut house is because basketball became my thing. I watched the Knicks and I developed heroes and I practiced. I played high school basketball and college tennis. In _____ there weren't too many girls except Lil who I went out with once when I was in eleventh grade. You see, my parents never slept together. I had two parents. There was only one time that I had seen them kiss.

Doctor: They must have had intercourse twice anyhow.

Patient: I keep wondering. You know, it's not the immaculate conception. I don't know, it's just that at the age of twenty I, no, seventeen, I was teaching _____ , this Israeli girl, her name was Jean. I was interested in her, but it was nothing. My first affair was with a prostitute in Philadelphia, Pennsylvania. I don't remember in detail, because it seemed so unimportant.

Doctor: How old were you at the time?

Patient: I was twenty-three. Then there was Bea. Bea was a French teacher at the school where I was teaching. We went together for a couple months.

We had a little affair, I guess you call it. She went to Europe for a year. We were supposed to think about becoming more serious with each other, and then I met Ann. I kept telling my landlady that I wasn't going to marry her. For two years I kept saying I'm not going to marry her, I not going to marry her, not going to marry her. We went to Europe together, went to Jamaica together, and I kept telling her, "We're not going to get married." We were engaged on April Fool's Day. I broke off the engagement in June. We went to Europe together, broke up, went home for Yom Kippur, came back. I was working for Mr. Smith and my aunt's brother-in-law who was just breaking up with his wife. We were talking and I showed him a picture of Ann. He said, "You should call her up, send her some flowers, box of candy and tell her you're going to marry her." And that's what I did. John was conceived on our honeymoon, _____ came in rhythm. And Fred was, I think, December 17, 1969. Fred was a ten-pound baby.

Doctor: _____ you weren't using any contraceptives?

Patient: No, I think it was a plot to make sure she had me.

Doctor: She tricked you into it?

Patient: No, I fell.

Doctor: You fell, voluntarily.

Patient: I became an innocent victim of love.

Doctor: So you don't trust love very much then?

Patient: No, I don't trust anybody, except Dr. G.

Doctor: Do you trust me?

Patient: Yes.

Doctor: That's two people you trust anyhow.

Patient: Well, you're a Freudian. It's very funny, this guy I went to so long was a Freudian. He was a nice guy, you know, he helped me. It's not that he didn't help me, but I became his son and he became my father. I ended up having a therapist who was my father with criticism, and a wife who became my mother who castrated me so completely. Every obsession was a castration symbol. And you see, in one second I told Dr. G. that I was losing my mind. I started taking Elavil, and my depression was so extensive that my mind was like a rock. It wasn't rock, but it felt that way. Because my obsessions became so intense, I thought I was losing my mind. I thought I was regressing into childhood. I thought I was going to kill myself. I had all those things. In the fall I came back from camp when my father died. I had known he was dying for a long time, because a man has a certain thing. I said to myself on his death bed, "I'm going to find a way to beat my depression." Well, between my pill and my doctor, I am a lot better than I was last year. With the Elavil I felt like my mind was expanded, it was like a door was opening up. Whenever I couldn't understand feelings, I immediately thought I was losing my mind, and whenever I had a problem Dr. G. was always available. I called him and he said, "You're not losing your mind, you're losing something else." For a year and a half I had been convinced I was losing my mind, but when he said that, that was it. I stopped worrying about losing it, not that I know I have it. I know that I'm here and I know that I'm better. I know that I need a lot more. I know where I was; I was on the path to self-destruction. I had guilt—guilt about losing, being a schmuck and losing my kids, my wife, the whole bit. We had a beautiful home. We had two beautiful kids and my whole wheel fell apart.

Doctor: You seem to be afraid to enjoy women. Have you ever thought of your marriage as a defense against sex? She must have been a good lay anyhow.

Patient: That she was. I think after a while practice makes perfect. Practice enough and it has to improve. You known I like sex. Right now I feel like I could live without it if I had to, and I can get it when I want to. I had a very interesting experience. I went to Jones Beach and I met a person, a man in his seventies. You know, when you go to different places, people begin to talk to each other. This man made an interesting comment. He is one of those guys who go into the water with nothing on when it's like zero degrees. He told me when he goes into the water he thinks about something pleasant. Well, that's great. And he told me about his situation. He said he was a very, very happy man. I couldn't understand why, because his wife was in a hospital, his family, two children, were free, and he was alone. I couldn't understand what he meant. But he said when a woman gets you, you get what you give her. It's good and bad. I've reached a point where I don't want to be dependent upon anybody for my jollies or my happiness, because if I am, then I'm going to have problems. That's the way I lived my life—my wife and my two kids. I began to realize that the most important thing you have is your brain, and if it's clear and if you're not feeling, if you can come off that cross. . . . This man used to say in a very interesting way, "Get the hell off the cross, stop playing the Jesus role of suffering." But as one of Dr. Goldman's books, *The Joy of Suffering* claims, there is a repetitive joy in despising yourself when you spend your whole life because you've had a father who criticized and a mother who screamed and yelled and a retarded sister who is just not normal.

Doctor: You're afraid if you fall in love with a woman again, that she'll take you.

Patient: No, I'm not afraid. I just don't want to relive another experience. I just relived my whole life in the last three years of marriage and the breakup of my marriage. I don't want to, right now I'd be willing to live the way I am for a while. I'd like to remarry, because I think that's the best relationship there is between a man and a woman.

Doctor: Why can't you enjoy yourself without being married?

Patient: Well, I said the best type of relationship. You can enjoy yourself without being married. You can enjoy yourself many different ways, but I think the best relationship is between a man and a woman with children. However, there are all those wonderful middle class values, a nice home, kids to look at, a wife to talk to. I don't know, maybe I'll do it again. I don't know how I can ever trust another woman after my mother and my wife. I went from one barracuda to another. My mother calls Ann a barracuda, and she should know, because she is one. I have an aunt and mother who are very castrating. My aunt, in December before I went to Martinique. . . . I told her I didn't want to go out to Suffolk County to be with some people because I was tired, and she gave me a barrage that was so overwhelming I couldn't speak. I could speak, but my voice was so hoarse from all this castration and overpowering criticism that I just. . . . And she said to me, "Why don't you say something?" I just sat there. I went from one barracuda to another. I thought I was marrying a nice sweet, loving, compassionate woman of character. I ended up with a female _____. She isn't quite it, but she is a female _____ . It's funny, I took the kids home a couple weeks ago, and I told John, "I want to watch you play baseball on the weekend." I have them every other weekend, which was allright when I wanted to get back together, but now that I don't , I want to see my sons every second I can. And she starts with this shit, "You can't see them. You can't go to the baseball game because your father is going to be there." I had a bat in my hand and I asked her to walk outside, but there was Fred who is the young kid, whenever we go through this criticism or arguments, he gets destroyed. So I decided, as much as I'd like to blow her brains out, which I would never do, because I never touched her or hit, because I'm not violent . . . but there are times in my mind when I can do it. Theory. Because, you see, my thing with the fantasy is that I couldn't accept the fact that I could be violent. I mean, a knife fantasy is the most violent form of whatever, and I always conceived of myself as the most passive individual. . . . But the point is that when you're angry at somebody, and it's like anger extensively. . . .

Doctor: Did you ever think of the knife as a substitute for fucking her?

Patient: Yeah, well I found that out, but after I'd been through the fantasy. You see, the problem with this man was that he wasn't clever enough or creative enough to transplant the knife with something else. He was very vague and that's what my problem was. I was so confused, and his vagueness perpetuated my difficulty. What I wanted to do was break my depression without him. He was so God damn vague and uncreative I just couldn't do it and, you know, that's part of it.

Doctor: Well, I still get the impression you're afraid to enjoy women at this point.

Patient: I'm not afraid.

Doctor: Some fears with other women. . . . Well, suppose you can find a woman who you don't have to become so dependent on.

Patient: Well, I don't ever want to be dependent on a woman, that dependent anyway.

Doctor: So that you will have to work out with the analyst. Once you work that out you have a great life ahead of you. Seems to me you've come a long way.

Patient: I've come from hell.

Doctor: Thank you very much then.

Patient: Is that it then? Okay.

Discussion

Reuben Fine, Ph.D.

In general, I would say that the present interview conforms to my usual style, although I had to make certain educated guesses because of the time limitation and the absence of previous knowledge about the patient. In the present case the attentive interest of the interviewer produced a mass of useful material that easily lent itself to meaningful integration.

In order to clarify this technique, the classical one introduced by Freud, it is necessary to understand the concept of *dynamic inactivity.* Usually the Freudian analyst is accused of being too passive. What is not grasped is that it is not passivity, but readiness to receive—a warm, empathic openness which allows the patient to pour his heart out. It will be noticed that the patient did, by far, most of the talking, and came away with a good many insights.

While the notion that you have to listen to patients may seem simple, it is still hard for many on the current scene to grasp. It so happened that this patient had seen a number of therapists, none of whom except Dr. Goldman had taken the trouble to try to find out what was happening to him. Fortunately, he had the good sense to get away from the gestalt therapist who was doing breathing exercises with him.

In one of the classic cases histories of psychoanalysis, the Russian who is called the Wolf Man in the literature relates how he went around from one eminent psychiatrist to another before he went to Freud in 1910. One suggested he relax, another made a diagnosis and hospitalized him, a third did suggestive therapy. All agreed that he was too "sick" to relate to a woman. Freud, he tells us, was the first man who paid careful attention to him, and also the first to accept the possibility that he might find some love in his life. It is not so very different today, when analysis is compared with other techniques.

The second focus of the interview was on the patient's love life. This too is typical of my technique. Love is the central experience of every human being's life, and the sooner you can get to it the better off you are. In a very real sense, psychoanalysis is a way of teaching people how to love.

The childhood memory that came out immediately was one where he had bitten an older woman who worked for his mother when he was a little boy. Obviously this was displaced hostility toward his mother, and, just as obviously, this displaced hostility must have seriously interfered with his later love relationships. While there was no time to go into it in too much detail, the connection between his early anger at mother and his later conflicts with women soon became very clear.

In recounting the story of his love life and the obsession with the knife, the patient to some extent relived the hell that he had been through; at the end he verbalized it in that way. That too is necessary for therapy to be effective; the patient must somehow become aware of what he did to himself in the past, and how it compares with what he is doing to himself now.

Significant also in the whole theory of technique is the positive transference. He says he never trusted anyone until Dr. G. came along; then he says he also trusted me, because I am a Freudian. Then he goes on to talk about his Freudian analyst who was like a father to him.

All of this reflects the curative nature of the positive transference. Over and over in our clinic we have observed how seemingly very disturbed patients make a dramatic recovery when they form positive transference toward their therapists. Again, in terms of theory and my usual technique, the case presents one more piece of justification for the basic stress on the positive transference.

Chapter 3

EXISTENTIAL PSYCHOANALYSIS

Sabert Basescu

Sabert Basescu, Ph.D.

Sabert Basescu is Adjunct Professor of Psychology in the Doctoral and Postdoctoral Programs at New York University. He is Director of Training at the Westchester Center for the Study of Psychoanalysis and Psychotherapy. He studied philosophy at Dartmouth and psychology at Princeton prior to psychoanalytic training. Since then he has combined teaching with a private practice.

Almost all existential philosophers and psychologists at some point in their careers disclaim identification with existentialism. They do that because they tend to be **anti-system**. The whole existential movement came about through a negative reaction to oversystematized, rigidified thought. Therefore, as soon as anybody who starts out aligned with existentialism begins to feel that he is being put into some kind of mold, he gets very uneasy and disengages himself from being categorized. Furthermore, the designation "existential psychoanalysis" is confusing, because there really is no systematic therapeutic approach, no body of techniques, no organized way of doing therapy that can in any sense be called "existential." What could be said is that there is an attitude that might be called "existential," which can influence the work of therapists no matter what their more formal theoretical or conceptual or psychotherapeutic allegiances might be.

The two best known European existential analysts, Binswanger and Boss, both claim that when it comes to psychotherapeutic practice they are more or less orthodox Freudians. (1) They take that position for somewhat different reasons. (Incidentally, when Binswanger writes about existential analysis, he is not referring in any sense to anything psychotherapeutic. He is referring to analysis as a way of understanding different modes of being-in-the-world. He sees his work essentially as what he calls "philosophic anthropology." His main studies are of the different life structures of the individuals about whom he is writing. He does not write about their therapy. In the case of Ellen West, (2) for instance, she was not a patient of his, but was dead before he ever heard of her. She had committed suicide before he wrote the analysis that constitutes the published case history from the notes of her previous therapists. His interest was not in the psychotherapeutic process, but in the life structure that constituted her world. (So his use of the term "analysis" refers to analyzing life structure or mode of being-in-the-world rather than anything to do with psychotherapy.) Binswanger considers himself a Freudian, because psychoanalysis deals with pathological modes of being-in-the-world, or the life of persons as determined. He thinks Freudian analysis makes sense in dealing with such determined aspects of existence. Boss, on the other hand, partitions Freud's work into the therapeutic and the metapsychological. He rejects most of Freud's metapsychology, but thinks that Freud was a thoroughgoing phenomenologist and existentialist in his therapeutic writing. Thus, these two well known existential psychoanalysts do not consider themselves as utilizing a mode of treatment different from the classical model.

I do consider my work as different from the classical model, although I do not feel that I can represent my work as in any way typical of what might be called the work of existential analysts. I do not think I am going to be less representative than anybody else might be, but since there really is no systematic position or body of techniques, I do not see how anyone could fairly represent himself as standing for the position of existential psychoanalysis. What I will present, then, is my own personal understanding and conception of, and feeling about, the kind of work I do. I will relate my attitudes to what might be called attributes of the existential approach to understanding. These attributes are not exclusive to an existential approach. People working in many modes and with varied backgrounds function in ways that I would consider to be quite existential.

The first attribute is what might be called observation in the phenomenological mode. To elucidate that, I would like to distinguish between understanding and explanation. To understand a person is to approach the person to be understood on his or her terms, to see in that person the structures which emerge from his or her side, not from my side. In explanation, phenomena as they appear are transformed in that they are subsumed under laws that relate them to other phenomena, or they are broken down into parts that are taken as more real than the whole. (3) In the mode of understanding, the person is the model; in the mode of explanation, the explanatory system is the model.

I recently read an article entitled "Musings on the Trained Incapacities of Scientists." (4) It reported a study done in England in which advanced science students were asked to describe simple phenomena to which they were exposed. The study was particularly striking in revealing that these student scientists found it extremely difficult to simply describe what they saw. I think this illustrates one of the dangers in our work. We come from backgrounds in which theoretical, conceptual training is very much a part of our learning experience, and too often our models are interposed between us and the people with whom we work, so that we see the operation of our models rather than the people themselves. What's most important for us is to understand what the world is like from the point of view of the explanatory model. We have been schooled in a tradition that emphasizes causation; and we look for the causes of behavior. We find those causes largely in our theories. More recently, and partly as a function of the influence of existential thinking, we have begun to switch from causation as the explanatory concept to a focus on meaning and intention. That is, now we focus more on what people are intending and what their worlds mean to them, than primarily attempting to spell out how they got to be the way they are.

The second attribute is the experiential mode of knowing. Our scientific backgrounds foster an emphasis on objective knowledge and truth. The task in psychotherapy is to understand the subjective world of the people with whom we work. The focus in psychotherapy is on subjective knowledge and truth. "Existential truth is neither the truth of abstract propositions, nor the objective facts of reality. It is concerned with the nature of a person's relation to objective fact or subjective reality and their meaning to the individual. Existential truth exists only as a person produces it in action, only as it is lived. Similarly, existential knowledge is not familiarity with facts about someone or something, but rather direct experience through meaningful participation. The facts may become existential in the matrix of a meaningful relationship, at which point they contribute to widening the scope of the experience. However, until that time they turn up mainly on final exams, television quiz shows, and case reports. To explain human behavior, it must first be understood in terms of its meaning to the experiencing person, in a sense, by participating in his or her world. The attempt to fit observations of an individual into a preconceived conceptual framework, whether it be physiological or Freudian, runs the risk of serious distortion.'' (5) In the experiential mode of knowing, we as therapists must come to experience the worlds of our patients, and our patients must experience their defenses and character style as something they live.

The goal of therapy, as I conceive of it, is the fuller awareness of one's being. Changes in behavior and the alleviation of symptoms are obviously desirable, but I think psychotherapy is designed to deal with the enabling conditions, that is, the conditions which enable change. Change is the person's private option. What enables change is the fuller awareness of one's being and one's experience.

A young man in his early twenties frequently talked about his experience of failure in his relationships with women. He had a very limited heterosexual history. He frequently dated, but rarely dated the same woman more than once, and experienced his dating in terms of failure. This was a frequent theme in our therapy sessions: his experience of failure in many aspects of his life. Therapeutic progress was slow, and we began to experience failure in the therapy sessions themselves. One night he had a dream which had to do with his family witnessing an eclipse of the sun. When I asked him how he spelled "sun," he laughed and said, "s-o-n, I guess." The dream seemed to, again, be a reflection of his experience of failure. He was the son who was being eclipsed. The dream portrayed, however, a rather grandiose way of representing one's failure. Even an eclipsed sun is an imposing symbol. That thought lead me to say to him, "Well, you may be a failure, but you are a terrific success at being a failure." He looked at me and started to guffaw in a way that was more spontaneous than I had ever seen him. He said, "You know, I never talked about this, but every time I go on a date, when it's over I think to myself, 'Boy, I succeeded in getting out of that one.' Or riding home by myself I think, 'Thank God, I didn't have to take her home.' " That led him to talk about his experience of success on his dates. Every time he failed on a date, he walked away with some feeling of having succeeded in carrying out his plan. I think in that session he experienced his failure for the first time. Prior to then, he had experienced his depression, his despair, his discouragement, but not his commitment to failure, not what it meant to him. Some therapists feel that everyone is a raving success in his own terms. The most seriously disturbed people are raving successes at carrying out their intended life plans. This was an instance that brought that home very vividly to me.

I have also said that the therapist must experience the world of the people with whom he or she works. There is an increasing awareness in our discipline of the value, even the necessity, of the therapist's using his own experience to elucidate, and get in touch with, the world of the people with whom he works. However, there is the danger that we may too readily dump our feelings onto the people with whom we are working. That is, we may, if we feel bored, for example, blame it on our patients: "I'm bored; you must be trying to bore me," is the paradigm for what I am referring to. I think that is a mistake and does not really further the process of understanding. If you are bored, it is your responsibility that you are bored. Your boredom may arise out of reactions you have to the interchange, but I think it is very risky to put the responsibility for your experience on the other person. However, I think it is crucial to use your experience, to take it seriously, and to see in what way it can help you understand what is going on. In what way can it help clue you in to what it is like to be in the world with this other person.

I received a phone call from someone who wanted to make an appointment with me, someone I did not know. We discussed her situation briefly for a few moments and arranged an appointment. I said, "Goodbye." She said, "Goodbye, Sabe." I was startled by her use of my first name. This was somebody I did not know. After this phone call I thought, "This person moved in so quickly! It isn't even somebody I know, and here I am being called 'Sabe.' " In the first session I had with this woman, she did not sit down in the chair where it was. She pulled the chair so close to mine that I could not put my feet on the floor without almost stepping on hers. I am not exaggerating. The session went very well in the sense that I felt quite in touch with what was going on. I felt that we got started effectively. I pondered whether or not to articulate my reactions to the phone call and her physical closeness in the session. I decided not to at that time.

In the second session she told me about a dream she had in the period of time between the first and second sessions. In that dream, she said that we were having a therapy session. At the end of the session in the dream, she and I left and met another therapist. She threw her arms around him and hugged him, but was very disconcerted by realizing that he did not seem to know her. Then she awoke. At that point I said to her that in our first session I felt like I had been hugged by a woman I did not know. This led to an exploration of the extent to which she needs to experience intimacy and manipulates it, rather than experiencing it as growing out of something more substantial. I am attempting to illustrate that I used my own experience of what it was like to be with her, but I did not tell her that she was doing something to me.

The third attribute is emphasis on the here and now. That does not mean the exclusion of an exploration of the past. I think that what is significant about the past is active in the present in such a way that a full understanding of what is going on now is sufficient without an understanding of how and why it got to be that way. I realize that oftentimes a person's history can be helpful to the therapist in clarifying the structure of present behavior, especially if the therapist is interested in how things got to be the way they are. But that just is not a major interest of mine in psychotherapy, and therefore not one I frequently resort to in my attempts to understand the nature of the other person's world. I think a knowledge of history is necessary for a theory of development, but not necessary for expanding one's awareness. However, I believe that there are a number of routes to the same goal, the goal being the increased awareness of oneself and one's experience. Dreams, fantasies, personal history, current experience, and the patient-therapist relationship are all relevant areas deserving of attention. Different therapists use them differently, because of varying interests, sensitivities, and skills. My own interests are less in the area of personal history than in other areas. Therefore, I do not as often rely on a person's history to shed light on what is happening with that person as other therapists might. That is not to say that I never do. But I think that when we are exploring the past, we are exploring only our recollections or reconstructions of the past. These are always a function of one's orientation in the present, and they change with changes in the present. It is interesting to ask people in therapy to give a description, for example, of their mothers. If you ask them at the beginning of the therapy, in the middle of the therapy, and at the end of the therapy, you are likely to get quite different descriptions. It is not that their mothers have changed in that time. It is not even that their memories have changed in that time. But the meaning of their acts, the meaning of their relationship with their mothers, has changed.

One historian has said that the history of a period tells us as much about the period in which it was written as it does about the period about which it was written. That is why we will never in this country cease writing histories of the Civil War. Although the war itself ended over one hundred years ago, the meaning of it for us changes as a function of what is happening to us in the present. My own preference is to work with what is going on now.

A fourth attribute is the focus on therapy as primarily a creative experience rather than as an uncovering process. That is, I do not see therapy as primarily an attempt to get at the traumatic experiences of the past, to find the points of fixation, or to relieve the repressions of past experiences. Rather it is an opportunity to understand the way in which one structures his (or her) being-in-the-world in his current life, and to what extent he can involve himself in examining that structure from the viewpoint of how well or poorly it meets his needs, and his problematic life goals, and to what extent he can experience change. Arieti writes that the task in psychotherapy is not to show the patient how the past has determined the present, but rather how it need not determine the future. I think it is the future that is the primary temporal modality for psychotherapy, and the future is not to be uncovered, but to be created.

Fifth and last, and perhaps most important of what I consider the attributes of the psychotherapeutic process that are existential, is the emphasis on will, choice, and responsibility for oneself. Will is the great neglected area in the literature of psychoanalysis. I think there are a number of reasons for that. One is that psychoanalysis grows out of an essentially natural science model of understanding or explanation, and will does not play a role in the natural sciences. Psychoanalytic literature almost never deals with will. (The work of Otto Rank is one exception, and more recently, Leslie Farber's work is another.) In addition, the concept of unconscious determinism as a primary explanatory mode leaves no room for the operation of willing and conscious choosing. Although I adhere to the concept of unconscious processes and their influence on behavior, I think they are often dealt with in psychoanalytic work in a way that induces passivity and a discounting of the effectiveness of a person's will. I believe, incidentally, that this is what underlies the meaning of the statement that psychoanalysis is the disease for which it purports to be the cure.

Someone I see, a psychologist and therapist himself, said to me in one session, "I haven't done a lot of things I know I ought to do, because it would take a conscious decision and a struggle to do them. That seems unnatural. I've been waiting for them to happen spontaneously." On the one hand, it is striking that consciously deciding something and struggling to implement it gets equated with unnaturalness. On the other hand, it is exactly what could be expected from the omission of will. Most often, unconscious content is seen to be the consequence of childhood repressions. I think it is also the consequence of conscious choices. That is, the way in which one chooses to structure his or her world influences the nature of one's unconscious experience. What is unconscious is a function of the self and its projects and is determined by them. Unconsciously determined behavior is the result of prior choice and commitment. In that sense, the unconscious influences consciousness and consciousness influences the unconscious. Psychoanalysis has traditionally concerned itself with the former, not the latter. I try to emphasize the latter without neglecting the former. Wheelis put it nicely. He said that too often, when putting our backs to the couch, we neglect putting our shoulders to the wheel.

There was a study some years ago comparing a group of experienced so-called Freudian analysts with a group of experienced so-called existential analysts. (6) The existential analysts were so designated because of their belief in free will as opposed to the Freudian commitment to psychic determinism. Among the findings in that study were these. All therapists, regardless of theoretical orientation, made no reference to deterministic control at times when a change in the patient's behavior was being contemplated. All therapists, regardless of theoretical orientation, tended to accept determinism when speaking of infancy, childhood, and the past in general. And all therapists assumed freedom of choice when referring to the present and the future. The investigators concluded that psychotherapists adopt a scientific, i.e., deterministic, frame of reference for the past and a humanistic, or freedom-oriented, frame of reference for the present and the future. We seem to regard different sets of factors as relevant when we deal with possible events as opposed to actual events. (7) When we examine the past, our concern is with actual events that have already occurred, and we take their existence for granted. Our focus is on making sense of the events. When we consider the future, we deal with possible events, and our focus is on whether or not they will occur, specifically on the choices one makes. To make sense out of human experience retrospectively by connecting the facts and factors in a coherent, understandable pattern never fully explains the occurrence of the event. It is limited to making understandable the events, given the fact of their occurrence. To account for the fact that an event occurred, an additional consideration is required—namely, the part played by the person's world of choices. William James said, "Will is whatever you do just before you do it." The past consists of things done, so that the just-before is not considered. The future is the realm of the not-yet-having-occurred, and consequently focuses our attention on the just-before.

Farber (8) maintains that although we recognize the presence of many causes for our behaviors, we attribute the motive power to a particular aspect of the causal nexus, for example, libido or anxiety. The only prime mover, however, which is held accountable, i.e., responsible, is will, the power of volition. When a personality theory does not deal with an explicit, accountable will, it smuggles it in under another name and this is an irresponsible, i.e., unaccountable, prime mover. Behavior then seems to be determined, rather than chosen. In dealing with the material world, body facts and environment facts are sufficient to account for everything about an event including its occurrence. In dealing with the human world, body facts and environment facts are insufficient. Human consciousness demands that a stance be taken toward the constitutional and environmental determinants. Then the stance for which the person is responsible becomes a factor in a causal nexus. In the same study I referred to previously, the major difference between the Freudian and the so-called existentially oriented therapists lay in the emphasis on choice and will and responsibility. The existentialists, as you might expect, had many more of their interventions around the issue of choice and responsibility than Freudians.

I am going to turn now to some comments about the nature of the therapeutic relationship. What we are experiencing in our analytic work is a changing conception of ourselves as therapists and of the kind of work we do. This is not surprising. Psychoanalysis is every bit as much a product of its time and culture as any other manifestation of our cultural heritage. Particularly in the role of the therapist, we are undergoing an evolution in conception from the therapist being seen as a blank screen or mirror, through the therapist as a participant observer, to what might be called the conception of the therapist as human being. Subsequent conceptions of the therapist do not replace former ones; they are simply added on. One of the problems in our field is that we very rarely discard excess baggage; we simply accumulate more and more, and add on new ways of thinking and new conceptions without ridding ourselves of the old. There are advantages and disadvantages to that way of functioning.

Within the context of the more current conception of the therapist as human being, there are still distinctions which are important to note between the kind of relationship that exists in psychotherapy and other human relationships. For instance, the psychotherapeutic relationship is an asymmetrical relationship. It is not a relationship of equals. Equalities exist, but, I think, it is a gross mistake to overlook the asymmetry involved in that relationship. The two people are not there for the same reasons; and it is important that at least the therapist not lose sight of the fact that the reasons that bring the patient and therapist together are quite different. They are not there to focus on the same things. The therapist's personality and problems are his important concern, but the therapeutic work must focus on what is going on in the patient's life, not in the therapist's.

The therapeutic relationship is an asymmetrical relationship, just as a parent-child or student-teacher relationship is asymmetrical. The therapeutic relationship is not a friendship or a love relationship or a parental relationship, although it may very well, and often does, encompass aspects of friendship, love, and parenting. But it is not in its essence any of those relationships. What is unique about the therapeutic relationship, as opposed to other human relationships, is the way in which the two people come together, the way in which the therapist orients himself or herself to the experience. In other relationships two people mesh their neurotic needs, more or less working out some balance and living out their respective neurotic patterns with each other, getting into trouble or not. They may relate to each other in terms of hostility, rejection, or withdrawal. The therapist, ideally, does none of these. He does not mesh neurotic patterns, nor respond or react in terms of hostility, nor withdraw, nor reject, but maintains his presence as fully as possible. By that I mean you are all there. You don't rule out aspects of your being, but you do not respond to what is going on in terms of how it meets your needs or how it gratifies you. You might be aware of how it makes you angry or rejecting, but that becomes something for your own awareness rather than something to be acted upon.

With the emphasis placed upon the therapist as human being, a new dimension of therapist behavior comes into focus—self-disclosure. Is it desirable for the therapist to be as open and as free with his own feelings as he expects patients to be with theirs? I think there are many pitfalls in that. I think that self-disclosure plays an increasing role in the work of the therapist, but, because it is a relatively new aspect of our way of working, it requires us to be more attuned to the consequences and impact of the use of ourselves as tools in our work.

Levenson (9) has written about the concept of transformation in the work of psychotherapy. The therapist, by participating with his or her own humanness in the relationship, becomes vulnerable to being transformed, or acted upon, by the other person in such a way as to be drawn into the structure of the other person's world. This bears a resemblance to Boss' (10) contention that counter-transference can never be avoided, only denied. Levenson describes the task of the therapist as that of resisting transformation, although he maintains that one cannot avoid it. That, in a sense, is desirable in that it offers the therapist a first-hand experience of the world of the other. However, at the same time as it is experienced, it must be resisted, since being totally drawn into the world of the other leaves one involved in the same way everyone else in this person's life is involved, i.e., unable to articulate and observe what is really going on or to understand and experience with some perspective. The task is to resist being transformed by attending to the structural characteristics of the relationship in which you are involved.

The therapeutic relationship has traditionally been viewed in terms of the concept of transference. Traditionally, we have explained many distorted interpersonal perceptions as intact attitudes from the past transferred whole to present relationships. But the trigger for every so-called transference is perhaps the patient's realistic perception of some characteristic of the analyst. The patient's perception is then acutely narrowed to pin point focus. The particular pin point is a function of the patient's significant past experience and the therapist's personality. The germ of truth in the patient's perception is then magnified to fill up the whole space of the relationship, and everything is cast in its light. Acknowledging the germ of truth deprives the patient of the prop for his self-limiting perception. Those aspects of the relationship that are also present but omitted in the patient's view of the analyst can then be explored. But the analyst must have enough self-awareness to be in touch with the germ of truth before he can acknowledge it.

I see the psychotherapeutic process existing between two poles: the initial pole is that of the person as victim, and the final pole is that of the person as responsible for the world in which he or she is victim. I refer to them as "initial" and "final," because I think that the therapeutic process itself moves from an initial focus and concentration on the experience the person has of being victimized, into the arena of the person as responsible. The ultimate value of psychotherapy lies in the confrontation with the ways in which one perpetuates a self-limiting world. There are many constraints placed upon our behavior and experience which are beyond our control. However, even in situations of most extreme limitation, we are at least capable of some degree of freedom, and therefore responsibility, in determining how we orient ourselves to those experiences. In most life experiences we play a considerably larger role in creating our worlds.

The confrontation with one's own responsibility may be painful, anxiety provoking, and enraging, although it is ultimately liberating. The therapeutic relationship is what cushions the pain, anxiety, and anger. It is the experience of being in a relationship characterized by understanding, trust, and mutual respect that allows for the confrontation of oneself.

References

1. Basescu, S. Phenomenology and Existential Analysis. Chapter 4 in *Progress in Clinical Psychology,* Vol. VI. Edited by L. Abt and B. Riess, New York: Grune and Stratton, Inc., 1964.
2. Binswanger, L. in *Existence.* Edited by R. May et al. New York: Basic Books, Inc., 1958.
3. Needleman, J. *Being-in-the-World.* New York: Basic Books, 1963, 38-9.
4. *A.P.A. Monitor.* April, 1976.
5. Basescu, S. Human Nature and Psychotherapy. *Review of Existential Psychology and Psychiatry,* 1962, II (2), 153.
6. Gatch, V., and Temerlin, M. The Belief in Psychic Determinism and the Behavior of the Psychotherapist. *Review of Existential Psychology and Psychiatry,* 1965, IV, 16-33.
7. Basescu, S. The Concept of Freedom. *Contemporary Psychoanalysis,* 1974, 10, 2, 236-7.
8. Farber, L. *The Ways of the Will,* New York: Basic Books, 30-32.
9. Levenson, E. *The Fallacy of Understanding.* New York: Basic Books, 1972.
10. Boss, M. *Psychoanalysis and Daseinsanalysis.* New York: Basic Books, 1963, 287.

Chapter 4

PATIENT INTERVIEW

Case History: "Bill"

Patient has been in treatment on three different occasions for different reasons. At the present time he is in psychoanalysis and has made considerable progress. However, he seems to be in conflict with the here and now frame of references as compared with psychoanalysis, and this leads him to want some treatment in terms of existential considerations. However, he has cooperated very well with psychoanalysis using the couch and has made considerable progress.

A. The patient first appeared for treatment on February 19, 1965 and remained in treatment until August 31, 1967. At that time he was married to Lillian and seemed to be in a severe depression with anxiety panics. These panic attacks were precipitated by extra-marital relationships. Each time he was involved in such a relationship, he would punish himself by bouts of alcoholism and severe depression. However, alcoholic bouts and depression did not prevent him from continuing his work. He was employed as a professor at a local college and seemed to do a good job in teaching. Usually he would sober up so that he was able to go in to teach the next day.

During this period the patient was in analytic psychotherapy on a once-a-week basis individually and later entered a group, so that the therapy consisted of once a week individually and once a week in group. He made considerable progress, and it was not until the end of the treatment that he requested to be referred to a colleague, Dr. D., a psychiatrist, who had him on Antabuse. He cooperated well with this, and from then on the alcoholism was under control. He terminated this period of treatment when he received a Fulbright scholarship in an Asian country and went there with his wife and two children.

B. The patient reappeared for treatment on June 11, 1969 and stayed in treatment until January 26, 1971, again on a once a week individual and once a week group analytic psychotherapy basis. On this occasion he had **returned from Indonesia. During his stay there he and his wife had met** *another couple with whom they had become very friendly. On their return to this country they kept in touch with this couple who lived in Washington, D.C., and that initiated an affair with the wife of this couple. Eventually they would get together for some weekends in which there was an attempt to switch partners. Bill and Mary, the woman of the other couple, were enthusiastic about this, but Lillian reluctantly participated a few times but did not react positively to the idea and eventually after a few weekends, this* *stopped. However, there was much marital difficulty between Bill and Lillian, and Lillian was referred to a colleague for psychotherapy. As a result of her therapy and Bill's continued therapy, they mutually decided upon divorce. After the divorce Bill and Mary got together, and they have been living with each other and Mary's three children.*

After the separation and the new arrangement with Mary, Bill began to improve rapidly, and the alcoholism and depression remained under very good control. During this period, Bill developed rapidly professionally. He always was considered a good teacher, and at one point he received the award for "the best teacher of the year" at his college. He was involved in many college activities and, in general, made excellent progress.

Because of financial problems and because he was somewhat improved, Bill discontinued treatment around January 26, 1971. The financial problems were realistic in that now he has to pay child support and also maintain a new household, although Mary receives some support from her former husband. However, Bill felt very strongly that when he could afford it again, he would return for complete psychoanalysis. It was our mutual feeling that this was a good stopping point, because if he wanted to go any further it would require his being in psychoanalysis rather than psychotherapy. Bill came for a short period of time from March 15, 1972 to May 8, 1972 and resolved some problems relating to his new situation.

Bill entered analysis on February 19, 1975 and has been in analysis on a three time a week basis and is still under this treatment, which now includes twice a week individually on the couch and once a week in group psychoanalysis.

C. During the analytic treatment Bill has been dealing mostly with his long-standing conflict about masculinity and has definitely strengthened his masculine identification, although he never acted out homosexuality except for one or two isolated instances. He has had a need in the past to verify his heterosexual drive and masculinity through extra-marital relationships. However, since he has been living with Mary he has been completely faithful, although they never did have a formal legal marriage. Somehow, their being in a "living together" relationship without marriage enables them both to remain more committed to each other. Some time has been spent in analyzing this. Bill seems to be in love with Mary and has assumed a father role toward her children. He gets along well with two of the children but has some problem with one. He has also been in close touch with his own children, and Scott, up till last June while in college, was doing very well. Scott left college for one year in order to get some work experience, and he and Bill had numerous conversations about this. Bill approved this plan, and Scott expects to return for his degree after the year is up. Bill has a good relationship with Scott, and they meet together weekly and have close discussions. Bill is very much involved with his daughter Peggy who has graduated from college with honors and has been an excellent student. She has now been admitted to law school and intends to pursue a legal career. She lives in New York and Bill meets with her weekly. With her he also has a very close relationship, although some of the problems which have come up in analysis relate to his personal overinvolvement with her.

Peggy periodically calls Bill when she is in a state of depression. She has developed a drinking problem similar to the one Bill had. Bill begins to feel extremely guilty about her problem, feeling that his having divorced Lillian and leaving her and the children contributed to that problem. Furthermore, Bill unconsciously identifies Peggy with a deceased older sister, also named Peggy, who died before Bill was born. One of the things that came up in Bill's analysis was the fact that his mother was in constant mourning for Bill's sister, whom Bill never knew, and Bill always felt that she did not accept him as a substitute for the sister. She tended to emasculate Bill and to treat him as if he were female rather than male. Bill's mother was an extremely religious, conventional person who seemed to disapprove of sex and "vices" of any kind. She dominated the family, including her husband who was passive and distant from Bill, so that Bill had difficulty in identifying with his father and seemed more involved and concerned with his mother. The etiology of Bill's problems seems to have been in these earlier relationships in which he was dominated and emasculated by mother. He was emotionally and deeply involved with her, and sensitive to the feeling of rejection he felt from her. Bill felt he could only love himself and develop more or less of a narcissistic personality. His identification with his father was very poor, and he negated his father's influence almost completely. However, he did have some masculine contact with an uncle on a farm whom he admired and got close to.

During the analysis Bill has brought in many dreams which have been analyzed and have brought out much pertinent material. The analytic therapy of years ago brought him out of the narcissistic personality disorder to a state where he developed sufficient ego strength to withstand analysis.

Recently, during the course of analysis, Bill became very much interested in psychoanalysis as a possible career for himself. The previous ambivalent transference became more positive, and Bill started taking courses at an institute with which the countersigned is connected. This institute does accept a few creative people who are interested in pursuing analysis with the idea that they might later use it in their present work or possibly become practitioners if they show aptitude for it. Bill has taken a number of courses at the institute and has done well in them. He holds a Ph.D. degree in English Literature. During the course of his treatment with me, Bill wrote two books which were published. One dealt with problem life styles, and another was based on his interest in existentialism and was done as a research project on people with a here and now orientation to life. Both of these were published in paperback and seem to be excellent contributions. During the term of analysis Bill has written a novel which is more or less autobiographical, but he expects to polish it up before submitting it for publication.

D. The transference relationship has been more or less ambivalent, but lately has been more and more on the positive side. Bill has become so interested in psychoanalysis that he has applied to the institute for approval to handle one or two patients under supervision at its low-cost clinic. Bill is now at a point where he seems to be well integrated and has developed considerable insight into his inner processes. He is very adept at self-interpretation. It would seem that the analysis is proceeding quite well. Bill participates enthusiastically and actively both in individual and group analysis.

E. The major evidence of some countertransference seems to occur in the group situation in which Bill is in competition with other group members. He becomes more fatherly and passive in this competition when he senses any kind of positive reaction on the part of the analyst for any one or two of the other members with whom he feels competitive. Bill has much difficulty in expressing anger and hostility whether it is toward the other members of the group or the analyst. However, one gets the impression that some anger is present.

The present consultation was requested by Bill when the analyst mentioned the Conference at Adelphi. Bill is interested in exploring existentialism, and I thought he might get some further insight from an existential consultant. However, he has not expressed any marked dissatisfaction with his psychoanalytic treatment and expects to continue and complete psychoanalysis.

This case history prepared by Samuel B. Kutash, Ph.D.

Patient Interview
Sabert Basescu, Ph.D.

Doctor: Perhaps we could begin with how you come to be here.

Patient: I was at class a couple weeks ago which my analyst teaches in a psychoanalytic institute, and he announced that this conference was looking for patients. He mentioned the styles of therapists and that one was existential. I have always had some flirtation with existential psychoanalysis. Like, I still have a couple books in my library which I borrowed from my analyst about three years ago and haven't given back, and I was interested. I immediately volunteered.

Doctor: Well, what did you think would go on that would meet your interests?

Patient: I didn't know. Maybe I ought to add a little bit more to this. I have another class in the institute on the human life cycle, and we're now dealing with old people, and I certainly wasn't interested in old people. It was great talking about babies or talking about Melanie Klein, but old people just weren't interesting me, until I read an article the teacher gave me. I don't remember the name of the article. Somehow this article made old people sound as though their problems had a continuity with our problems. I don't know if this writer is an existentialist or not. He did quote Vince Longer in the article. But anyway, having read the article, which is all about pathology, it struck me, Jesus, it's just as important to give an old man a good day or a good week as it is to give a thirty-year-old graduate student a good day or a good week, and it represented a kind of a. . . . It seems simple, but it was kind of a crucial thing for me, partly because I want to have enough for openers to deal with any kind of patient if I become a therapist, and partly because I'm going to be an old man before very long. I'm not all that young now. This represents something I think about a lot. I think that was important to bring back maybe nothing that is specifically existential, maybe nothing that specifically interests you, but at least for me representing a point of view that I missed. I hadn't thought enough in my life. I still don't think enough in my life, in terms of whether I had a good day. It's whether I'd gone somewhere, whether I'd blown a day. That kind of thing plagues me more than it ought to. I guess I wanted help in having a good day without worrying about whether or not it's going to lead somewhere, without worrying about the fact that I'm one year closer to forty-seven and haven't produced as much as I want to produce, and that kind of thing.

Doctor: Well, I missed how you get from that desire to volunteering to be a patient.

Patient: All right. That desire I think sparked, that desire set a feeling sparked by that article I read with _____ name in it, that had me ready for the moment when my analyst said, "There's an existentialist going to be at my program." And I said, "Hey! Wow! Maybe this guy can give me some kind of new perspective that would allow me to be more comfortable with my life."

Doctor: Did the fact that you'd be seeing this new guy in front of an audience influence your reaction, your feeling?

Patient: I don't think so. I'd prefer to see you alone.

Doctor: Gee! It influenced my reaction! I thought of interviewing, seeing, someone in front of an audience. It's hard for me to imagine how it couldn't also influence yours.

Patient: It didn't influence my reaction. It influences me now.

Doctor: In what way?

Patient: I'm self-conscious. I'm trying to cut them out. I took pains to put on a new suit I bought just about two weeks ago in order to come here. I wish I had a comb because my hair is messy. All these things are happening to me now. It didn't happen to me when I thought about it.

Doctor: It sounds to me that you thought it would be like some kind of theoretical exposure, almost like an opportunity to take another class.

Patient: Yep. One more thing I asked was if I came here if I could attend the other meetings. This has worried me a little bit. One of my approaches to life is intellectual. I'm trying not to be. I'm trying to be authentic, and I know that's the word, or at least some existentialists use it. So those are the intellectual things coming in, even when I'm just trying to be ordinary and honest. It's hard.

Doctor: Yeah, I think it is.

Patient: I stood outside waiting for you, because I wanted to avoid your theoretical presentation before talking to you.

Doctor: Why did you want to avoid it?

Patient: Because then whatever I said to you in here would have been a response to that, even if I'd have tried to keep it down some way or other.

Doctor: And that's what happens too often with you?

Patient: Yeah. I'm overanalytic. Even as a teacher I try to fight it. I teach literature, and the real danger and the real temptation is to work at literature so analytically that you lose the experience. You lose the experience for your students. Recently, and I think it's part of my analysis, I've been trying, I don't know how you can try this, but I do try, to surrender myself to experience. Plays, dances, novels, I try a little bit more to read literature that I'm not going to teach, to forget the analysis, to just let myself have the experience. It's not easy for me. I sometimes think as an English teacher, a teacher of literature, that I (inaudible) if I approach it so totally analytically as I'm tempted to. I'm good at it, good at analyzing things. But if analysis were my game, I should have been a philosopher, not an English teacher. In all of life, I said, this is probably part of where I'm at in analysis. I don't know. I'm trying to learn to experience. Analysis can come after. I'm not opposed to analysis, but I defend myself against experience lots.

Doctor: Well, let's try to see how far you can break through the defense you feel you've erected against this experience. Well, you didn't say you erected the defense against this experience, but my slip indicates I think you did.

Patient: Yeah, I agree.

Doctor: And your volunteering and not really taking into account that it would be before an audience. Let's see if we can tune in on, as much as possible, the impact of your sitting here now. What else occurs? What else comes to you about what you're feeling, aside from your appearance?

Patient: Well, immediately, I'm looking at you hard to avoid what I think is a kind of pull to scan the audience.

Doctor: You gave a pretty quick scan.

Patient: Yeah, a gesture of a scan. But the audience is there. If I scan it more. . . . Well I was. I was sitting right over there during the early part of the day, and one of the things I do when I glance over any audience is to look for attractive women. And I probably, if I wanted, could point to four right now in the audience.

Doctor: Only four?

Patient: Four that I noticed quite specifically. My vision was limited. I couldn't see that part at all. I got a bit of an ego boost by overhearing a couple of people saying, "I think he sounds interesting," as they were reading my case study. I'm aware that you got the case study. I was very much tuned into the fact that Dr. Goldman, I think, asked who had read the case study. I thought, gee, they're reading about me. Yeah, I was ego tripping on that sort of thing too. On the way out one of the members of the audience said to me, I'd been sitting right behind her, that it was unfortunate that the names of the books I had written were included in the case study, because that's a key to my identity, to Bill's identity. She didn't know I was Bill. I said, "Let me tell you something. I'm Bill." She said, "Oh! Wow! You sounded interesting." So we went out to lunch together. It was a very pleasant lunch. I'm aware of that.

Doctor: How did you feel about. . . . Were you here this morning through the whole presentation?

Patient: I was here for Dr. Fine's presentation.

Doctor: I wonder if you made any comparisons or did any anticipating about the patient this morning and yourself.

Patient: Oh, yes.

Doctor: What about that?

Patient: Well, I suppose in a way I envied his (inaudible) by himself, conscious problem. He had a` real problem that involved real sexual adjustments and love adjustments, and he had a straightforward story to tell. I stayed up a good deal of last night ruminating about what I would say and rehearsing, and knowing I shouldn't have been rehearsing, and feeling kaleidoscopic possibilities. He just seemed like a better patient than I am. I feel phony. I know I am not. I don't think I am. But I don't feel like a good patient.

Doctor: Is that true in your therapy now too?

Patient: I really get into binds. If I go in and say I want to be a good patient, I do the good patient bit. I know that I'm doing the good patient bit, but that's not really being a good patient.

Doctor: That really is a bind.

Patient: I'm too conscious about being a good patient. And so maybe the analyst says, "Gee, Bill, you're making progress, really good. A lot of material came out." Yeah, well, a lot of material came out, I was a good patient. I feel a little bit phony about it. Trying to be sincere, trying to be authentic, and trying to be spontaneous is a pain in the ass. It's hard for me, and it's a bind.

Doctor: Incidently, how are we doing in terms of the rehearsal last night?

Patient: Just dredged up so many problems. God, I'll never get out of analysis. I'm really sick. I said to Mary, whom I'm living with, "Give me some respective. I've got all these problems." She said, "You're crazy, you don't have any problems lying around in your life." That made me feel better.

Doctor: Did you say give me some respective or perspective? I heard respective.

Patient: No, perspective. I hope I said perspective. So I shift in and out of feeling problems, or a little bit as though I were coming to a new therapist for the first time, and I want to tell him everything about myself. It got me a bit depressed, a bit anxious. Oh, hell. I was reading Freud's *Problems of Anxiety* yesterday for another class, so yeah, I'm going to be anxiety-laden.

Doctor: Are you anxiety-laden now?

Patient: Right now? Yeah.

Doctor: Let's hear more. Tell me what you can about it.

Patient: When I feel what I think of as anxiety I have a kind of tension or pain in my upper thigh. My analyst says that's sexual tension. He did some years ago when I complained about it a bit. Freud says that anxiety has to do with breathing and heartbeat, but I get it in my legs. I used to be a cross-country runner when I was in college, and running, until fairly recently, symbolized a lot the way I did things. I wanted to run, both literally and figuratively, escape. So leg movements, leg twitchings, that sort of thing reveals anxiety. I'm also anxious because you make me talk.

Doctor: You wanted me to talk?

Patient: I rather hoped after all of the ruminating, maybe he'll do all the talking, maybe he'll ask questions so that I just respond to his questions. And then I thought of what my analyst put in the case history about passive problems. Yeah, passive active conflict. You're not talking, and forcing me to talk, and that's where I get my anxiety.

Doctor: You read the report?

Patient: I read the case history, yeah. I was almost afraid to do that. I never asked my analyst for a diagnosis.

Doctor: Had you thought about it? I mean, what your diagnosis is.

Patient: Too much. I have to agree with Fine's feeling that diagnostic labels are often not very useful. And recently, like medical school students, I've gone into self labeling trips in terms of what I'm reading. I was into a narcissism trip for about six months. God knows, I've got plenty of narcissism, but I read (inaudible) and found my symptoms all over the place. I guess I'm afraid to ask him for that kind of label. I'm glad he didn't give me one.

Doctor: You know, I just had the thought that I wonder if you really wanted me to talk, as opposed to your doing the talking. I guess I wondered about it because you brought up narcissism.

Patient: I don't think I wanted you to talk. I wanted you to ask questions that were more directive so that I wouldn't have to reveal myself or, yeah, I guess something like that, so that I could reveal myself in terms of your structure.

Doctor: Well, what kind of questions could I ask that would do that?

Patient: Or you could have taken the case study and asked about specific points in that . . . asked about my relationship with my wife, with my children, with Mary, one at a time and give me about three minutes for an answer. You could ask about my professional goals and hopes. It would be like a questionnaire.

Doctor: Yeah, and that would have both pleased you and displeased you.

Patient: It would have made life easier for me. I don't think it would have pleased me, not in a deep sense, but it would have made things easier for me, and at this moment I would take anything that would make it easier for me. On the other hand, I appreciate it that you're not making things easier for me. I used to have a college wrestling coach who when we looked pained would say, "Do five more push-ups. When it hurts it's good for you." I guess I always believed that.

Doctor: Incidentally, my name is pronounced Basescu. (Patient had previously mispronounced the name that was omitted from the transcript.)

Patient: Basescu, thanks.

Doctor: That's a thing of mine.

Patient: All right, I don't blame you. I correct people who mispronounce my name too. It's strange you're letting me be quiet. One of the things I've been doing in analysis recently has been lying quietly on a couch for a little bit. It's new for me to be able to simply be quiet. (inaudible) If there were a fellow in the audience too and I'm not on the couch. It's tough.

Doctor: Tougher here than there.

Patient: Tougher here than there. For a good while it was tough on the couch too. I just didn't allow it to happen. I didn't know it was tough. I just didn't allow silence to happen.

Doctor: It's tougher for me here too, than there.

Patient: Yeah.

Doctor: Well, what's it like? You say partly it makes you anxious. What else? You seem to say it like you wish you could do it more. Just be quiet.

Patient: Yeah.

Doctor: What else does it feel like for you?

Patient: My mouth gets a little bit dry. My hearing gets very, very keen. I can hear all kinds of things. Something very good about it. I suppose, it feels I ought to do something. I find an impulse to do something.

Doctor: Analyze something?

Patient: No.

Doctor: What?

Patient: Reach out, touch maybe. If you were a woman I would have powerful, erotic impulses to reach out and embrace you. Maybe I have some anyway, even though you're a man.

Doctor: Do you feel that often?

Patient: Feel what?

Doctor: That impulse to touch?

Patient: Yeah. My parents were non-touchers, feeling they were non-touchers. I touched my kids a lot, touched, embraced and held, rode on my back, and squeezed them, maybe too much. I don't know. I even spanked them. I don't think I would if I started all over again, but my parents didn't spank me. They simply disapproved or withdrew or something like that. I think it's terrible. I used to envy kids whose parents spanked them and it was all over. So partly it was right that I spanked the kids. Then we hugged a lot, very primitive stuff, I guess. But I'm still something with non-touching, I suppose, for whatever reason I combine non-touching with impulses to touch, to reach out, to embrace. (inaudible) Sometimes, but that is very rare.

Doctor: You know, from what you said about your envy of this morning's patient and your impulse to touch, it sounds like you really want to be touched, and that that's an experience you don't have often enough, for you.

Patient: Yeah, if I don't have it often enough it's probably because I don't let it happen. Yeah, I think you're right. You know, I'm capable perhaps of sometimes shrinking from a touch, being nervous about a touch. But I get touched. Mary touches me. We embrace a good deal. We sleep touching. It's kind of important to put a leg over there, be in contact.

Doctor: I wasn't thinking so much of that kind of touching as of touch in a feeling way.

Patient: Yeah, I know what you mean. Yeah, I will, but I'll fight it too, and I'm afraid of it and I do want it.

Doctor: See, I felt that a few moments ago when we were touching and we lost it.

Patient: You mean when we were silent?

Doctor: Yeah.

Patient: You know it might be easier for us, me, here in front of an audience than it would be in your office, the two of us now.

Doctor: Yeah, how so?

Patient: The audience keeps us safe. If there were just the two of us, feelings might get too strong for me to handle, and I really don't think I'm talking about homosexuality here. Maybe I am, I don't know. You're the analyst.

Doctor: You're the feeler.

Patient: All right, I'm the feeler. I'm having strong feeling now. About a minute and a half ago, just looking at each other, I found it very, very powerful.

Doctor: Yeah, and what?

Patient: I think if we were alone in an office I wouldn't let it happen. I really think these silences, I would have plugged them up more quickly if we were alone.

Doctor: Yeah, by talking?

Patient: By talking. There's also the fact, you know, that we're looking directly at each other. It's interesting. Now I intellectualize, because I think the couch allows things to happen. I'm usually on the couch. My analyst is behind me. Things that happen are perhaps less intense than in a face-to-face relationship. It's always seemed to me, at least to me, two people in direct eye contact are having a very strong relationship. I find that powerful. I never used to be able to look at people in the eyes, you know, like I'm looking at you now. I can do it now and I do do it now. In teaching I used to look about six inches above the shoulders of my students rather than looking down at their faces to see what was happening in them as I talked. Now I can look at their faces for a little bit.

Doctor: Just a little bit.

Patient: Well, I'll look at one person for a little bit, then I'll shift to another person, scanning the room. I won't fix on one student for very long. I think that's more for them than it is for me.

Doctor: You mean, to give them the feeling that you're connecting with them?

Patient: To give them the feeling that I'm connecting with them, but not to make them feel stared at and vulnerable. Occasionally you've been in a class, or I've been in a class, where a student will ask questions and the teacher will then stare at him for the next half hour. So I was talking about a technical thing. Now I'm wondering what it would be like if you were my therapist, if you were my analyst. What would be happening? Now we're talking about feelings, sort of immediate, personal, strong feelings. Where do those go? What am I going to do with them? God, I better keep up the fences.

Doctor: You think that's what would happen if I were your therapist?

Patient: I don't know. I suppose not. I wonder, if I were in therapy with you, what we would get into. You know what I'm feeling is a feeling from my point of view, is a powerful set of feelings that are being generated, emanating out there. I think, Jesus, three times a week at this! What would happen? In a way it's what I want, but obviously I find it a little bit frightening too.

Doctor: Tell me, do you remember your dreams much?

Patient: Yeah.

Doctor: What did you dream last night?

Patient: I don't remember last night's dreams.

Doctor: When was the last one you do remember?

Patient: The last one I remember was about a week ago. Do you want me to tell it to you?

Doctor: Yeah.

Patient: I dreamt that a neighbor had loaned me a fish net. It was a crab net, you know, with a long pole. I had returned it, and he pointed out that there was a hole in it, and that two knots had been tied in it, I think by my step-children. He was critical about the hole in the net, and the knots that were tied in it. And I said something to the effect of, "Well, it's more hassle having to put up with your criticism when I give the net back than it would have been to buy my own net, and after this I'll get my own net." I had this image of handing it back to him over a wall between the two properties. For some reason, I have a powerful association with Robert Frost's poem, "Mending Walls," and the best known line in that is "Good fences make good neighbors."

Doctor: But it didn't seem to help with you.

Patient: No, it didn't help with me. I should have bought my own rather than depending on him, because he criticized the shape it was in when I handed it back to him.

Doctor: Did you discuss that dream in your own therapy?

Patient: No, I didn't.

Doctor: How come?

Patient: I'd been discussing a lot of dreams with him, and the dreams had all related to the therapy. I decided I was going to, rather than discussing dreams, which was something like an intellectual exercise that I enjoyed very, very much. . . . While discussing dreams I was going to try simply to lie there and talk about my relationship and feeling with him for about two or three sessions and try to get into that relationship as deeply as I could. So I put dreams aside for a while, although I did suspect that dream had something to do with that relationship. I didn't try to analyze it at the time.

Doctor: Did your suspicions go beyond simply suspecting? Did you have any ideas what it might have to do with the relationship?

Patient: No. That's not quite right. I think I did at the time, and I forgot.

Doctor: You know, I guess when you borrow a net to go crabbing, you end up with crabbing.

Patient: I assume you meant the pun out of that. It's interesting because one of my. . . .

Doctor: But that is where you ended up in the dream, crabbing.

Patient: Crabbing. One of my life changes recently has been going to try to pretend that everything is fine when it isn't fine, or if it's not fine it's horrible, but to accept some things in life and just go ahead and grumble a bit. I'm allowing myself to grumble. Strange way to find growth, maybe it's temporary, at least I do a bit of crabbing about things. I suppose, too, that the hole in the net might have represented things I didn't tell him, that I might have told him but chose not to from time to time, so that's the hole that things leak out of. Something like that. Perhaps an assumption that he is sort of omniscient and knows there are things I haven't told him and he is unhappy about that. And partly also, I suppose, my wish to get out of analysis, to give it back, and do my own work after this. Dredge up my own stuff from wherever it's got to be dredged up from.

Doctor: Is that something you're thinking about now, getting out?

Patient: No, I'm going to stay in it, and crab and grumble my way through the rest of analysis, I suppose. But I'm committed to it, I'm going to stay in, but I'll complain more and I'll fight with him more. I'll fuss more about things than I have in the past. Some commitment like any other commitment, I suppose. I'll accept it for better or for worse. If things aren't perfect, nothing's perfect.

Doctor: How would you like things to be different right now with you and me at this point?

Patient: I would like you to give me a brilliant interpretation of that dream.

Doctor: That's funny. I thought I did.

Patient: Okay, it was a brilliant partial interpretation of that dream. It was good. It really was. Yeah, I would like you to be more active, but I know I have that ambivalence about that kind of thing.

Doctor: Why do you think you would like a brilliant interpretation of the dream? What would you do with it?

Patient: I don't know if I would do anything with it. One of my fantasies, one of my wishes which is opposed by all kinds of other wishes is to be a patient, or a student of, or a son of a brilliant authority figure who solves all my problems without my having to work for it. Of course, if I ran into one of these people I'd fight and rebel and kick and so forth.

Doctor: So my brilliant interpretation would be like a trophy on a mantel piece than?

Patient: Yeah, a trophy, but let me tell you about this brilliant interpretation. Actually what you did, I think, was pretty good. I feel kind of bad now that I didn't give you more credit, because it is good. I see a trophy over my mantel piece, because I'm capable of being proud of my dreams, the pungent dreams. I wish I could be half as creative in writing as I am in dreaming.

Doctor: Well, in dreaming you're not trying so hard.

Patient: Yeah, that's right.

Doctor: You know, I feel that the one thing I really want to say to you about what we discussed and my reaction to what's going on, is that I think one of the reasons you have such a hard time experiencing things is because you're trying so hard to experience things. You've posed it as a problem for yourself. Experiencing things comes from letting them happen, and I think it's pretty hard for you to let it happen.

Patient: That's something of a bind isn't it? To try to let it happen.

Doctor: I feel a little bit like I just got kicked.

Patient: Do you really?

Doctor: Yeah. Well, I guess I experienced your saying, "That's a bind," as really kind of patronizing like, you know, you kind of wanted to agree with me. But, after all, what did what I said amount to?

Patient: Suppose I was _____ . I don't know now what to do with it. Since I do agree with you, I agree strongly with you and, as I said earlier, it feels to me like a bind, my own bind that I put myself into.

Doctor: Well, okay. Maybe that's about as far as we can go with the bind for now.

Discussion

Sabert Basescu, Ph.D.

To what extent can an interview held on a stage in front of a live audience of a few hundred people, with a man I've never seen before, know almost nothing about, and who is in psychotherapy with another analyst, be considered representative of the way I work? I approached the situation very skeptically, expecting something more resembling show business than psychotherapy. However, I thought that the way to make the interview meaningful was to at least deal in depth with Bill's feelings about the immediate circumstances—what led him to volunteer, what anticipatory fantasies he had, and what he actually experienced about being on stage. Primary attention to the here and now is typical of the way I work.

I was aware of a number of ways this unique situation influenced me. I had to contend with my impulse to "make something happen," since it was a demonstration session. I was less comfortable with silences than I ordinarily am. When I introduced the subject of dreams, I was aware of being partly motivated by the desire to show how I worked with dreams. I was also reacting to my feeling that the tension had gone out of our interaction at that point, and that Bill had reverted to intellectualizing. But changing the subject, as I did with asking about a dream, is not something I ordinarily do.

The only intervention I seriously regret may have also been influenced by the public nature of the session. When Bill said he had an impulse to reach out and touch me, I asked him if he felt that often. His impulse came out of a highly charged, intimate, and meaningful interaction with me. My question turned off the further development of that personal experience at that time. I bit my tongue as soon as my words came out, because I knew their impact. Perhaps I was made anxious by the intensity of that degree of intimacy in front of an audience.

My summing up comment at the end of the session (. . . "the one thing I want to say to you. . . .") was prompted, I think, more by knowing this was our only contact, than by anything else. I am generally skeptical about the value of such remarks.

Although I was conscious throughout the session of the importance of avoiding any participation in Bill's intellectualizing, there are two points where my avoidance is especially evident, with his slip of the tongue ("give me some respective"), and my response to his dream (if you set out to go crabbing, you end up crabbing). In both cases, my intention was to simply underline or emphasize something for him to think about or stew about. I did not want to risk analyzing away whatever meaning these interchanges could have for him. I think that is a major risk inherent in the therapeutic work with this man.

In retrospect, I am surprised by the degree of my involvement with Bill. My skepticism was not born out. A show business feeling certainly did not predominate. Whatever its consequences, I have the feeling of something substantive and meaningful having occurred.

Chapter 5

MODERN PSYCHOANALYSIS:

AN OPERATIONAL THEORY

Hyman Spotnitz, M.D., Med. Sc.D.

Hyman Spotnitz, M.D.

Hyman Spotnitz is a graduate of Harvard College and received his M.D. from Friedrich Wilhelms University, Berlin, and Med. Sc.D. in Neurology from Columbia University. He is engaged in the private practice of psychoanalytic psychiatry (individual and group) in New York City. He has written and lectured extensively on analytic psychotherapy in the severe psychiatric disorders, analytic group psychotherapy, and neurophysiology. His books include *Psychotherapy of Preoedipal Conditions, Modern Psychoanalysis of the Schizophrenic Patient,* and *The Couch and the Circle.*

The term "modern psychoanalysis" has been applied to various systems of psychoanalytically oriented therapy that have been introduced or formalized in recent decades. Illustrative of this usage are the statement that "modern psychoanalysis is primarily concerned with the analysis of 'ego defenses' " (Strupp, 1972) and *Modern Psychoanalysis: New Directions and Perspectives* as the title of a bulky book encompassing the whole field of psychodynamic theory and practice (Marmor, 1968). But the term is not used here in that general sense. The subject of this chapter is a specific theoretical approach which has evolved from my own work and that of colleagues in treating severely disturbed patients whose problems could not be resolved through the classical method.

In the first published reference to the operational theory discussed here, it was stated: "Ultimately, I believe that the special approaches being developed for the treatment of the preverbal personality will facilitate the emergence of a more efficient form of psychotherapy for both verbal and preverbal personalities—a modern form of psychoanalysis" (Spotnitz, 1963, p. 24). The first book devoted to the theory of the technique of modern psychoanalysis was oriented to the treatment of schizophrenia (Spotnitz, 1969), but the basic principles are being applied in the treatment of patients in other diagnostic categories (Spotnitz-Meadow, 1976; Clevans, 1976; Dato, 1975). Successive stages in the elaboration of the theory and the major clinical concepts and techniques utilized, as well as the nature of the training and supervisory processes, have been reported (Spotnitz, 1976; 1976a).

Viewing this ongoing development in historical perspective, one may say that modern psychoanalysis begins where Freud left off. Incorporating recent advances in theory and technique, it extends Freud's method of treating patients with oedipal problems—"of treating certain kinds of patients in a certain way" (Menninger, 1938, p. 16)—into a broad psychotherapeutic science for the treatment of all psychodynamically reversible illnesses, including psychosomatic conditions (Brody, 1976).

Modern psychoanalysis adheres to Freud's definition of psychoanalysis as "any line of investigation" that recognizes transference and resistance and "takes them as the starting point of its work" (1914, p. 16). While conducted within that framework to resolve the nuclear problem of the patient, modern psychoanalysis amplifies the basic theory of technique. The major working concepts of transference and resistance are utilized in a more discriminating way. The technical implications of the existence of different transference states are recognized, the focus being on the narcissistic transference of the preoedipal patient. Both concepts are substantially expanded, and effective strategies for dealing with resistance are formulated.

Modern psychoanalysis differs from classical psychoanalysis in sanctioning an extensive range of interventions rather than relying primarily on interpretive procedures. The practitioner intervenes to promote verbalization as an integrative and connective process. In a sense, the standard approach of striving to make the unconscious conscious is reversed; insight emerges as a by-product of the connections established between impulses, feelings, and words when the patient is trained to convert the ingredients of internal speech into spoken words.

The emphasis on verbalization revives the notion of "talking cure," as Anna O. characterized her treatment by Josef Breuer nearly a century ago. It will be recalled that she was instructed to talk about what was on her mind and that, as she talked out her feelings, her symptoms subsided. This first case in the annals of psychoanalysis (Freud and Breuer, 1893-1895), is now regarded as the first successful treatment of a psychotic patient. Anna O. eventually recovered and became the first social worker in Germany— Bertha Pappenheim.*

Other differences between modern psychoanalysis and classical psychoanalysis center around contractual arrangements and the working alliance. The former usually begins on a non-intensive basis (one or two sessions a week) but session frequency may vary during the case. The contract reflects the degree of purposeful participation that may reasonably be anticipated of someone at the emotional level at which the patient enters treatment. The baseline requirements are that he come to the office at the appointed hours, lie on the couch, talk, and pay for the treatment. Violations of these terms do not lead to termination, provided that the patient consciously attempts to function in the spirit of the agreement. As long as the relationship continues on this rudimentary basis, the analyst assumes responsibility for results until the patient has progressed sufficiently to share it. Accepting whatever contribution the patient is able to make in the initial stage, the modern analyst works systematically to transform their relationship into a full-fledged working alliance.

General Strategy and Goal

Patients enter treatment in various stages of emotional immaturity. A lack of essential growth ingredients in the environment or exposure to forces that militated against their behaving as their impulses dictated—in some cases both factors—were incriminated. The earlier the maturational failure occurred, the more damaging its impact. Disruptions of the maturational sequences that unfold during the first two years of life—the preoedipal period—are more difficult to reverse than those occurring in the third, fourth, and fifth years of life—the oedipal period. The spectrum of functional disorders, ranging from mild psychoneurotic conditions to the

*Vicissitudes in the relationship, which Breuer did not report but disclosed to Freud (Jones, 1953), are instructive in terms of transference and countertransference (Spotnitz, 1969).

various forms of psychoses, thus reflects the highly specific reactions to maturational failure that have been classified.

The curative process is viewed as one of investigating and nullifying the forces that hampered the patient's emotional growth and of catalyzing personality maturation. Operating on the assumption that the patient's maturational needs were improperly or inadequately met in his interchanges with his natural objects, the analyst, in the role of therapeutic object, provides a supplementary series of interchanges to help the patient reach, as quickly as possible, the high level of development associated with emotional maturity. All psychological tools at the practitioner's command are utilized for that purpose.

The treatment relationship activates two distinctly different types of interferences with personality maturation—deficiency states which resulted from the improper meeting of maturational needs, and the patterns of maladaptation that eventually resulted from the patient's early attempts to cope with these states. But the analyst addresses himself only to the maladaptations. In the process of working on these pathological defenses, some maturational needs which were not met early in life may inadvertently be gratified—symbolically—by the analyst, but he operates only indirectly as a maturational agent.

Major Developmental Factors

Approach to Aggression

The operational theory integrates post-Freudian findings on the role of aggression (aggressive impulses) in the early evolution of the mind (Spotnitz, 1969).

Freud formulated his system of treatment before he recognized that aggressive impulses were separate from libidinal impulses, rather than libidinal impulses transformed into their opposite. Both types are mobilized by the frustrations inherent in the analytic situation, but aggressive impulsivity is considered to be the primary force leading to illness; in preoedipal conditions, it is observed to have strong hereditary or constitutional components.

The working hypothesis pursued in the treatment of schizophrenia identifies aggression (internalized in an ego-damaging way to protect the object) as the primary problem to be dealt with. In other preoedipal conditions, such as psychotic depression, hypochondriasis, severe obsessive-compulsive neurosis, and in some psychosomatic illnesses, emotional deprivation may emerge as the primary problem throughout or at various stages of the case. However, emotional deprivation tends to mobilize aggressive impulses. Consequently, the fate of these impulses is regarded as more important than that of libidinal impulses.

When aggressive impulses are activated in the treatment relationship, the analyst focuses on removing the obstacles to their verbal discharge while providing the necessary safeguards against destructive behavior. The release of hostile feelings to the transference object facilitates the creation of new action patterns for the healthful and productive discharge of impulsivity.

This task is compounded if the transference develops on a predominately positive basis; the patient then tends to bottle up feelings of resentment and anger. A negative transference climate is essential for resolving the primary problem of the preoedipal patient. To secure the full development of negative transference as expeditiously as possible, without exposing the patient to undue pressure to act on aggressive impulses he is unable to verbalize, the analyst maintains an attitude of reserve and limits his interventions.

To resolve the obstacles to the verbal discharge of hostility (negative transference resistance), the analyst conveys the message: Words do not damage me; they are acceptable. At times, he may have to explain the distinction between verbal abuse for therapeutic purposes and for sadistic gratification; the latter is not acceptable. The patient is free to develop more positive transference reactions to the analyst as destructive aggression is transformed into constructive aggression.

Narcissistic Transference

Practitioners of modern psychoanalysis attach great significance to the phenomenon of narcissistic transference, and to its exploitation for therapeutic purposes.

Although Freud understood that the infant did not feel separate from the mother, he did not recognize that this would lead to a narcissistic transference in preoedipal patients. When he stated that "they have no capacity for transference or only insufficient residues of it" (1917, p. 447), he had in mind transference to the analyst as a separate object. This is now referred to as "object transference" or "oedipal transference" to distinguish it from transferential reactions to the analyst as part of the self, or like the self; a severely disturbed individual may also relate to the analyst as non-existent. These primitive attitudes suggest the symbolic revival of clusters of experience during the first two years of life or a re-experiencing of the ego in the process of formation.

Narcissistic transference is also viewed as the patient's unconscious attempt to reveal the basic maturational needs for objects that were not met in his interchanges with objects during the undifferentiated period of life. These needs arouse impulses, feelings, thoughts, and memories. As these become attached to the analyst, he applies himself to the task of liberating the patient from their pathological influence.

To resolve the nuclear problem of the preoedipal patient, the analyst investigates (silently) the various mental operations by which the patient in a state of narcissistic transference often tries to prevent the release of frustration-aggression to the analyst. He does not work systematically for the resolution of these resistances until the narcissistic transference has fully evolved; its maximal development usually takes place after six months but may require two years. Thereafter object transference phenomena become increasingly prominent, though more fluid; the patient typically oscillates between the two states.

Narcissistic transference gives way slowly to object transference. With the establishment of object transference, the patient, having passed the emotional age of two, relates more consistently to the analyst as a separate object, someone different from himself. Dissolution of the narcissistic transference initiates what is commonly regarded as the middle phase of an analysis.

To get rid of damaging object impressions, the preoedipal patient needs to re-experience the emotional charge of his earliest object relations. The narcissistic transference provides that opportunity. But it invariably operates as resistance in the sense that the patient, when in that state, denies the reality of his interpersonal relationship with the analyst (Abrams, 1976). The dissolution of narcissistic transference is therefore worked for as soon as it has served its purpose. Object transference, on the other hand, is retained as long as it is needed. It is the source of the analyst's decisive influence.

Countertransference

The analyst's feeling-responses to the patient's transference attitudes and behavior are extensively explored in modern psychoanalysis. Countertransference is viewed not only as a source of counter-resistance, but also as a phenomenon from which therapeutic leverage can be extracted. Since the effective treatment of the preoedipal patient calls for emotional as well as intellectual commitment, the operational theory focuses on the countertransference reactions induced by the narcissistic transference, the nullification of their resistance potential, and guidelines for the utilization of these reactions.

The terms "countertransference" and "countertransference resistance" are used in modern psychoanalytic literature as reciprocals of "transference" and "transference resistance." The term "objective countertransference" is applied to the feeling-responses that are realistically induced in the analyst—the predictable response of an emotionally mature observer. Transference manifestations may also arouse feelings that the analyst developed for persons in his own life. These idiosyncratic feelings, referred to as "subjective countertransference," account for most deleterious forms of countertransference resistance.

The student analyst is trained to sustain the realistically induced feelings (objective countertransference) until their communication will be helpful in resolving an immediate resistance of the patient. Freedom to experience these feelings is contrasted with selectivity in communicating them. It is also pointed out that the impact of the induced feelings on the patient is directly proportionate to their genuineness.

The emotions induced by the patient in a state of narcissistic transference are often difficult to account for. It is presumed that they encompass the feelings that he experienced from others during the first two years of life as well as his own pre-ego feelings. Other narcissistic countertransference reactions are not comprehensible in these terms. At times the preoedipal patient communicates the need for feelings that he did not experience sufficiently as a young child; the analyst may then become aware of a strong desire to "nurture" the patient. Anxieties that seem to be totally unrelated to the patient may eventually be recognized as feelings that he has induced.

Dominant reactions at each stage of the narcissistic transference have been described. As it begins to unfold, the analyst may feel impatience or contempt if the patient complains or cries, or mild anxiety or indifference when the patient talks without affect or feels anxious. Feelings of indifference or unrelatedness may be induced by a patient who experienced much emotional deprivation early in life. When, on the other hand, the patient denies his murderous feelings for the analyst and says he wants to kill himself, the analyst may feel like killing the patient and become preoccupied with a personal problem. He may feel compassionate, or hopeless when the patient feels hopeless. By and large, the analyst's initial attitude is one of kindness and forebearance, which may operate as a defense against anxiety.

As the anxiety is mastered, these attitudes may be submerged in annoyance. The repetitive verbalization of the patient's self-attacking attitudes may induce feelings of aversion, and the analyst may experience revulsion and a need to protect himself when the patient explodes with rage. The analyst may get to feel that the patient is a "terrible nuisance" and become aware of urges to dismiss him in the middle of a session. When the patient expresses suicidal wishes freely, the analyst may wish to talk at length. Interventions that serve the purpose of self-reassurance may be rationalized as assurance that the patient needs.

At the height of the narcissistic transference, the analyst may oscillate between states of self-preoccupation and anxiety. The patient's autoerotic feelings and delusions may make the analyst aware of desires to appease or "tranquilize" the patient. A more or less realistic sense of danger may be experienced as the analyst is exposed to the patient's expressions of rage or suicidal wishes, especially when these are accompanied by bodily contortions or the clenching of fists.

But such anxieties dissipate later when the patient lies on the couch and maintains a relaxed posture no matter what he is feeling. The analyst then experiences a strong sense of security and control, as well as growing interest in helping the patient understand what has been going on in their relationship. The analyst becomes aware of admiration and genuine affection for the patient, becoming aware at times of strong desires to "mother" or "father" him.

Resistance

No value-judgment is attached to resistance. Neither good nor bad, it is simply the best adjustment the patient was able to make at the trauma level. Resistance is a force that needs to be recognized and dealt with, for without it there is no cure!

The modern psychoanalyst is less interested in resistance as an artifact of the treatment situation than as an expression of the living personality—the patient's characteristic modes of functioning. Any impulse or behavior may create resistance, but it is prominently identified with the early defenses patterned by the ego in the interests of psychological survival and mastery of the environment. These protective and helpful devices are activated in treatment by the charge of transference. When their mobilization prevents the patient from engaging in progressive communication, the patterns are identified as resistance.

Although originally equated with the blocking of communication, resistance is now recognized as communication in symbolic form, provided that someone is present to decipher its meaning. To the analytically trained observer, the resistance of the preoedipal patient often conveys, in a primitive or disguised way, otherwise unobtainable information about his psychic history. By giving clues to the developmental stage in which a maladaptation was formed, the pattern of the resistance also suggests the type of therapeutic intervention needed to influence it.

Recognition of these survival and communication functions has engendered a more tolerant attitude toward resistance. The idea of abolishing or cutting through it—overcoming resistance—has faded; the modern analyst tries to resolve it, which means helping the patient become fully capable of mastering it, analyzing it, and giving it up voluntarily when it is no longer necessary. In theory, a resistance is gradually diminished in force so that, as a by-product of emotional growth, it eventually loses its compulsive grip on the personality. Meanwhile, the patient gets to understand that his right to resist is respected.

The modern analyst departs from the customary practice of dealing with whatever resistance pattern crops up. Most urgent attention is given to serious violations of the treatment contract, and to any mode of behavior during the sessions that would, if continued, make it necessary to break off the treatment. These "treatment-destructive" patterns are responded to on an emergency basis to nullify their immediate threat, but the behavior is not interpreted until the patient is capable of modifying it.

When treatment-destructive resistance is not operating, other patterns are dealt with in a sequence that will facilitate forward movement in the case. Listed in the order in which they command attention, these patterns are categorized as status quo (inertia) resistance, resistance to analytic progress, resistance to team work (cooperation with the analyst), and termination resistance.

Explanations of the ordinary functional resistances are withheld until they become transference resistances. All components of transference resistance are investigated, and it is dealt with at all levels. Obstacles to the verbalization of hostile feelings for the analyst (negative transference resistance) are dealt with first.

Techniques and Interventions

In modern psychoanalysis techniques and interventions are viewed as tools for transforming immature patterns of resistance to more and more mature patterns. Effective treatment of the preoedipal conditions requires many and diverse tools, but all of them are dedicated to the management and mastery of resistance. The principle of intervening when and only to the degree necessary to resolve transference resistance is observed.

A therapeutic range and sequence of interventions are emperically determined for each case. By and large, symbolic, emotional, and ego-reinforcing communications are implicated in the management of preverbal patterns of resistance. The higher the level at which it operates, the more responsive it becomes to interpretation. In a sense, this progression observes the principle of infant feeding—no solid food on a regular basis until it can be easily digested.

Some commonly used techniques and interventions are described below.

The preoedipal patient is initially instructed (really commanded) to talk, and permitted to do so, on any subject he pleases. This instruction, which helps to minimize resistance, is the first step in educating him to free associate and discourages overly regressive tendencies (Spotnitz, 1969).

Early in the case, interventions are timed by the patient's contact function—that is, his verbal attempts to solicit information or advice. The analyst reflects each of these attempts in a brief communication. These verbal feedings on a self-demand schedule are motivated by the need to limit the amount of frustration-tension to which the patient is exposed.

In sessions during which the patient does not make contact, the analyst usually asks him a few brief questions about current events or other impersonal matters. Object-oriented questions represent a disguised form of verbal feeding and educate the patient (by identification) to the idea that he may ask questions. Similarly, in a period of protracted silence when the patient is tense, suffering, or in a state of conflict, the analyst may himself talk for a while about external realities.

Questions focusing on the patient's intrapsychic problems are not asked early in treatment, because he often experiences them as attacking and damaging. After his self-dissecting tendencies have been mastered, the analyst begins to pose ego-oriented questions.

When the patient reveals disturbing feelings and delusions, the analyst does not express interest in such material or give information about it. As the narcissistic transference develops, the patient's impressions of the analyst, however distorted, are accepted as valid. No attempt is made to correct them.

Preoedipal patterns of resistance are frequently "joined" (psychologically reflected, mirrored) to bring such a pattern into focus, to manage it, or to help the patient outgrow the need for it. By reducing the pressure for impulse discharge, joining interventions indirectly serve the purpose of reinforcing the preoedipal personality. Thus, the joining of the patient's own resistance to acting on his destructive impulses is viewed as an essential safeguard against explosive behavior.

In reflecting the repetitive communications of the patient in a state of narcissistic transference, the analyst helps the patient relate to an object like the ego. Various types of joining approaches have been described and illustrated (Spotnitz, 1969, 1976).

Explanations of unconscious mechanisms may be provided when the patient requests them after the first year of treatment. But they are given primarily to control the frustration level, rather than to promote understanding, while the narcissistic transference is evolving.

Interpretations are the dominant intervention after the establishment of object transference, and eventually the patient gets total explanations of his significant patterns of transference resistance. The general principle of progressing from object-oriented to ego-oriented interventions is observed; the latter type are provided when the patient is able to talk of himself with some detachment. But the artful use of "why," which gives him the opportunity to verbalize his own insights, is often preferable to formal interpretations. The analyst then limits himself to placing a stamp of approval on correct self-interpretations at an opportune moment.

The joining procedures that proved most effective in resolving resistance patterns early in the case are reverted to at this late stage when the patient reactivates these primitive patterns. (Though drained of their compulsive force, they are still at his disposal.) Interpretations rarely help the patient give up these infantile modes of functioning; he is usually aware of his backsliding and discouraged by it. But the joining procedures to which he was most responsive when these patterns were originally activated now resolve them with relative ease.

As termination approaches, the analyst tests out the permanence of behavioral change and tries to immunize him against the return of his old resistant attitudes in stressful life situations. In a series of so-called toxoid responses, carefully graduated to prevent undesirable reactions, the analyst feeds back to the patient the feelings induced by his transference behavior (objective countertransference). These emotional confrontations are engaged in on suitable occasions until the patient recognizes their therapeutic intent and indicates that he has had enough of the "old stuff."

References

Abrams, E.K. The Narcissistic Transference as a Resistance. *Modern Psychoanalysis*, 1976, 1, 218–230.

Brody, S. Somatization Disorders: Diseases of Communication. *Modern Psychoanalysis*, 1976, 1, 148–162.

Clevans, E.L. The Depressive Reaction. *Modern Psychoanalysis,* 1976, 1, 139–147.

Dato, R. Modern Psychoanalysis of a Borderline Patient. Doctoral thesis (unpublished), 1975.

Freud, S. On the History of the Psycho-analytic Movement (1914). *Standard Edition of the Works of Sigmund Freud,* Vol. 14.

———. Introductory Lectures on Psycho-analysis (1916–1917). *Standard Edition of the Works of Sigmund Freud,* Vol. 16.

Freud, S., and Breuer, J. Studies on Hysteria (1893–1895). *Standard Edition of the Works of Sigmund Freud,* Vol. 2.

Jones, E. *The Life and Works of Sigmund Freud,* Vol. 1. New York: Basic Books, 1953.

Marmor, J. (ed.). *Modern Psychoanalysis.* New York: Basic Books, 1968.

Menninger, K. *Theory of Psychoanalytic Technique.* New York: Basic Books, 1958.

Spotnitz, H. The Need for Insulation in the Schizophrenic Personality. New York: Psychology Dept., Stuyvesant Polyclinic, 1963. (Also Chapter 11, Spotnitz, 1976).

———. *Modern Psychoanalysis of the Schizophrenic Patient.* New York: Grune & Stratton, 1969.

———. *Psychotherapy of Preoedipal Conditions.* New York: Jason Aronson, 1976.

———. Trends in Modern Psychoanalytic Supervision. *Modern Psychoanalysis,* 1976a, 1, 201–217.

Spotnitz, H., and Meadow, P. *Treatment of the Narcissistic Neuroses.* New York: Manhattan Center for Advanced Psychoanalytic Studies, 1976.

Strupp, H.H. On the Technology of Psychotherapy. *Archives of General Psychiatry,* 1972, 26, 270–278.

Chapter 6

PATIENT INTERVIEW

Case History: "Chuck"

Chuck is twenty years old and is in a therapeutic community (24-hour residential) for drug addicts and abusers. He continues to act out his feelings impulsively outside his sessions, instead of expressing them within session. While he is in the session, he is closed off, he has enormous resistance to talking about his feelings; everything is external and nothing is personal. I'm concerned as to why he won't share them with me and what it is I'm doing to prevent him from sharing anything really personal. He avoids historical material. He also only expresses positive feelings about me. He recently made an example of how he is treated like a dog. He stated how protective he was toward one of the two dogs at the Program. He said, "The dog gets picked on and picked on and picked on. He barks to a staff member. You don't understand him because he is talking in a different language. Then he gets frustrated, so he takes things into his own hands by biting and getting in trouble for them, and it is threatened that the dog will be gotten rid of." Among the things that have been given to me by Chuck, are a number of poems. On three different occasions, three copies of the same poem have been given to me by him. It goes as follows:

"As I sit here
And look your way
I try and think
Of things to say.

Because I want so bad
To be accepted by you
No matter what happens
There's nothing I won't do.

Why can't you see
I lonly (sic) and blue
And when I'm down and out
I need someone to turn to.

No matter what I say
Or how nice I try to be
It doesn't help
You just reject me.

Wanting to give up
And not knowing what to do
Turning away
And trying to forget you.

Changing my mind
Is what your (sic) trying to do
But no matter what you say
I'll feel the same way about you.

I try to understand you
I think you try to understand me
But we always get lost
Somewhere in between."

This case presented by Kenneth J. Katkowsky

I believe the above is relaying something about the barrier in the sessions.

A. *Prior to his admission into therapy, Chuck was a transient. He had been living in the streets, abandoned buildings, and in and out of relatives' homes. He was on probation due to a number of arrests including burglaries, grand theft, criminal trespassing, and more than 180 traffic violations. He was also an occasional alcohol abuser. He was admitted for treatment in January and has been seen twice a week in groups and once a week for private sessions. He was externally motivated by the choice of jail or therapy; he chose therapy.*

B. *When Chuck was two years old, his parents separated. Along with his nine-year-old sister, he went to live with his father. His mother was on the verge of a nervous breakdown and allowed the father to have custody. Chuck feels his mother never really wanted him. In reality, his sister raised him. Chuck talks of his father with pride and idolizes him. "He was a self-made man." His father often went to school functions with Chuck. In reality, his father had a criminal record. He served time in prison for armed robbery. When Chuck was twelve, his father died and Chuck went to live with his mother. His behavior since then has always been inconsistent. He was a constant acting-out problem at home, and his mother threw him out a number of times. Chuck's functioning in school was also inconsistent; he had behavioral problems, and his grades were slightly below normal. Chuck states that he really loves his mother, but his actions indicate otherwise. His attitude toward his father is consistent with the strong love he feels for him. Chuck has been very protective toward the women in his life except for his mother. This parallels his father's behavior and attitude. Part of the image Chuck has of his father is the gangster: a strong, masculine figure, with antisocial tendencies.*

C. *When Chuck entered therapy he was hyperactive, with much excess energy. He didn't develop many interpersonal relationships initially. He often flirted excessively with new female residents in the Program. His first caseworker was a female who developed strong feelings about him. She suggested, "I feel Chuck needs a male caseworker in order to develop a more sane image of a man." She left the Program to get married and moved out of state. During this time, Chuck developed an attachment to another female caseworker who was quite seductive. When she left, he carved her initials and her name on his arms numerous times. He was then transferred to the present caseworker.*

During his early months he had many court appearances to attend to prior matters. Many residents were intolerant of him and didn't hide the fact that they wanted him to leave. When Chuck was able to give material things, he successfully bought relationships. These, over a period of time, yielded true reciprocal friendships. After about eight or nine months,

Chuck began assuming responsibilities and earning status positions within the Program. However, once he'd receive official recognition and titles with authority, he would begin to regress. Like his father, Chuck has a strong need to gain attention and recognition through unacceptable and inappropriate means. His treatment has been interrupted many times by his leaving the Program against the staff's advice. Currently, he is extremely ambivalent about his ability to benefit by continuing treatment in the Program. He leaves often, but does not go far and keeps in contact. Chuck is presently working his way back into the Program, having recently returned after a two-week unauthorized leave. Generally Chuck's behavior in the Program has been impulsive, exhibiting very little self-control. He uses his caseworker's name or the director's name as having given permission to do wrong things. He confuses both names and sees both persons as the same. When he is in control, he can be a very well-liked, productive resident. When he is acting out, he is despised and hated by other residents.

D. He openly says only positive things about the caseworker and his boss, confusing their names often and using their names to give approval to act out. He rarely says anything negative about them, like with his father. Chuck constantly tries to get us to reject him, like with his mother. He displays unacceptable behavior toward the Program's rules.

E. The therapist has difficulty controlling his personal hostility to Chuck, particularly when there has been some difficulty with the therapist's superior or when Chuck's behavior has been extreme. This countertransference reaction has at times impeded the progress of his treatment, and at times has threatened Chuck's continuance in treatment.

Patient Interview

Hyman Spotnitz, M.D.

Doctor: I want to welcome Chuck here. We've already had a few words, and he said he's been in front of audiences before. What kind of audiences?

Patient: Mainly for my band and what not. You know, playing and singing.

Doctor: You play in a band? What kind of band do you play in?

Patient: Musical band.

Doctor: And what kind of instrument do you play?

Patient: Drums.

Doctor: Does the band have a name?

Patient: Not really. It's like, you know, we just like to play for people and play for parties. We thought up many names but we didn't like them so we never used them that much.

Doctor: Do you think anybody in this audience could become a customer of yours?

Patient: At this present time, no.

Doctor: You don't think they're a good audience for that?

Patient: Not that I don't think they're not a good audience, it's just that I ain't got the privilege of leaving that place that much.

Doctor: Haven't had the privilege of what?

Patient: Leaving that place. You know, you have to be there a certain time and have a certain privilege before you can go out for a weekend or whatever. But I don't have the time to get away from there to play.

Doctor: You mean, that place won't let you go out to play with your band?

Patient: I haven't played for about two years now.

Doctor: Holy mackerel, sounds like you're in prison. Do they treat you like a prisoner?

Patient: Not really.

Doctor: Hell, if I knew how to play and couldn't play for two years in a band I would feel very resentful about that. Who keeps you there?

Patient: Well, mainly myself, because I ain't doing nothing to get out of there.

Doctor: What has to happen for you to get out of there?

Patient: I have to get certain privileges. That's what they call it. I want it, so, if I ask for it and I deserve it, I get it. If I don't, they say no, and I don't get it.

Doctor: Well, how did you get put into that prison?

Patient: I would like not to have to refer to it as a prison, because if I do I might get more resentful. I'm resentful enough as it is.

Doctor: Well, I'm already resentful to begin with.

Patient: In that case, maybe you can get me out of there, right?

Doctor: I sure would like to get you out of there, and I'd like you to play in your band, for God's sake. How did you ever get in there, get locked up there?

Patient: Well, a person named Phil suggested the place for me, because I was getting into trouble a lot in the street. Violence and stealing, stuff like that.

Doctor: Isn't it more fun to be out in the street engaging in violence and stuff like that than to be tied up in that place?

Patient: Not really. It's just that the choice was there or jail.

Doctor: Oh, you mean that jail or another jail. Is that it?

Patient: Yeah, in a way. In that sense.

Doctor: Who's your jailer in that place?

Patient: Frank.

Doctor: Is that Frank in the chair over there?

Patient: At least you got something in common.

Doctor: He doesn't like to call it a jail, and you don't like to call it a jail either. What does he like to call it?

Patient: Therapeutic community.

Doctor: Oh, therapeutic community. With no privileges of getting out.

Patient: Well, if you earn it, you get out.

Doctor: If you earn it. But you're still in jail. You earn it if you have good behavior.

Patient: If I just wanted to get up and leave, I could get up and leave. I don't have to break out of any bars.

Doctor: Oh, that's an advantage then. You can break out any time you want. In jail you can't break out. I'm glad to know that. What does your therapist have to do with your breaking out? I met him before. What's his name? Ted what?

Patient: I'm not sure.

Doctor: What does Ted have to do with your getting out?

Patient: I don't know. I guess he gives the O.K. When I have treatment groups on Friday, treatment meetings, they decide on what treatment a certain individual should receive, and if he deserves it, they bring that to all staff and they take a vote on it.

Doctor: Who decides whether you deserve it or not? Who makes that decision?

Patient: All of them. It's like a group decision.

Doctor: They share the responsibility, so you can't really be sore at any one of them. Is that it?

Patient: All of them.

Doctor: You're sore at all of them, I see alright, but you really can get out any time you want. You can break right out without any trouble. What happens if you break right out?

Patient: It depends. Last time I left, I was gone for two weeks, and I had no problem with my P.O. or anything like that. But I guess if I were to stay out any longer, my P.O. might have come and told me I had to come back or do my time in jail.

Doctor: Who is your P.O.? Probation Officer?

Patient: Yes.

Doctor: So the probation officer makes sure you go back there, and they make sure you stay there. If you're out you have to go back; otherwise, you have to go to jail.

Patient: I'm not sure of that really, whether I go to jail or not. He might give me a break or let me stay out there. It depends. I haven't actually gotten his opinion on it.

Doctor: And what does Ted have to do with your staying there? What's his role?

Patient: He's my case worker. Like if I have any problem, I can talk to him about it. If I have any questions, I ask him. Like, he goes to the right procedures for it.

Doctor: Well, does he say you have any problems?

Patient: An awful lot of them.

Doctor: He says you have a lot of them. What problems does he say you have?

Patient: Problems of not wanting to move in the program, and not wanting to do the right thing, as they call it, to get out of the program.

Doctor: It doesn't make sense to me. It seems to me you want to get out, you want to fulfill the program, you don't want to go to jail. Is that right? It seems to me you want to cooperate in every way possible, and you're proving that by coming here today. It seems to me that Ted tells you you don't want to cooperate. What the hell is wrong with him? How does he dare tell you you don't want to cooperate when you're cooperating? Aren't you here today for that reason?

Patient: First, get to know me a little better; don't say that.

Doctor: What would I get to learn if I knew you better?

Patient: How I fly off the handle and catch attitudes and. . . .

Doctor: Fly off the handle? But not without provocation?

Patient: I don't like to be put in positions where I have restrictions on me or where the authority which I don't even feel is authority. It's like in the residential place I'm at, there's a lot of residents, about seventy-two, I believe, and each resident has his own job function, and I feel that I'm a lot better off and a lot smarter and a lot more equipped than a lot of residents there. When I'm given a direction to do something by somebody I don't feel is equipped to give me direction, who doesn't deserve the responsibility, I rebel and I ignore his direction, and I'll tell him where to go and where to fly.

Doctor: Is that normal?

Patient: Yeah, in that place I'm supposed to be able to deal with these feelings and do it anyway.

Doctor: If they tell you to do something, and you don't think they're right in giving the order and you hate the order, do you have to swallow all that rage and anger and go ahead and do what they tell you anyway?

Patient: Right.

Doctor: Sounds like the army.

Patient: Believe me, I've been there too, and you're right.

Doctor: Either you're in jail or in the army. Haven't you got any freedom any place?

Patient: At this point, no.

Doctor: Tough luck. Anything I can do to help you become a free man? Is that what you want, or am I making a mistake? You really want to be a free man?

Patient: I want to have my own say-so. I want to do what I want to do when I want it, depending on what it is.

Doctor: You really want to do what you want to do when you want to do it as long as it doesn't harm anybody else, right?

Patient: Right.

Doctor: That's the kind of guy you are. You like to be straightforward, have your freedom, and do anything you want to do. Have I got it right? Do we understand each other?

Patient: Right.

Doctor: And all these people around you are preventing you from doing that?

Patient: Right, you can say that.

Doctor: What's the matter with them all?

Patient: They don't see it my way.

Doctor: I see it your way.

Patient: Yeah, you can be my therapist.

Doctor: Okay, I'll be your therapist. Can I help you? Right now.

Patient: You can't.

Doctor: How can I help you?

Patient: You can't, because you ain't got the authority.

Doctor: You mean, if I had the authority I could arrange it for you to be free?

Patient: In a sense, if you had the authority what you could actually do for me is just give me a job, position in the house where I'd be working and getting my money, you know and going out at night seeing the people I want to see. That's what I really want. Just a little freedom and a little responsibility where I can go out every night. Well, not every night, you know, but like some of the other people in there who earned the privilege of working during the daytime or going to school or going out at night or on the weekend or something like that.

Doctor: Well, why the hell doesn't Ted arrange that for you? He's got the authority, hasn't he?

Patient: Why don't you ask him that question?

Doctor: I want to ask him that question. Is it all right, Chuck, to bring him up here? Come on, Ted, we want to find out why you're keeping this poor guy in jail. He wants a little freedom; that seems to be a reasonable request. Why don't you grant his request? He has the authority, doesn't he, or am I wrong? Chuck, set me straight. He has the authority?

Patient: He should.

Doctor: He should have the authority. Well, why don't you grant Chuck's request? I like him. He's a nice fellow, straightforward, says what he wants. He makes a reasonable request, he wants his freedom, wants to have a decent job, to do something worthwhile. You don't want to harm anybody?

Patient: No. I say he should listen to you.

Doctor: So why the hell shouldn't you listen to me, Ted? What's wrong with you?

Ted: (Inaudible.)

Doctor: He gets himself into trouble? He's in no trouble here. He's behaving very well. Are you doing anything wrong here, Chuck?

Patient: Nope.

Doctor: He's no trouble here. So far he's behaving perfectly. Anybody in the audience find anything to criticize about Chuck so far? Has he done anything wrong here so far today? No. The whole audience is on his side. The only one who says he does anything wrong is you, Ted. What makes you think he'll do something wrong? Right now.

Ted: (Inaudible.)

Doctor: Well, why can't you use your authority and give him what he wants?

Ted: (Inaudible.)

Doctor: Do you know what he's talking about Chuck? Explain to me what he's talking about, Chuck. He said later on you'll do something. What does he mean by that?

Patient: Well, like he said, I'll be acting out. Like when I go back to the house, somebody would give me a direction I probably wouldn't like and I'd ignore it. Nine times out of ten I would do that, because if I don't I'd be put in a bad position. But usually I do it.

Doctor: It seems to me if they're reasonable and they make a sensible request and don't push it too far, you'll do it. The only time you get out of hand and you get resentful and you don't obey them is when you get pushed too far. Am I right?

Patient: Right.

Doctor: Seems to me that's their fault, not yours.

Patient: It's not his fault they don't give me the directions.

Doctor: Well, who gives you the direction?

Patient: The other residents in the house. They're people in my position who tense up the whole community. I feel if they can't run their own life and they have to be in that place, who the hell are they to run mine?

Doctor: I agree with that. So why does he support them and give you orders?

Patient: Because they tell me I'm going to find a lot of the same so-called idiots in the community, and I will have to deal with them. Like if I have a boss and I don't actually agree with what he tells me, I'll have to swallow my pride and do it anyway despite everything else, or I'll lose my job. That I can see. You know, if he's my boss, I'll have to put up with his grief. But at 5 o'clock, after my job is over, I don't have to see his ugly face. Over here I live with them twenty-four hours a day and I've got to see them twenty-four hours a day.

Doctor: And a lot of ugly faces twenty-four hours a day.

Patient: Yeah.

Doctor: Well, why can't he be in that place just till five o'clock and be free after that? Why can't he go out then? Why does he have to have these ugly faces around twenty-four hours a day?

Ted: (Inaudible.)

Doctor: Ted is saying that if they let you out after five o'clock you'll get into trouble outside. Is that right?

Patient: I really couldn't answer that question. I don't believe so, and I wouldn't plan on it, but there are a lot of things that happen in this world that people don't plan on, that people don't want to do. Outside I could go somewhere and mind my own business; but if something happened I could get picked up just for being at the scene of it. Then I just might plan to do something wrong, but after being in therapy two years I wouldn't go out there to do something wrong on purpose. I wouldn't, like you know, go out there to plan to commit a murder or burglary or hit somebody or whatever.

Doctor: I don't understand why you wouldn't go out and commit a murder if a guy deserves to be killed or deserves to be robbed. Why wouldn't you do it?

Patient: See, if somebody deserves something, during his course of life he'll be dealt with. Why should I put myself in the position. . . .

Doctor: Can't you commit the perfect crime? Can't you rob or kill somebody and get away with it?

Patient: I probably could.

Doctor: You could? Well, why wouldn't you do it?

Patient: Because then I'd have to live with myself afterwards.

Doctor: Your conscience would bother you?

Patient: Yeah.

Doctor: You have a conscience too. That's tough. If you didn't have a conscience, you could go out and rob and murder and wouldn't let it bother you. Want to have one of those operations? You know, the kind that can take your conscience away. Then you could go out and get away with what you want.

Patient: Let's get off that subject.

Doctor: You don't like the operation, or you don't like robbing and killing? Which is it?

Patient: Both. Got me in enough trouble.

Doctor: Who got you into trouble?

Patient: Doing all that stuff got me in enough trouble.

Doctor: What kind of trouble did it get you into?

Patient: If I hadn't done all that stuff, I wouldn't be in this seat with this mike and this audience today.

Doctor: You mean this is trouble right now?

Patient: No, but after this I have to go back to that place, and I don't want to say that's trouble, but I actually don't like the restrictions of being placed there.

Doctor: Yeah, but being here right now with this audience, is this trouble for you or is this something you enjoy? Do you like showing off like this in front of all these people with me?

Patient: Right now I'm being myself. Showing off is like when I have my drums or something like that, then I'm being somebody I'm really not.

Doctor: You don't feel you're showing off here?

Patient: I feel I'm being myself.

Doctor: You're just being a genuine guy. Why are these people looking at you?

Patient: I am being observed.

Doctor: What are they observing you for?

Patient: Therapy.

Doctor: How are they observing you being in therapy?

Patient: Because right now they are observing what I'm saying, what questions you're giving me, how I'm answering them. And when I leave here, you will have a conversation with them and they will interview you in a sense. This is what I was told, also that I won't be able to listen to it when they interview you.

Doctor: Why not?

Patient: Why, because you don't want me to hear, they don't want me to hear their opinions of me.

Doctor: They don't want you to hear their opinions of you or my opinion of you?

Patient: Probably both.

Doctor: Both. Well isn't that pretty rotten?

Patient: Well, it might be in my mind, but there's always a reason . . . (inaudible).

Doctor: I didn't agree that you should not stay on and listen to the discussion.

Patient: You've been in this field for a long time, you know how it runs.

Doctor: I know how it's run, but if you'd like to stay here and participate in the discussion, I'd be very happy for you to stay.

Patient: Okay. So after we finish our discussion, I'll sit up there and listen.

Doctor: Is that all right with you, Ted? Is that all right with the audience? Does anyone have any objections to his staying here and listening? No? See, I'm not passing the buck, I told you. Ted's the authority. He's running the show. He's the boss.

Patient: Well, that's life, that's life.

Doctor: Well, shall you and I give him hell and try to punish him in some way?

Patient: Would it change anything then? Would I be able to sit up there then if I gave him hell?

Doctor: I don't think so.

Patient: So what's the sense of giving him hell? It ain't going to change anything, so why argue?

Doctor: We might feel better.

Patient: We'd be acting off my feelings.

Doctor: That's not desirable.

Patient: Right.

Doctor: Have you taught him that, Ted? Have you tried to teach him not to act on his feelings, to start to feel them but not act on them? That's a very good lesson if he taught you that.

Patient: It depends. Sometimes I like to act off my feelings.

Doctor: You always like to act out your feelings. You have a lot of fun acting out your feelings.

Patient: I have to agree with that much.

Doctor: Sure, it's a lot of fun. But if you act on your feelings and somebody else gets hurt, that's tough on the other person.

Patient: Mainly I won't act off of anything that's going to hurt anybody else. If it hurts me, well, I want to do it anyway, that's my prerogative. But I usually don't do anything to hurt anybody else.

Doctor: Well, if you murder and rob, isn't that hurting somebody?

Patient: Well, first of all, I don't believe I will go outside and murder somebody.

Doctor: But if you felt like it, why wouldn't you do it? Plenty of people around deserve to be killed.

Patient: I'd rather be caught for a burglary if I ever did a burglary than get caught for murder. Because like burglary, I could always get that reduced. You ain't getting murder reduced. That's a lifetime felony. If I don't like being in that place for two years, I ain't going to like staying in jail for five or fifteen or whatever it may be.

Doctor: You know, I'm getting the impression that if there weren't a danger of your getting into trouble, you'd really enjoy robbing and murdering. You'd get a kick out of it.

Patient: Not really.

Doctor: No?

Patient: I'll be honest. If somebody did something to my family that I didn't like, like I done in the past, I'd go out there and take care of them my own way, like I've done many times before. I wouldn't go as far as murdering someone, unless it's a life for a life or a tooth for a tooth thing. Like if somebody messed with my sister or my girl or my family and I felt they couldn't handle themselves, I'd have them backed 100 percent.

Doctor: Well, suppose when you were with your girl, a guy came at you and wanted to attack your girl. Would you murder him?

Patient: I would defend her and myself as far as necessary, and if this meant my life for his, well, I'd do my best to protect mine.

Doctor: Get rid of his?

Patient: If that's necessary to save my life, yes.

Doctor: Now that's smart.

Patient: That's survival.

Doctor: Sure. . . . (Inaudible)

Patient: I wouldn't quite appreciate that, or like that either, whether it was my girl or anybody else.

Doctor: We agree on that. How about you, Ted? Do you agree on that?

Ted: Yeah.

Doctor: We all agree on that. What about the situation where you really feel like killing somebody, even though there is very little provocation, what are you going to do in that situation? If you felt like killing somebody and there was very little provocation, what would you do under those conditions? Suppose this guy Ted gets a little obnoxious and you feel like killing, what would you do then?

Patient: If somebody was getting obnoxious with me and I felt like killing them, that's not a good enough reason for me. Well, naturally, you're going to feel like that. Right now you came up with a question I don't like to answer. I will say I would like to get right up and walk right out. But that's not dealing with my feelings; it's like showing that I'm not man enough to sit here and take whatever abuse or take the feeling I'm going through. That would be acting like a baby and chickening out.

Doctor: Well, am I saying anything or raising any questions that you would rather I didn't ask?

Patient: If you did I'd let you know.

Doctor: You'd let me know, sure. Because I don't want to say anything that would offend you. I don't want to get myself murdered. If I went too far, would you murder me?

Patient: Nope, I don't think so.

Doctor: Why not?

Patient: Like I said before, I don't like to hurt anybody unless it's necessary.

Doctor: Suppose I provoked you enough, called you bad **names?**

Patient: I wouldn't necessarily hit anybody unless I was being assaulted in one way or another.

Doctor: Well, how would I have to assault you now to get you to feel like killing me?

Patient: Physically.

Doctor: Just by words, I couldn't get you to kill me?

Patient: Not really, because I was always told by my father that old saying sticks and stones will break my bones, but words will never hurt me.

Doctor: You don't think I can hurt you with words? Enough to want to kill me?

Patient: No, not enough to want to kill you. But it's happened in the past where people pushed my button to the point where they needled me and needled me. If somebody walked up to me and rapped me in the jaws a lot of times, I could probably walk away from it, but I can't take that little baby slap of antagonizing. I fly off the handle at the littlest things instead of the biggest things.

Doctor: If I came over now and slapped you in the jaw, would you feel like killing me or not?

Patient: I would want to hit you, but I say it's more of a man to walk away from that fight than it is to hit you. But if you came up to me and started antagonizing me and needling me and you're my buddy, but behind everybody else's back you want to stab me, it's like I'd get very resentful for that and I'd call you like . . . I forget the word used for it. It's really being a two-faced person. It's that I don't like.

Doctor: Suppose I'm a two-faced person and, when you walk out of here, I say all kinds of awful things about you. Would you feel like killing me then?

Patient: If I didn't hear you, I wouldn't feel any anger toward you. But if I'd know you were talking behind my back when I walk out of the room, and you turn around and say here's this and here's that and contradict yourself, it wouldn't provoke me enough to conflict any pain against you in any way. But the next time you talked to me, I would just turn around and walk away and make believe you don't exist.

Doctor: Oh, you mean you wouldn't kill me physically, you'd just kill me psychologically, act as though I were dead already. You'd want to murder me, but you wouldn't kill me.

Patient: Right.

Doctor: So if anyone in this audience sees you afterwards and says, "Dr. Spotnitz says you're awful. He said some harmful things about you," the next time I meet you you wouldn't recognize me.

Patient: It's not that I wouldn't believe it; it's that how do I know they're not lying? That's something I'd have to find out for myself.

Doctor: How could you find out for yourself?

Patient: I've got ways. I find out everything one way or the other.

Doctor: Well, is that a secret or are you willing to tell us?

Patient: It's no secret. I just happen to be in places at the right time, or I happen to know how to snoop a little bit for my own benefit.

Doctor: But suppose I say the worst things I can think of after I leave here. How are you going to get that information?

Patient: You got to tape me too. You're recording this whole session, aren't you? Well, if I really wanted to find out bad enough, I'd get access to the tape.

Doctor: I'd better be careful after you leave here, huh?

Patient: You'll have to use your own judgement.

Doctor: That's right. So you people in the audience, remember, after he leaves here we have to be careful not to say anything too wrong. It's going to be on a tape, and if he gets it, whoever says the wrong thing here is going to be in trouble.

Patient: No, it's like everybody has their own opinion. If one person says they like me and the other person says they don't, well, everybody is entitled to his own opinion. But what I'm trying to stress is that I don't like somebody saying he's all right in front of me and, when I turn my back, saying he's a skunk and everything else.

Doctor: But after you walk out of here and I say he is a skunk and it gets on the tape, you're not going to say hello to me the next time you see me. Am I right?

Patient: You won't see me.

Doctor: Do any of you plan to call him a skunk after he leaves here? If anybody here makes me call you a skunk under duress, I was forced to do it. I don't intend to call you a skunk.

Patient: Take the fifth amendment.

Doctor: Yeah. I don't intend to call you that at any time. I don't intend to say anything you wouldn't want me to say to you. You don't want me to call you a skunk. Anything else you wouldn't want me to say?

Patient: I'd rather not go down the list. I'd be here forever.

Doctor: You mean there are a lot of things you wouldn't want me to say about you?

Patient: Say what you feel. Just don't contradict yourself, that's all.

Doctor: Yeah, but I have a lot of contradictory feelings. That's my problem.

Patient: Well, talk about it.

Doctor: I'll be glad to talk about it, come on. What do you want to know about my feelings?

Patient: What do you think?

Doctor: What do I think about what?

Patient: You taught me all I know about therapy too.

Doctor: You want to know what I think about what, anything?

Patient: Anything you think, feel, or remember. It's okay with me.

Doctor: Well, I'll tell you the first thing I think. I think you're doing a very good job here. I think you're presenting your ideas very well. I think you have a problem yet of what to do when you're angry at people. That seems to be your major problem, from what I can tell. When people abuse you, mistreat you, or call you very bad names, I think they can provoke you into behavior you wouldn't like to engage in. I don't think you've worked out the problem yet of what to do when you're totally provoked.

Patient: I know what to do. It's just that I don't feel justified in doing it. If somebody does something wrong to me, I don't feel like I could let him get away with it. In a sense, like if somebody does something to me . . . It's like the incident when I went down to . . . there was a dog on the property the other day. Somebody conflicted pain against the dog and I told him to stop it. And he did it again. I wanted to show him how it felt to be hurt like the dog. I felt like hurting him and saying how do you like it, and when he says he doesn't, tell him the dog feels the same way. Because I feel the dog is being misjustly treated, because the dog cannot express his feelings. And when the dog went back to bite the guy or snap at him, he punched him in the face, and I didn't quite appreciate that. But if somebody conflicts pain against somebody, the normal reaction, especially in an animal, is to defend itself.

Doctor: Yeah, but see what I don't like about the situation; I'll tell you honestly what I don't like. I don't like the idea that you would protect a fellow, even though it would hurt you. I think you're vulnerable to that. If some bastard would come along and mistreat a dog, you'd get so angry that you would want to protect the dog, and you would then go and attack the other fellow even though it would be to your disadvantage.

Patient: That's my problem. It's like I look up to other people's behalf before I look up for my own. It should be forget about everybody else, I'm number one, but there are a lot of times I don't feel that. I grant you, I misuse myself in a lot of ways when I protect other people and it's going to hurt me in the long run, in one way or the other.

Doctor: That's what I think is your major problem. That you don't put yourself first all the time. It seems to me that your job in life is to put yourself first all the time, no matter what. I think you're inclined to put other people first; even a dog you put above yourself.

Patient: Mostly about the people I care about the most. Right now if I was in that place, and I know if I leave I'll get in trouble, but if Carol or any of my close friends outside needs help and I'm the only one that can give it, I will leave and help them out. And when my task out there is done I will come back, place myself on the chair, and take any punishment necessary.

Doctor: Well, that's what I think is your major problem. See, I don't have to say it behind your back. I'll discuss that with them later. I think that is your major problem, that you will do what's good for the people around you, even though it's toward your personal disadvantage. I don't think you say Chuck's number one all the time. I don't think you say that.

Patient: You know, I analyzed that myself in the past years. And what started that, you know, is that when I was a little kid and I lost a tooth, my father always used to give me a dollar, a dollar fifty, something like that. One time I lost a tooth, and my sister gave me two cents, and right away I thought of like, hey, it's only two cents. So I went and told her "Give me my tooth back. Daddy gives me $1.50." She started crying and I felt like so high. Ever since then, no matter what she asked me for, if I had it, she had it. And ever since then I've felt justified in my own feelings that hurting somebody else wasn't worth it.

Doctor: In other words, it hurts you to have your sister hurt?

Patient: Right.

Doctor: You don't want your sister to get hurt and feel a lot of pain, and you don't want to feel the pain that your sister feels, so you do all you can to avoid that kind of painful situation for you and your sister, or anybody you care for. If you really like somebody and care for them and they get hurt, it hurts you too. Then you want to protect them. Right? So, in a sense, you are really looking out for yourself too.

Patient: Well, I could say something else. When my sister stole something, like she stole some rollers and brought them into the house. This was quite a number of years ago, and my father asked where they had come from. She said, "I found it there." My father knew one of us had stolen it. So we started getting a lashing. Here's an Italian the old-fashioned way. He believes in punishment the old-fashioned way, severe, and we both got lashed and whatnot until one of us confessed. I said I did it until, like fifteen minutes after I was taking a beating, I said, "I can't take it no more. I didn't take them, she did." He broke down and cried, because I had taken the punishment for her because I couldn't see her as a female getting the same lashing as I did. I feel that if one is going to get in trouble for something, it might as well be one and not two.

Doctor: Between your sister and you, you're the one who gets it. So you're really a very good guy. You're really a very good person. Is that right?

Patient: I like to think so.

Doctor: You seem to be good to your sister, but not so good to your father.

Patient: I'll agree with that sometimes. Normally I get what I need.

Doctor: Yeah, but when your sister's going to get hurt and he's going to hurt you, you try to see to it that your sister doesn't get hurt.

Patient: Right.

Doctor: It's a very difficult situation you were placed in with your father, that he was punishing both of you because one of you. . . . Who had committed that, who had stolen that?

Patient: She did.

Doctor: She did?

Patient: What do I need stolen rollers for? What am I going to go out and steal rollers for?

Doctor: She stole the rollers? Then why did your father hit you?

Patient: Because he didn't know who did it, and I took the blame for it. I said I did it.

Doctor: Oh, you were protecting her.

Patient: Right.

Doctor: Well, didn't he have enough brains to know you wouldn't go steal rollers? Sounds a little stupid.

Patient: I wouldn't say it was stupid of him, because he had his own ways of trying to teach honesty and trying to show a lot of other things. It's like, all right, I lied to him. He didn't quite like me lying to him, even though I was saving my sister's back.

Doctor: Oh, he was punishing you for lying to him really.

Patient: Actually, you might say he was punishing me for lying to him. He knew what was going on and it hurt him more, in a sense, psychologically; it hurt him more to take it out on me for saving my sister's back. I was always taught to defend the family, you know, no matter what the case may be.

Doctor: It seems to me you were doing an admirable thing. You weren't trying to deceive your father; you were just trying to protect your sister from getting a beating. The beating wasn't going to do her any good. What you did was protect her. You lied in order to get the beating on yourself so she wouldn't get hurt, so you were doing a good thing.

Patient: If you weigh both sides, you see it levels out. All right, I did something good. I did something bad. I did something good so this is the good side. It goes down.

Doctor: How can you call it bad?

Patient: I lied.

Doctor: But that's called a white lie. . . . (Inaudible) That's the right thing to do. That's admirable.

Patient: But it's a white lie. Is that a lie?

Doctor: Everybody tells a lie.

Patient: But it's a lie. A lie is a lie, no matter whether it's a big lie or a small lie.

Doctor: You should be beaten for a white lie? If you were a man and you had a son who lied to protect his sister, would you beat him?

Patient: Right now I would say no, but if I become a parent, I don't know. Things change.

Doctor: If you knew your son was lying to protect his sister, I don't think you would beat him up.

Patient: But this is not like, you know, twenty years ago. I mean times have changed. Many years ago they were very strict. Right now if you had wine at the table and you put it over your shoulder to pour it into a glass, they wouldn't say nothing to that. But when I did it when I was a little kid, my father slapped the hell out of me, you know, right away. That wasn't proper for me to do.

Doctor: But I have the impression that you don't want to make your father look bad.

Patient: Well, right now whether he looks bad or not doesn't really. . . . He's dead now. I loved him. He's been dead for about five or six years. Whatever opinion the people here get, it's not going to hurt him one way or the other. I know how good of a man he was, so whatever they say now, it's not going to change my opinion of my father. Whether he was the best man in the world or the best crook in the world, he's still my father.

Doctor: And you're loyal to him?

Patient: That's right.

Doctor: And even though in your opinion he did the wrong thing in hitting you because you were trying to protect your sister, you still are loyal and devoted to him and don't want to upset that.

Patient: That's right.

Doctor: Is there a lot of loyalty in your family? Is your mother loyal, your sister loyal?

Patient: It's a hard question to answer.

Doctor: If I had your sister here and she was talking, would she also defend your father the way you do?

Patient: Yes.

Doctor: She would. How about your mother?

Patient: That's very hard, because my mother was divorced from my father when I was two years old. My father always defended my mother. If I was like to say, "I wouldn't go live with that slut if you paid me," my father would always tell me, "She's still your mother. No matter what differences we had, she is still your mother." And that's true. I shouldn't knock her down to hell, because she didn't do anything wrong to me at those times. But whatever she would say about him, that's her opinion. I really don't know how she feels about it. But my father did defend her like she was there.

Doctor: She was living?

Patient: When he died, she and her husband and her son came down to the funeral and the wake and everything. They were there constantly, to show their last respects, I guess it was. She must have had some feelings for him.

Doctor: Where did your father die?

Patient: He died in New York.

Doctor: Did he die in a hospital, did he die at home?

Patient: He died in a hospital.

Doctor: Was your mother there at the time he died?

Patient: No.

Doctor: She wasn't there.

Patient: Ironically, I was living alone, I was paying my own bills, and working and going to school at the same time. That night I had a fight with my sister for some off-the-wall reason. I went over to live with my mother for that night, to spend the night there, so I didn't have any conflict with my sister and brother-in-law. It was that morning I was told he died. I always looked at it that something or somebody or whatever is taking a lookout for my back, because letting me be with someone who could handle me, who could break the news to me. I guess nobody wanted me to be alone. It's very hard. I don't actually believe in the spirits or anything like that. There's something that made me fight with my sister, because normally I wouldn't fight with my sister. Something made me fight with my sister so that I would be brought over to my mother's house.

Doctor: What I don't understand is why nobody was with your father at the time of death.

Patient: He was in the hospital.

Doctor: He was all alone when he died?

Patient: It was like visiting time was over. I used to stay there twenty-four hours a day at times, but that particular weekend he gave me permission to go upstate with my friends. I came down early and I was going to see him the next morning. I didn't have to be there till the next day. And it was that morning, 5:35 A.M., he passed away.

Doctor: You really wanted to be with him when he died?

Patient: Well, I was told by the doctors the day I left that in about three or four days he would be home . . . that they just did exploratory tests for the screeners, and three days later he was dead.

Doctor: But if they had told you your father was going to die, when he died you would have been there.

Patient: Yes, I wouldn't have left his side. I think being I was the youngest in the family, they didn't want to tell me anything because maybe I would have been heartbroken. But I feel it would have been a lot better for me, because I could have been prepared and known that he didn't have much of a chance. But this way they brought my hopes up high that he was coming home. I had a downfall.

Doctor: Well, whose fault was it that you weren't there? I mean did the doctors mislead you or did your father mislead you? Who misled you? Your father told you to go upstate. The doctors. . . .

Patient: You could look at it many ways. Maybe he didn't want me to be there and he told the doctors to tell me he was going to be all right, or the doctor didn't figure he should tell me. Or a freak accident did happen and he did die and they all thought he was going home. Or maybe he told my friend to take me upstate. There's a million things that could have gone on. I don't believe in analyzing it and finding out the real reason why I wasn't there. I couldn't change anything. It doesn't matter. I wasn't there, five years ago, six years ago. He's dead.

Doctor: But it really hurt you that you weren't there when he died.

Patient: It did. And six years ago, if I knew what I know now, I would have been by his side.

Doctor: Okay. Thank you very much. You're very helpful in getting me to understand the problem around the situation with your father. . . . It's really a tough situation, because you're very loyal to your father, you're very devoted to your father. You want to maintain his standards, uphold his standards. You have some of the things he had that you don't approve of. You don't want to do what he did. So you have a conflict situation, conflict. And, I guess, they're trying to teach you not to do everything your father did because that puts you in a conflict. You're very loyal to your father. All right?

Patient: Uh-huh.

Doctor: I'm sorry you're having such tough times. Did I help you any today; did this help you any today?

Patient: Well, I can't answer that question now. It remains to be seen, that's all.

Doctor: You're not sure whether this was helpful or not.

Patient: Hey, what can I tell you? Do you want me to pump your heart and say yes, or do you want me to tell you I don't know?

Doctor: No, I want the truth.

Patient: I don't know.

Doctor: You're not sure whether it helped you?

Patient: It could have.

Doctor: It helped me. I found it very helpful. I wanted to understand you, so I found it very helpful. It gave me a lot of understanding about you that I didn't have before the session started. Thank you very much.

Discussion

Hyman Spotnitz

This time-limited encounter with the patient of another therapist illustrates the ego-syntonic manner in which an initial interview is conducted in modern psychoanalysis. It shows the primary attention given to dealing with obstacles to progressive communication and a few of the techniques commonly employed. However, the rapid-fire tempo at which the interview was conducted and the broad scope of the questioning were atypical.

In the initial contact with a prospective patient in my own office, I proceed more slowly and tentatively. At least half a dozen sessions may be devoted to eliciting the information compressed into the demonstration interview presented above. Moreover, had I been forming a treatment relationship with Chuck, I would have conveyed my sympathy for him in a more reserved manner.

On this occasion I tried to cover as much ground as possible without damaging his ego. Emotional communication was employed to help him talk rapidly and comfortably before an audience which he had anticipated would react unfavorably to his disclosures—his main concern. I was striving to help him make a good impression and also to recognize that he was making it.

Rather than operating objectively to ferret out facts, I focused throughout the interview on resolving Ċhuck's resistance to verbalizing what he thought and felt and remembered in the immediate situation. Thus indirectly, the first thing I tried to do was to help him talk, and specifically to talk about external realities. As much as possible I avoided asking him questions about himself, inquiring instead about the band he played in, his impressions of the audience, the therapeutic community to which he belonged, his caseworker, probation officer, and myself; later I asked him about his father, mother, and sister. This object-oriented approach was intentionally adhered to unless I really understood what he was feeling; then I asked him to confirm my impressions. Usually he did so; when he did not, I pursued the investigation until he clarified the situation.

Some of my questions early in the interview, such as "What has to happen for you to get out of there?" and "What's the matter with them all?" as well as my verbalization of the feelings I would have had in his situation, were asked to help Chuck verbalize hostility. These interventions illustrate the major operational principle of dealing with resistance to releasing aggressive impulses in language before addressing oneself to the verbal release of libidinal impulses. This strategy militates against the bottling up of aggression in ego-damaging ways, a strategy that is encouraged when libidinal impulses are dealt with first. The pattern of resistance I was primarily interested in working on in this interview—Chuck's objections to verbalizing his reactions to expressions of disapproval—was too strong to resolve in this encounter. Consequently, whatever resistance he might have had to favorable comments were not touched on.

In the course of the interview I intervened to help the young man verbalize his feelings, thoughts, and ego attitudes and to help him state his own problems accurately and draw the logical conclusions. In brief, the opportunity to interview him was utilized to provide him with a therapeutic experience.

Chapter 7

GESTALT THERAPY:

THERAPY WITHOUT RESISTANCE

Erving and Miriam Polster

Erving Polster, Ph.D.

Erving Polster is Director of the Gestalt Training Center in San Diego and has co-authored *Gestalt Therapy Integrated* with his wife, Miriam. He received his Ph.D. degree in 1950. He became interested in gestalt therapy in 1953 and has been exploring, teaching, and writing about it ever since.

We are living in an age of amplification. Movie blood is redder than life's blood; LSD trips have outdone the wildest of Hieronymus Bosch's fantasies; electronicized sound dwarfs conversation; hyped-up terror captures moviegoers; and a beer commercial advises us that we only go around once, so we should go for the gusto. Our culture is inundated in sensation-mongering.

Understandably so, because these exaggerations make us attend to what is otherwise overlooked. They reverberate from a valid need to recover lost experiences of sensations and feelings and the accompanying respect for personal awareness.

The so-called third force in psychotherapy was spawned by these concerns. Its contribution to a new level of personal awareness in our culture is considerable and long overdue. Nevertheless, the consequences of the long period of stunted awareness which preceded the recent psychotherapeutic developments are evident in indiscriminate and poorly integrated behaviors which have made caricatures of some of these techniques. The grim beating of pillows, for one example, is an attempt to sensitize awareness of aggression and anger. What is frequently overlooked, however necessary these forced marches may sometimes be, is that there is *also* a more organic way into the sensate experience. Amplification of experience emerges organically when one pays attention to what is *already* happening. One of the great recognitions of gestalt therapy is that attending to one's own personal experience from moment to moment mobilizes the individual into a growth of sensation and an urgency for personal expression. As this momentum gathers greater amplitude from each moment to the next, it impels the person to say or do what he must. This progression leads to closure, to the completion of a unit of experience. With closure comes a sense of clarity, as well as an absorption in fresh developments without the preoccupation which unfinished situations call forth.

In working toward behavioral change, therefore, there are two paradoxical (1) principles to follow. The first is *What is, is;* the second, *One thing follows another.* Instead of trying to *make* things happen, the psychotherapist following these precepts must focus on what is actually and presently happening. The present moment offers an infinite range of things which may interest the therapist: the patient's beguiling voice, dramatic story, contradictory statements, perspiration, glazed eyes, flaccid posture, unfounded optimism, ad infinitum. The therapist's own attitude, imagery, sensations, etc., are also fair game. From this range the therapist chooses a focus. When the therapist is absorbed with what is current and brings the patient's attention to current experience, a resuscitative process is started which brings liveliness to very simple events. A therapeutic fairy tale will illustrate. A man complains that he is unable to enjoy himself at picnics. He feels neurotic and dull. While he is talking his face is screwed up in a painful expression. The therapist suggests that the patient attend to his face. He is surprised, when he focuses on his face, to notice a tension there. As he stays with this sensation he begins to feel warmth developing in the tense area, and he experiences a slight movement. It is an involuntary grimace, he says. As he concentrates on the grimace his tightness grows, revealing a pain. When the therapist suggests that he make a sound that would fit his particular sense of tension and movement, he screws his face up and grunts several times. When asked what that sound feels like, he says it feels like he has to take a shit but can't quite get it out. He feels weird about this fantasy but also feels some relief from the tension. Also, he likes making the sound, but is embarrassed and blushes as he speaks. "Suppose," says the therapist, "that you just make the sound, temporarily setting aside any meaning it may have for you." He goes into the sound again and this time his hands begin to move slightly as though in rhythm with the sound. Asked to notice how his hands are joining in, he now says, in surprise, that they are giving a beat to the sound and he then begins to snap his fingers. Soon, laughing, he says this is incredible fun. He goes into a lively song. Finally he is overcome by hilarity and falls to the floor saying this is more fun than shitting. Furthermore, he can do it publicly. He is aware of absorbed internal excitement and is also aware of being carefree, with no concern about either shitting or any other mistake which free expression might lead him into.

This fairy tale took seriously the simple events which were happening. The process of moving from each event to the next had natural amplification powers and moved on to climax and closure. In the stalemate between the fear of shitting and having fun, new ingredients were recognized which changed the chemistry of the struggle. Such ingredients, in this instance tension on his face, grunting, snapping his fingers, song, etc., always change the chemistry of a situation so as to form a new configuration. *What is, is. One thing follows another.*

Beyond Resistance

Fairy tales are not reality, of course, and some of you may object that there is a complex set of forces, usually including resistance, which interferes with such easy resolution. This concept of resistance has, of course, had a useful history. Through it, contradictory motivations inhibiting behavior and feeling have been recognized. People do interrupt behavior and feelings which *seem* to be in their best interest. People *should*, after all, enjoy themselves at picnics. They should succeed at work, cry when sad, play with their children, have orgasms when sexually engaged, etc. When it is obvious to us as therapists, and to the patients themselves, that they should be doing these things but are not, we look for resistance. Ideally then, the resistance would be obliterated, leaving the individual free to be the person he or she could or should be.

The troublesome implication is that resistance is, first, alien to the individual's best interests, and second, like a germ its removal would permit healthy function. Psychological leeching of the unhealthy organism does not work, however, because what is called resistance is, after all, the individual's own behavior, not a foreign body. It is through re-incorporation of the alienated energy bound up in this behavior that the individual achieves fuller functioning.

Reformulating the concept of resistance along these lines requires an altogether open mind about the priorities in people's feelings and behavior. Not assuming the person is behaving wrongly, resisting, leads up to stay with each expression of the person, as it arises, moving always with the actual experience, innocently witnessing the unfolding of fresh drama.

There are several basic difficulties in encompassing such an attitude, and it is hardly likely that any therapist would wholly succeed. Some of the difficulties are discussed here:

1. It is only natural for people to look ahead in any process and to set goals for themselves. This is true, of course, for both therapist and patient. If not for the inspiration of personal goals, there would be no therapy in the first place. People want to get better in specific ways. The task of the therapist is to be able to bracket off these goals so as to function in terms of present experience—even though at heart wanting the patient to give up alcoholism, improve relationships with people, find good work, say goodbye to dead parents, etc. The difficulty of coordinating goals with immediate process is not unique to psychotherapy. A homerun hitter will tell you he cannot focus on hitting a homerun. He must attend to the ball and to his own stroke. Great novelists do not foreclose their own surprise at how their characters develop. Psychotherapists also must tune in and remain faithful to what matters in the unfolding situation.

2. In the age of the psychological detective, the uncovering of the hidden has been magnetically attractive. Most of us are fascinated by following clues until we find a hidden ingredient. The temptations of psychotherapeutic detection are supported by fact that we often *can* discover that which has already been there. Mother bakes a pie. Child hopes it is a pecan pie. It is covered though. Child lifts the cover and sees a pecan pie. The excitement irradiates the child. It is a new delight. The pie *was* already there. Only the discovery is new.

For these reasons it is difficult to transcend the magnetism of the uncovering phenomenon and to replace it with the creativity phenomenon. The creativity phenomenon is the development of that which has never existed before. It is more like what mother experiences when she bakes the pecan pie. Though she may have a lifetime of experiences with pecan pies, this new one never existed before, and her pleasure, if she is not already jaded, comes from the process of the creation and freshness of experiencing an altogether new pie. So also in therapy, do we discover that which is created anew. We discovered in the earlier illustration that the person unable to have fun at picnics did something which was initially reminiscent of shitting. We were not oriented toward uncovering the "original" and now anachronistic trauma about shitting. Instead we were oriented to follow the sequence of experiences which culminated unpredictably in lively song. There are also, of course, uncovering aspects in the experience, and those who prefer viewing it from that perspective are not "wrong." We just prefer to follow the freshly unfolding process itself rather than to view the process as uncovering something previously obscured. We would rather bake a pie than look for one.

3. The psychotherapist must exercise considerable "connoisseurship" in distinguishing between what is happening in the present moment and what is distractingly preoccupying. The distinction is a subtle one; rules about what is a present experience will only clutter up one's good sense. The very act which appears to be a preoccupation, when focused on, may turn into present occupation. For example, the woman who looks around the room when talking seems preoccupied rather than presently engaged. When the therapist suggests that she notice how her eyes wander and tell what she sees (rather than telling her she is resisting), what may be revealed is inordinate curiosity which, when acknowledged and accepted, results in lively visual experience. So, although the original inclination of the therapist may be to consider looking around the room as irrelevant to the current process, a mere deflection, the fact may well be that looking around the room is basic, and that talking to the therapist has been a deflection. The basic propellant to change is the acceptance, even accentuation, of existing experience, believing that such full acknowledgement will in itself propel the individual into an unpredictable progression of experience.

4. Though it is true that simple experience teaches, it is also true that people have an inherent reflex to assign meaning to events in their lives. This meaning gives dimension, support, and context to events. Without the context which meaning provides, events are torn out of their natural settings, empty and discontinuous, as with the labile manic whose pressured liveliness accelerates into forced moments, each unrelated to the previous moment, springing in frantic isolation from any personal context. He walks on air, like the cartoon characters who, when they notice they have walked off the edge of a cliff, suddenly fall.

According to the gestalt theory of figure/ground relationship, there is an inherent integration of experience (figure) and meaning (ground). When this integrative function is impaired, it may be necessary to formulate a verbal context for the immediate experience so that the harvest of the experience may find a place within the daily existence of the individual. To recognize the relevance of a current experience to other experiences in one's life gives coherence and continuity which are crucial to a sense of security and general well-being.

The proportions of experience and meaning vary from person to person. Some well-integrated individuals could not articulate the meaning of certain events in their lives even though the unity between figure and ground is, for them, quite sound. Others could articulate it well. Sometimes insistence on meaning upstages experience and interrupts the pure flow of involvement. On the other hand, sometimes the experience can be desultory and futile, because there is no development of the sense of fit into personal context which would provide ownership and dependability. The therapist's artistry must take this into account when establishing the direction and the emphasis of work at any given moment.

Composition

When a therapy views expression as creative rather than resistive, how does the consequent internal struggle between two parts of the individual move toward closure? No need of the individual exists alone; its counterpart also exists, and the composition is only rarely peacefully achieved.

The gestalt concern with polarities addresses itself to this internal struggle. Each faction in this struggle wants to dominate, but each is also subordinate to the individual's struggle for internal unity. The course of these internal struggles is varied; where two parts of the person seem incompatible with each other there may be out-and-out ambivalence, or one side may be submerged in deference to the other. The subdued part may appear ineffectual or it may work underground, frequently in disrepute, sabotaging the dominant faction but making life uneasy at best, and panic-stricken at worst. Frequently the struggle is frozen in anachronistic concerns or in personal horror stories about the consequences of allowing full expression of one or the other of the competing forces. To bring the interaction up to date, the warring parts must confront each other, the struggle must be expressed and articulated. The neighborhood tough guy may, for example, also have a soft side which once plagued his existence. Showing his soft side may actually have gotten him into trouble, or he may have internalized the standards of his childhood scene and so views his periodic moments of softness as threats to his own self-esteem. So in the interest of survival, as he sees it, he covers over and subdues his soft responsiveness. He got the message of toughness-uber-alles early and forgot what he had reflexively wiped out of existence.

The therapist must be alert to the surfacing of polarities, because, although they are sometimes obvious, they are often discerned only through sensitive attention. A moist quality appears around the tough guy's eyes when he is talking brusquely about his mother being exploited by her employers or beaten up by his father. There may be only a flicker across his eyes, a swelling in his lips, or a relaxation of his wrist. At first the disowned soft side would be easy to disregard; he has been doing it for so long. Even if the person is willing to engage the two parts of himself in dialogue, there would at first be a poor quality of interaction, including mutual disregard, scorn, low energy involvement, and a sense of the futility of any interaction; what could they have to say to each other? The therapist, however, enters his observations and brings to the patient's awareness the chronic discounting and stand-off. The patient is intrigued, and some vitality enters into the dialogue. The two disputants address each other more vigorously, each insisting on recognition for what it contributes to the totality of the individual's experience. Gradually the acknowledgement comes, that each does something to define the person in full dimension; rather than being a one-dimensional stereotype of a tough guy, he can be a compassionate tough guy, a tender but outspoken professional, etc. He is free to invent for himself all the possible permutations of being tough *and* soft. When this happens, he is whole and more open than before to doing what had once seemed unlikely and troublesome.

Contact Boundary

Bringing alienated parts of an individual back into contact with each other is a natural extension of the fundamental gestalt principle that contact creates change. We are all bounded in our existence by the sense of what is ourselves and what is not ourselves. We are also bounded by the need to make discriminations between these two, always imperfect but indispensible. Perls said, "Wherever and whenever a boundary comes into existence, it is felt both as contact and as isolation."

As always, paradox befuddles the soul. When the discriminations between self and other become most difficult to make, the individual runs the highest risk of either isolation from the world or such union that swallows him up, wasting his identity by living the will of another.

Since contact is to people as chemistry is to the relationship of physical elements in the universe, we must conclude that "through contact one does not have to *try* to change; change simply occurs." The philosophical equivalent of our chemical interaction is the Hegelian view that each thesis gives birth to its own antithesis, and contact between these two entities results in a new creation, a synthesis. We see human contact also resulting in mergers between that which is ourselves and that which is not ourselves. We are immensely affected by our environment, and we must sustain a sense of ourselves while at the same time remaining open to these infinite influences. We are continually confronted with the artful choice between assimilation and rejection of what we encounter.

The rejection of that which is not assimilable saves us from becoming what we don't want to become, from relinquishing individual identity. There are limits, however, to a person's freedom to stave off what he is steeped in. Non-smokers would have to hold their breath to keep out the noxious fumes of smoke-filled rooms. Accordingly, it is important for the individual to select or create environments which will make healthy assimilation or rejection possible without exacting too great a toll. The therapeutic environment, be it the one-to-one relationship of individual therapy, the therapy group, or the therapeutic community, must offer improved possibilities for making good quality contact. This may be accomplished in therapy through five pivotal elements. They are (1) creation of a new interactive climate, (2) personhood of the therapist, (3) the expansion of I-boundaries, (4) sharpening of contact functions, and (5) the development of experiments.

1. New interactive climate. People coming into a therapeutic situation quickly discover it is a very different world from the one to which they are accustomed. First of all it is a relatively self-contained unit of people with little seepage into the everyday world. This reduces, though of course it does not eliminate, the specter of catastrophic consequences. People are less likely to be shot, adjudicated, ostracized, flunked, ridiculed, or otherwise pilloried as a result of their actions or words. The general expectation is one of ultimate acceptance, even during painful interludes when acceptance may be in doubt. Only rarely is a person working on a problem not seen from a respectful perspective by at least some of the group. People are not crowded by the complex, contradictory requirements of the world out there. The climate is usually one of live and let live; there is a subtle optimism that the puerile, the confusing, the disgusting, the frightening, etc., will soon turn the corner and become vibrant, touching, revealing of inner beauty, and restorative. Consequently, there is less need to interrupt people. When one believes that what is happening will turn out well, even though presently painful or problematical, acceptance becomes easier. Each individual may discover a new extent of psychological space within which to function. Crowding of one's psychological space supports prematurity or delay, because these alien requirements impinge on the individual's range of possibilities.

The new community is, of course, not Eden. People do get angry with each other, misunderstand each other, trick each other, walk out on each other, and shower a whole range of kindred brimstone on their co-sufferers. Usually these mutual tortures are more readily recognized and dealt with because of the basic exploratory climate, the extended time opportunities, and the presence of a therapist who is commissioned to watch the store.

2. Personhood of the therapist. In a therapy where contact is seen as a major organ of personality, the personhood of the therapist is given central importance in the creation of behavioral change. Most excellent therapists we have known have been exciting people. They are readily radiant and absorbed. They encompass wide areas of personal experience. They can be tough or tender. They can be serious or funny. They change fast, according to the stimulations they receive. their articulations, and courageous in assimilating new experience and in facing the dragons of the mind. If patients spend considerable intimate time with such a presence, some of it will frequently rub off on them. Patients absorb a new way of perceiving, articulating, considering. They learn to seek new perspectives. They recognize alternatives to whatever is happening. They engage in a new partnership of feeling. They experience someone who knows how to accept, frustrate, arouse. They meet surprise and adventure. Hopefully, they imbibe a respect for what it is like to be a human being.

In the face of such an awesome pattern of characteristics, the reader may well ask whether humility is also included. Fortunately it is not indispensable that the therapist be such a marvel as we might all wish he or she were. What is more crucial than the specificity of desirable characteristics is the unavoidable fact that, social designations aside, the therapist is, after all, a human being. As one, he or she affects one. Once when referring a parent to a therapist for his 14-year-old son, the father was asked whether he would like his son to be influenced by this particular man. That is not a bad question for any person to ask of himself about a therapist. It is plain that the therapist's personhood ranks high along with technique and knowledge as a determinant of therapeutic direction. A kind person will affect people through his or her kindness, a demanding person through his or her demandingness, a person interested in power through this interest, a politically interested person through this orientation. Clearly, many of the therapist's characteristics or interests evident elsewhere might not enter into the therapy session. What is important, however, is that the therapist not be required to hide these characteristics or interests when they do organically appear in order not to unduly influence the patient. On the contrary, the therapist's influence is indispensable and unavoidable, and if the exercise of it risks putting inappropriate trips on the patient, this only reminds us that there is no guarantee of a good job. Permitting the influence to appear does not free the therapist of the transcendent requirement for exercising an artistry which unites his or her own personhood respectfully with the authentic personal needs of the patient.

3. Expansion of the I-boundary. People's I-boundaries include the range of contact experiences which their identities will allow. They will make only those contacts which do not excessively threaten their sense that they are still themselves. It is therefore important that they learn to experience aspects of themselves which they had formerly obliterated, so that as unpredictable stimulations arise they will not be unduly threatened by their reappearance. The prude endangered by forgotten sexuality, the macho man terrorized by his impotence, and the chronically supportive person engulfed by disquieting rage have all narrowed their I-boundaries and refused to accept certain alienated parts of themselves. The whining person, the saboteur, the leech, and the ogre may all be exiles from awareness calling for their right to be heard. Malaise ensues, because the risk of reappearances of these characteristics causes unbearable disturbances for the individual's self image. When unacceptable characteristics can be reassimilated and given a voice, individuals may discover themselves to be quite different in actuality from what they feared they might become if they listened to these alienated parts of themselves. Their sense of self expands, encompassing new possibilities in behavior and feeling, setting contemporary limits based on present experience, not past trauma.

Fixity of behavior and feeling always limits the world in which people may live nourishingly. Since there are limits to their control over the world and its confrontations, the more flexible people's acceptance of themselves is, the more securely they can live in a changing world. When their own worst fears about themselves are altered and they begin to assimilate the validity of these formerly alien characteristics, the possibilities for improved contact are increased. They can let the chips fall where they may, trusting their own ability to sustain themselves in the face of the unpredictable or customary.

4. Sharpening of the contact functions. We spoke earlier about the importance of making the distinction between what is ourself and what is not ourself. Basic to this ability is the rhythm which exists between the individual's *sense* of his or her own organic identity and the *functions* through which he or she makes and maintains contact. The seven basic contact functions (2) are talking, moving, seeing, hearing, touching, tasting, and smelling. In focusing on these functions, the gestalt therapist seeks to improve such qualities as clarity, timing, directness, flexibility, etc. All of these contact functions have been subjected to the erosive deteriorations of cultural prohibitions and interruptions. Growing up often seems like a long process of learning what not to see or touch or say or do. Each time a function is in-

rupted in its natural course, its impetus has been challenged. It is true that some others may be inspired by hardship, like Demosthenes; but more likely, most deficiencies are not so dramatic and will go unrecognized. Many people have overlooked their own contact functions for so long that, although dismayed about their lives, they have little awareness of the simple, but far-reaching, deficit. The gestalt therapist is alerted to these interruptions and deficiencies; he or she must develop a safecracker's sensitivity to what is missing as well as to what is too much.

In working with a man who speaks incessant gobbledygook, the therapist may ask him to limit himself to simple declarative statements. Or the therapist may respond to the circumvented meaning behind circumlocutions. The therapist might ask a verbally stingy man to add a few words to his sentence once he feels he has completed it. The therapist must have as much variety in his or her inventiveness as there are linguistic poisons. Following this tack, the therapist will almost inevitably meet the objections the patient has to the direct contact function; he will offend people, to be understood he has to give the full background to every statement; if people need more information than he gives, they should ask for it, etc.

These objections must be faced. The circumlocutious man may find it objectionable to say what he means to say for fear of discovering he is far more critical than he wishes. When brought face-to-face with his own critical nature he may feel pinched by anxiety. The therapeutic task is to turn this anxiety into excitement. How might the patient's critical facility be used right now, for example, in contact with the therapist? As the patient warms to his task he may discover a new clarity, a pungent sense of humor, or an affection that endures through the expression of criticism. Then the patient begins to respect the liveliness accompanying his critical faculty, he is on the road to magnifying his diminished zest. The original dread of himself as a tyrannical critic may evolve into the discovery of his genuine perceptual powers and the zing of not soft-pedalling them.

So also with the other contact functions. A man who was bombed out of looking because he couldn't stare at his mother's crotch may surprisedly discover the beauty of his therapist's eyes and no longer be willing to give up seeing. A woman having spent her formative years sitting stiffly with hands folded whenever company arrived may learn to fidget and feel the vibrant sensations which movement releases. People who have been rarely touched may be held or may explore the various textures in the therapy room or in their environment. Each time, the fresh recognitions of the excitement and fruition inherent in the exercise of these contact functions supports, even inspires, the person to try them out further.

Repetition is crucial for assimilation. It is rare that one experience solves a problem once and for all, but one experience may light the way. Alas, it is also true that full recovery of functions rarely happens. More likely the individual sets new thresholds for the exercise of function and for better recovery from temporary abandonment of functions. The circumlocutious man, for example, may return to his circumlocutiousness in situation which are especially difficult, but he comes back to clarity more easily. It takes more to throw him off the track and less to get him back on.

5. Development of experiments (3). The functional psychology of John Dewey espoused the primacy of doing something in order to learn. It is better to take children to a farm and to a dairy than just to tell them about milk production. So, also, in gestalt therapy we want to turn out "about-ist" habits into present action. The individual is mobilized to face the relevant emergencies of life by playing out his or her unrequited feelings and actions in the relative safety which the therapist's expertise and guidance provide. In gestalt therapy we call this "a safe emergency." Although the safety factors are present in the non-punitive and sensitively guided atmosphere of therapy, there is also a large emergency factor, because the individual is enabled to enter into areas of his or her existence which were formerly out of bounds and which are still laden with fear. For example, a remark about her grandmother easily passed over in ordinary conversation receives new focus when the therapist asks a woman to play her grandmother, whom she remembered sitting like a sparrow with head tilted to one side. She tilts her head, assuming grandmother's posture and regards the therapist with the same undemanding, completely loving expression which she remembers her grandmother had. Only now she feels what it is like to be such a loving person. She blushes with the animation brought on by the easy affection. Grandmother was like a star in the heavens beaming out from the deep reaches of the universe, but no longer an everyday part of existence. Now she returns to life within the patient's own skin. Reality begins to include unqualified loving. Mourning surfaces also for the lost birthright, misplaced when grandmother died. A lost right, because now as an adult everyone—spouse, children, colleagues—everyone needs her, and when she doesn't give them what they need she feels unlovable. Then she can't love them either. The therapist says, "Be your grandmother and tell them about you." To her spouse, grandmother describes how, as a child, the patient wanted to know everything and was constantly coming to her with stories about new discoveries she had made. Spouse, in fantasied dialogue, responds by saying that's just what he loves too and what he has been missing. To her children, grandmother tells how the patient could always make up games and toys out of the most unlikely materials, a wooden crate, an old quilt. The children respond, turning to mother (the patient) observing the fact that she never just plays with them and would she please, please, and who cares about dinner. The patient, realizing what she has dismissed

from her own adult function, is inspired to become again what she had once been, supporting herself, even though the support of her grandmother is gone.

This speculation is only one illustration of the consequences of recreating grandmother. The improvisational possibilities are endless. The action is open-ended, transcending accustomed modes for dealing with memories, fears, sadness, and moving the individual into untried and unpredictable directions. In the improvisational cycle which is played out in the experiment, the patient is moved to fresh ways of being. As we have said elsewhere: (4)

> . . . the patient in therapy . . . may tremble, agonize, laugh, cry, and experience much else within the narrow compass of the therapy environment. He . . . is traversing uncharted areas of experience which have a reality all their own and within which he had no guarantee of successful completion. Once again he confronts the forces that previously steered him into dangerous territory and the return trip (may) become as hazardous as he had reflexively feared. The therapist is his mentor and companion, helping to keep in balance the safety and emergency aspects of the experience, providing suggestion, orientation, and support. By following and encouraging the natural development of the individual's incomplete themes through their own directions into completion, the therapist and patient become collaborators in the creation of a drama which is written as the drama unfolds.

Two major forms which the gestalt experiment might take are enactment and directed behavior.

In enactment the aim is to dramatize, to enact some important aspect of the individual's existence. This could be a dramatization of an unfinished situation from either the past, the present, or the future. It could be the dramatization of a characteristic of the patient, as, for example, playing out the monster in himself or herself which he or she is otherwise afraid to reveal. It could be the dramatization of a polarity in dialogue, as where the tough and tender parts of one individual talk to each other. It could be the dramatization of an exchange with a fantasied someone sitting in the "empty chair." It could be the dramatization of a visual fantasy, or it could be the dramatization of the diverse parts of a person's dream.

In directed behavior, the individual is asked to try on a certain behavior. A man might be asked to try talking with his hands, to call a friend each day, to fidget in his chair while talking or listening, to say "dear" when he addresses the people in his group, to speak with the ethnic accent of the people who reared him, etc. This supports the actions-speak-louder-than words credo. The individual takes his risks through the action, giving him the palpable effect from which his previous gaps in experience have distanced him. Also, in present action, he is free to improvise, to take a new tack instead of the familiarly doomed course of action he may have tried before.

The experiment is also a route by which the unfinished business of the patient may be brought into the present. This not only fosters more than a dry narration of past events, it holds opportunities for action and improvisation and for the resolution of persistent but anachronistic limits on the patient's experiences. The woman who keeps her distance from all men, because her father kept her at arm's length, becomes freer to express her longing for closeness to a man and to find ways in which this longing can be satisfied. Not by sitting on daddy's lap, but she can fantasy sitting on his lap and telling him what that means to her, and express also what she would like to have received from him then. She could try moving, at first awkwardly, into an embrace or a supportive gesture that a man in her life is now willing and ready to offer, remaking her assumptions about the inevitable distance that must exist between herself and men.

These are some of the fundamentals of gestalt therapy which lead to behavioral change. The functional objective is to heighten present experience; the faith is that the ultimate objective, change, will be accomplished when one optimally experiences the present. Always, the return to experience, to the acceptance and re-engagement with what is, leads to a new orientation for behavioral change. Animating these principles is the move beyond the concept of resistance into the view of the individual as a population of ideas, wishes, aims, reactions, and feelings, which vie for full expression. Giving voice to these multilarities is like giving suffrage to a previously disenfranchised segment of the population. It allows these parts of the person to vote and to be attended to rather than relegating them to dissension and sabotage.

Gestalt therapy is a phenomenologically inductive system in which an individual's development unfolds from moment to moment, and in which we are more concerned with opening the person to a continuing process of discovery than with sending him or her back through time to concentrate on that which has existed before. This distinction is, to be sure, a subtle one. We believe that supporting a person's potentialities for creative improvisation with a contemporary focus, rather than an historical one, is basic ability that he or she needs now in therapy, and ultimately, out of it.

References

1. Beisser, A. The Paradoxical Theory of Change. *Gestalt Therapy Now.* Edited by J. Fagan and L. Shepherd. Palo Alto, California: Science & Behavior Books, 1970.
2. Polster, E., and Polster, M. *Gestalt Therapy Integrated.* New York: Brunner/Mazel, 1973.
3. Ibid.
4. Ibid.

Chapter 8

PATIENT INTERVIEW

Case History: "Ellen"

The patient was referred by a colleague as an intriguing challenge due to her handicapped physical condition and courageous reaction to a depressing life situation of illness, isolation, and financial insecurity. She is now the only one left of her family that consisted mainly of mother, father, and grandmother. She lives alone for the first time in her life and has trouble building a satisfactory support system.

A. Patient was born in 1930. Her parents told her that at conception she was a much wanted child of a large extended family. She has suffered from severe rheumatoid arthritis since she was 22 months old. Later, in 1947, she had a hip operation to correct her persistent limp, but this was unsuccessful, and she has been on crutches ever since. Her legs and hands are visibly affected by the disease. She weighs about 100 pounds. At five years of age, she also developed serious eye problems (uveitis) which opthalmalogists claim is arthritis-related. She has been blind in her left eye ever since.

Patient states that her father was the kindest influence in her life. Although he was not physically demonstrative, she felt he did the best he could for her. When she was refused entrance to handicapped classes, he got a newspaper reporter to come to the house to interview her. The reporter was taken by the seven-year-old girl and wrote a moving article. Within a week she was instated in an appropriate class. Her father also saw that she attended a camp for the handicapped. Later he procured a Division of Vocational Rehabilitation Scholarship for college. He died at 49 before he saw her graduate. He left no substantial estate (he had a business that failed and then became an IRS employee). Patient reports little physical reaction to his death with no extended grieving or depression. (It is interesting to note that patient never acknowledged to herself his benign influence until writing her history for this conference.) Although reaction to her father's death was minimal, there was a contrast when her grandmother died in 1958 (patient was 28). Her good eye became noticeably worse before remission came several months after. Again when patient's mother died in 1974 (patient was 43) her eye condition worsened once more. After several subsequent eye operations the condition has stabilized now to the opthalmalogist's satisfaction (and, according to patient, his wonderment).

B. Patient first consulted me in October 1975, after breaking several prior appointments. We have had once a week sessions with a total of 25 to date. Her presenting complaint was a reactive depression to the death of her mother whom patient felt always rejected her. Her grandmother openly told patient it would have been better if she had never been born, but since she was, couldn't she have been "good looking and lucky instead of just smart?" She claims that she is determined to live a "normal" life among non-handicapped people and prove them all wrong. She continued to live with her mother after her father's death in what appears to have been a love-hate relationship. The patient completed college, continued in graduate school, and became a psychiatric social worker. She then supported herself and her mother, who by then was ailing and semi-bedridden from rheumatic heart disease. According to the patient her mother was as rejecting and sharp-tongued as the rest of her family. She reports that her mother simply expected her to support and care for her. I got the impression that the mother considered it bestowing an honor upon the patient to do so. The patient claims that she always felt like an appendage of her mother. For example, greeting cards would arrive addressed to Mrs. T. and daughter. Invitations would be extended the same way, both written and verbally. She blamed her mother for having to limit her own activities in order to care for her.

The patient reports a love affair with a young man whom she met prior to entering social work school. She went with him for two years after which time he terminated the relationship because he found her "immature." She now sees a married man occasionally (every 2 months or so), whom she is fond of. She has sexual relations with him which are highly satisfactory, she says, but she feels worse than ever when he leaves, because then her loneliness becomes more acute.

She is now faced with abysmal loneliness, her physical limitations, and increasing financial insecurity. She claims that, with inflation, she now spends more than she makes even when she cuts corners.

Treatment at first centered on the patient's ambivalence between giving up altogether and living her life. She has gone through periods of severe depression, and several months ago she spent entire weekends in bed without eating. We discussed this option of slow death, and now she states that she has chosen to live.

After several months of treatment the patient admitted that when her mother was alive she had a good excuse not to make a life of her own. Now that her mother is dead she just can't find the strength to mobilize herself. She feels that it's too late. "Anyway, all my efforts come to nothing," she repeatedly says. "No one comes to see me. No one wants to be bothered. Even when I had the flu and was no longer contagious—just very weak— friends would still avoid coming." One said, "Why don't you train the cats to get you your dinner," or—"Tell the homemaker to leave a sandwich and thermos next to your bed so you don't have to get up." She feels lost,

*helpless, and without resources. Her continued complaint is, "I've suffered
enough. Now people should understand and put themselves out for me."*
    The patient's major strengths:

1. *Her sense of humor. For example, when we discussed her writing
    her own history as required for presentation at the conference she
    stated quickly, "Chronic Kvetch."*
2. *Her competency at work. She reports this, but there are other
    evidences. Once I asked for some advice as to appropriate agencies
    for another patient. She gave the information quickly and deftly.
    Her agency must think highly of her also. She has worked there 19
    years. They encouraged her to seek treatment in psychotherapy at
    this time. Since her strength has increased they have given her ad-
    ditional casework and showed her that they consider her a valued
    worker.*
3. *Her determination through the years in managing the daily affairs
    of living in her own apartment, getting help in her building re-
    cently during the maintenance workers' strike when she had to get
    assistance twice a day with the elevators, etc.*
4. *Her assessment of herself and her condition.*

D. *The transference focuses around the patient's demand for a magical
cure for her psychological problems. She negates the therapist consistently
with "I can't". "What should I do?" "I have no strength"; "I can't
manage"; "Nobody cares"; etc. With all this protest of powerlessness, she
resists the therapist with vigor. In this way the transference is the resistance,
in that the patient repels closeness to me, the therapist, by implying my
uselessness in affecting her life. Since preparing for this conference which
entailed a great deal of work for me as the therapist, it is interesting to note
that the patient said for the first time, "My goodness, what strikes me is all
the caring you put into this." Ironically enough, our participation in the
conference seems to be a crucial turning point.*

*We have looked most recently at the way in which the patient withdraws
or lashes out to avoid rebuff. She is catching glimpses of the ways he contributes to her isolation by defending against rejection through her "I
always knew you'd do this to me" attitude. Resistance also takes the form
of denying or minimizing her limitations due to her handicaps; i.e., she
refuses to live or work among handicapped people. On the other hand, she
demands special attention for her disabilities in dealing with others.*

*As a therapist I concentrate on the possibility of her integrating the pain-
ful effects of a rejecting, exploiting family and reparenting herself through
her own strength and relationship with me.*

E. *Countertransference aspects include my own fear that the reality of her physical and financial difficulties, as well as her isolation, are indeed insurmountable. Does her getting better frighten me that she will drain me in the process? Do I fear my own commitment to the enormous energy I need to solve my life problems? How much do I consider her plight simply a difference of degree in relation to my own struggle with living a significant life among and without others?*

Question: How much are psychogenic factors a part of a 22-month-old youngster's developing rheumatic arthritis?

In addition, how much do psychogenic factors also contribute to her eye condition? Since treatment, her eye condition has improved to the amazement of the opthalmalogist. Also, her agency has recognized her increasing ability to take on more responsibility due to her increased physical and emotional strength.

This case history presented by Gladys Natchez, Ph.D.

Patient Interview

Erving Polster, Ph.D.

Doctor: What's it like for you to be here?

Patient: Like you said before, my heart's not quite where it belongs.

Doctor: What do you think it would take?

Patient: I think for you to start to talk to me.

Doctor: Should I tell you a story?

Patient: No.

Doctor: Should I tell you about my life, or where I come from, or what I'm interested in now, or what would you like?

Patient: That would be easy if you did that.

Doctor: You object to things which are easy?

Patient: Not really, no.

Doctor: It's like most things won't do.

Patient: No, not now.

Doctor: Okay, I pass. Tell me what you'd like.

Patient: Well, I think there are two parts that go on for me now. There is the curious part that would like you to go on with your discussion of before, and then I could remain the therapist too and take it in. And there's a part that would like the contact to begin.

Doctor: Well, can you feel the contact already beginning?

Patient: Yeah.

Doctor: Can you describe how you feel that?

Patient: Well, I feel you're aware of how uneasy I am.

Doctor: Oh, you feel I'm aware of how uneasy you are.

Patient: I'm aware of it.

Doctor: Actually, that wasn't my awareness.

Patient: It's my awareness.

Doctor: It's your awareness, but I was aware of something else.

Patient: What?

Doctor: I was aware how excited you are. Just a different perspective.

Patient: Scared.

Doctor: Scared. So what does your scared quality say?

Patient: I wish I could run away.

Doctor: That would be quite something for you to be able to do, wouldn't it?

Patient: Yeah.

Doctor: What do you feel now?

Patient: I really want to run away.

Doctor: Let's see if you can imagine yourself running away. Just visualize yourself running away.

Patient: Right through those curtains and back home.

Doctor: Did you run all the way?

Patient: If I was through the curtains and back home without anything happening in between.

Doctor: Magic.

Patient: Magic.

Doctor: Blessed magic.

Patient: It would be nice.

Doctor: Yes. Suppose we would make a blessing on magic, how would we do it?

Patient: I'm not sure I know what you mean?

Doctor: Well, let's suppose you were a clergyman, and you were making a blessing on magic. How would you do it?

Patient: It's hard to imagine. I don't usually bless things.

Doctor: You don't usually imagine either?

Patient: I imagine a lot, I imagine a whole lot.

Doctor: What sorts of things do you imagine?

Patient: Well, being in pretty places. Mostly that I think. Where things are quiet and peaceful.

Doctor: Can you see one of those places now?

Patient: Yeah.

Doctor: Would you describe it to me?

Patient: I think the sky is very blue and cloudless, and it's kind of flat and easy to see and move around on. There are lots of flowers, and things are just very easy.

Doctor: What do you feel as you say that?

Patient: A wishing of being there.

Doctor: What do you prefer there as compared to here?

Patient: Only that it feels problem-free and peaceful, and this is scary and hard.

Doctor: What is scary and hard here?

Patient: I think several things, just being here and still having things to do and work on and unfinished business.

Doctor: Are you doing that?

Patient: At this moment, I'm still feeling my heart pound.

Doctor: Okay. Well, let's go to your heart pound. That sounds interesting. You smile when you say that.

Patient: I didn't think I'd be so scared so long.

Doctor: Oh, uh-huh, so you're still scared? Well, see if you can pay attention to being scared and feel what it's like, not what you imagine it would be like, but what it's actually like.

Patient: It's really trembly all over, with my heart pounding and being trembly all over.

Doctor: Tremble, tremble. Okay, pay attention to the tremble. See what's it like.

Patient: It's tight. It's tight and bumpy.

Doctor: Where is it tight?

Patient: In my arms.

Doctor: In your arms? Where?

Patient: In my shoulders, my upper arms.

Doctor: Well, pay attention to the tightness in your upper arms and see what you might want to do.

Patient: Drop this microphone.

Doctor: You could do that you know.

Patient: I wish there was a way to.

Doctor: (attempting to place microphone so that patient does not have to hold it): That's worse. . . . Is that any better?

Patient: Yeah. Better for my arms anyway.

Doctor: Well, one thing at a time. We'll get to the rest of you later. Okay, so your arms are better, right?

Patient: Yeah.

Doctor: Didn't take very much, did it? But you just didn't think of it, did you?

Patient: No.

Doctor: Let's see, what else are you overlooking? What are you feeling now?

Patient: Now I'm starting to get a little curious.

Doctor: See if you can exercise your curiosity.

Patient: That was a kind of curiously stimulating question or statement you made a minute ago.

Doctor: Which one?

Patient: Well, now your arms feel better, we'll get to the rest of you later.

Doctor: That's right, that's what I said. So now I want to hear more about your curiosity.

Patient: I wouldn't know how. . . .

Doctor: Just keep right on going. No way not to. . . . No way not to get to the other parts of you. Now, what are you aware of now?

Patient: The tension going out, really going out of my upper arms.

Doctor: Going out. Going out of it. Okay. What do you feel around your mouth?

Patient: A little dry.

Doctor: Feel any movement there?

Patient: No, I feel movement in my nose really.

Doctor: In your nose? Let's see it.

Patient: Yeah, that's where I can feel it.

Doctor: Yeah, I can see it now. Continue to let your nose move. What's that like for you?

Patient: It's something I like to do.

Doctor: Do you do it much?

Patient: I don't think I was ever aware of it, when I do it and when I don't do it. I don't usually pay that much attention to it, my movements that way.

Doctor: You have other things on your mind.

Patient: Usually.

Doctor: What's more likely to be on your mind?

Patient: All the things I think I have to do. How I'm going to get through the day. A lot of work things, heavy things.

Doctor: Very, very burdened, right?

Patient: More or less, yeah.

Doctor: Can you say that without moving your nose?

Patient: No, no.

Doctor: What's the difficulty?

Patient: I get tight in the throat when I say that, and that's different from moving my nose.

Doctor: You can't mix them, right?

Patient: No, I don't really think so.

Doctor: Well, let's see what happens if you try.

Patient: Well, one is a kind of very sad feeling, and the other is a kind of more adventurous feeling, and, they don't kind of go together.

Doctor: They don't go together. Well, what does the sad part of you say to the adventurous part of you?

Patient: Well, I usually take precedence.

Doctor: Uh-huh. And what does the adventurous part say in response?

Patient: Kind of doesn't say much, just quiets down and stays quiet.

Doctor: Up to now, you're characterizing her. I'd like you to let her speak now. What does the adventurous part say now to the sad part that says, "I usually take precedence?"

Patient: Okay.

Doctor: Okay? Some adventure. What are you feeling now?

Patient: Some adventure.

Doctor: What part of you says that?

Patient: The adventurer.

Doctor: So is the sad part in ascendancy now?

Patient: A little bit.

Doctor: A little bit. And the adventurous?

Patient: I think that's there too. I think that's there a little bit.

Doctor: There too. What does the adventurous say?

Patient: It's like, which one of us is really gonna do it today.

Doctor: Yeah. You smiled a little about that.

Patient: Yeah.

Doctor: What amused you?

Patient: It just came out very spontaneously. I don't know what amused me really.

Doctor: What does the sad part say?

Patient: We'll see.

Doctor: What's the tone of her saying that?

Patient: Heavy.

Doctor: Does she know the results?

Patient: At this moment, no.

Doctor: At last she doesn't know.

Patient: Don't say it so loud.

Doctor: Don't say it so loud.

Patient: She usually knows.

Doctor: Yes, but this time she doesn't know. How do you feel about that? You look like your breathing gained amplitude.

Patient: Yes, it's kind of frightening.

Doctor: Frightening? Stay with that feeling, see whether it's all fright.

Patient: Part of it's fright, and part of it is anticipation.

Doctor: What's happening now?

Patient: Getting tense back in the shoulder.

Doctor: And now you don't even have a microphone.

Patient: No.

Doctor: Stay with the tension in your shoulders and see what comes there.

Patient: I think that gets back to the feeling of heaviness again.

Doctor: Could you speak heavily? (inaudible)

Patient: Just feels very heavy.

Doctor: Can you make your voice sound heavy?

Patient: Just feels very, very heavy.

Doctor: Sounds more weighted down than heavy.

Patient: Yeah.

Doctor: So let your voice speak back to the heaviness.

Patient: I think the heaviness is kind of, you know, makes me voiceless and. . . .

Doctor: Well, let your voice say to the heaviness, "You make me voiceless. It's almost like I don't exist when you're on me." Say it.

Patient: It's almost like I don't exist when you're on me.

Doctor: Okay. What more do you want to say to the heaviness.

Patient: It kind of crushes out everything.

Doctor: Could you say, "You crush out everything?"

Patient: You kind of crush out everything.

Doctor: Can you say it again?

Patient: You kind of crush out everything.

Doctor: Yeah. What do you feel now?

Patient: Scary.

Doctor: Yeah, what else?

Patient: Sad.

Doctor: What else? I could feel the breath coming at times.

Patient: Yeah.

Doctor: Alright, speak again to the heaviness. How she crushes you.

Patient: She really, really keeps me down.

Doctor: Tell her, "You really keep me down."

Patient: You really keep me down.

Doctor: Are you saying it just the way you want to?

Patient: All I really feel I have the kind of energy in my voice has to kind of answer it back.

Doctor: Okay. Try this. Take a deep breath and say, "You crush me down." With your full air.

Patient: You crush me down.

Doctor: Yeah, it was a little different, wasn't it? Did you feel the difference?

Patient: It was less constricted.

Doctor: Would you be willing to try it one more time? Take a deep breath and say it.

Patient: You keep me down.

Doctor: What's happening inside. You feel any tremors?

Patient: No.

Doctor: What do you feel?

Patient: Some relief.

Doctor: What?

Patient: Some relief. I don't feel as teary.

Doctor: You don't feel as scared?

Patient: As teary.

Doctor: So that helped, didn't it.

Patient: Yeah.

Doctor: See if you can blow so that I can feel it. . . . I feel it, do you believe that.

Patient: If you say so.

Doctor: Oh, I might say so and you might not believe it.

Patient: Yeah, I believe it.

Doctor: You believe it. How do you feel about that?

Patient: That you can feel it?

Doctor: Yes. You can't believe that I was asking that?

Patient: No.

Doctor: Why not?

Patient: I usually think I can anticipate things, and when I can't I don't quite believe them.

Doctor: What's happening right now? You look like you might get a series of surprises if you're not careful.

Patient: Yeah.

Doctor: Yes, and what do you feel as you smile?

Patient: Curiosity.

Doctor: Alright. Would you express your curiosity this time.

Patient: Now I'm curious that you're into surprises.

Doctor: Oh. What, like what might be the next surprise?

Patient: Yeah.

Doctor: Well, I surprised you, didn't I. Now you surprise me.

Patient: That's harder.

Doctor: Well, I wouldn't ask you to do anything easy. You already said you didn't like easy things.

Patient: I wouldn't know what to do to surprise you. I really wouldn't.

Doctor: If that were true, that would surprise me.

Patient: How's that?

Doctor: I don't believe that you don't know anything that would surprise me. Even though you might not do it, see if you can think of something you might do that might surprise me.

Patient: I can't think of anything.

Doctor: Oh, bless you.

Patient: You're back to blessings again, huh?

Doctor: Yes. Okay. I guess it's my turn again. What are you feeling now?

Patient: I'm waiting.

Doctor: You're waiting for me to surprise you?

Patient: Yeah.

Doctor: That must be a vulnerable position to be in. Who knows what I might do. I'm a very strange man. Are you willing to depend on my surprising you, whatever way I want to.

Patient: Not entirely.

Doctor: I can see your heart fluttering. Does that surprise you?

Patient: Yeah.

Doctor: Don't tell anyone.

Patient: Now I'm not so sure I want to hear any more of these surprises.

Doctor: It's not all pleasure, right? But did that bother you?

Patient: Yeah.

Doctor: What bothered you about it?

Patient: I didn't know what you were going to see next.

Doctor: Oh. What's your objection to my seeing whatever I see.

Patient: Maybe something I don't want you to see.

Doctor: Can you think of anything you wouldn't want me to see? I'm not asking you to say what it is. Can you think of anything you wouldn't want me to see?

Patient: Yeah.

Doctor: Did you think of it? Do you expect I'll be able to?

Patient: Not if I don't let you.

Doctor: That doesn't quite answer my question does it? Because you might let me? Is there any danger of that?

Patient: There's always a danger in that.

Doctor: How do you guard against it?

Patient: I run away.

Doctor: Run away? How do you run away?

Patient: Either remove myself physically or. . . .

Doctor: I mean right now, how would you run away?

Patient: On a head trip, I guess.

Doctor: Do you want to do that?

Patient: Not really.

Doctor: What would you like to do?

Patient: I guess continue.

Doctor: Continue what?

Patient: Well, I guess the part that was peaking my curiosity.

Doctor: Which was what?

Patient: Well, partly I think it was wanting to know about the surprises and partly not wanting to know. I feel very two ways about it.

Doctor: All right, how do you suppose you can find another surprise? You think I know? I could obviously surprise you. That wasn't what I had in mind. How about if we turn things around and you ask me some questions.

Patient: Well, I think I would really like to know what you think about me.

Doctor: I feel warmed by you. There's a certain special _____ that I feel. I feel distanced. I feel like you would really dig being more open, but you're afraid of me.

Patient: Yeah.

Doctor: Is that true?

Patient: Yeah.

Doctor: That's some of what I think about you.

Patient: And?

Doctor: More?

Patient: I'll tell you when to stop.

Doctor: Okay. I miss you as I'm talking to you. I would like you to feel more, I sense a spunkiness in you which is neutralized. I think that you can spunk me out, or spunk me in, which ever way you want to put it. When I saw that I was going to be working with you, I was scared, because I saw in a case record that you were physically handicapped, and I have a son who has cerebral palsy. So I know something about that aspect of life. Not like your life, I don't know your life. I've seen some of what he can do and some of what he can't do. And I've seen my ogre and my beauty, and a whole range of things with him, that have been very important in my life. So there's something reminiscent for me, a part of my life, in talking to you. But that's not in my mind as I talk to you. I feel as though you ostracize yourself. Like, you could have as vigorous a contact with me as anybody in this room, and you God damn well won't. And I'm put off by that, and I'm sorry about it. I would welcome you giving me more than I ask for. Want me to stop you?

Patient: Well, I'm kind of sorry about that too.

Doctor: About what?

Patient: About not giving you what you want, or more contact, because I really want to. But it's something I'm very afraid of. But I think right now I could do it more, or try to do it more, knowing that part about you. Because now I feel that you have some special understanding of a special problem, that I don't feel most people have. So I hold back that part of myself, really, and hide. Well, now it makes me want to know my own feelings for you. The messages I have gotten from my own parents have been very much of being ostracized. I think I do it myself, and yet, what I hear from you now is something very warm and different about your son, and it makes me feel that there are different kinds of parents.

Doctor: Well, I don't know, I've been a shit with my son. But what I've experienced was you ostracizing me. Not me ostracizing you.

Patient: I don't know how to do that.

Doctor: You don't know how to do what?

Patient: I don't know how I do that.

Doctor: Okay. You do it by giving me only what I ask for. What I'd like you to do when you talk to me, when you think you're done, give me one more sentence.

Patient: It's hard to do too, because I have always felt that I talked too much, really talked too much. I've felt that I have talked my way in and out and away from relationships, rather than into them, or out of them. And I've gotten frightened of that too, because sometimes I feel the only thing I have to rely on is words, and often not the right words.

Doctor: Fantastic! Keep going. See if you can find the right words. The right words are the words that come out of you. Say whatever comes to you now.

Patient: I don't want you to feel that I'm ostracizing you or in any or most attempts I make out of a relationship, and yet it does come out that way, often without my awareness. That is what is very painful, and I think I sometimes feel that not talking will prevent that, really prevent that.

Doctor: Who were you looking at when you were just now talking?

Patient: I was closing my eyes.

Doctor: Yes. So let's see what happens if you keep your eyes open, if you look at me as you're talking.

Patient: I was kind of closing my eyes, because it kind of felt like a very global, universal, full-encompassing experience.

Doctor: You would like to get into that.

Patient: It takes me a long time to separate individuals out from it.

Doctor: Right on. Lead up several statements to me beginning with the word you.

Patient: You are listening to me and I appreciate that. When I say listening I mean really hearing me, and that's very important to me. You've already told me something positive about myself, and that makes it a little safer to try to be open with you. You also make me wrinkle my nose.

Doctor: You also what?

Patient: Make me wrinkle my nose.

Doctor: See if you can wrinkle your nose more. Okay, what do you see as you look at me now?

Patient: You're smiling at me.

Doctor: What do you feel?

Patient: I feel relaxed.

Doctor: Give me more detail. That more relaxed is in the same mold of giving me just what I ask for.

Patient: Well, I feel ready at the kind of. . . .

Doctor: You look like you're leaning toward me. You know psychotherapists take that as a very good sign. I don't want to do that.

Patient: Well, I feel ready to continue, and less ready to run.

Doctor: How does it feel to lean toward me as you are?

Patient: It was very natural. I haven't even thought about it.

Doctor: I know you did it spontaneously, but how does it feel? Does it make a difference?

Patient: Comfortable.

Doctor: What's a little movement toward a person.

Patient: I kind of take the positive or the good things I do for granted, and don't give them any special value.

Doctor: Exactly, exactly. So for you to move toward me in your position, is like if another person came over and touched them.

Patient: It's a small step. I think it's a small step. And if you're wrinkling your nose and blowing at me. . . .

Doctor: No, it's your mouth that you express a lot with, your mouth.

Patient: Right.

Doctor: I don't know what it is. I would like to. I don't think you're tuned into it enough to be able to do it now.

Patient: No, no.

Doctor: Okay. Now you tell me a story . . . about yourself. . . . You looked puzzled. Is that a strange question?

Patient: Yeah.

Doctor: What's strange about it?

Patient: I wouldn't know what story to tell you. I really wouldn't.

Doctor: That is so much bullshit. I can't believe how astute you are in that reflex, the nihilistic reflex. The story only means some event in your life. You can tell me the story if you want to. You don't have to, but you could do it.

Patient: I think of . . . I always think of problems, sad stories. I don't think people really want to hear them. So when someone says, "Tell me something about yourself," it doesn't seem very good or positive or exciting.

Doctor: The problem is whether it's interesting, not whether it's good or bad. You can tell me the saddest, most painful experience in your life, and if it were interesting, I would be glad you told me. And if it were dull, I would be sorry. You could tell me the most beautiful happy experience, and if it were dull I wouldn't care. The question is, can you be interesting.

Patient: I don't know.

Doctor: Well, let's try it out. Let's not go to the story first. See if you can tell me something that I'll remember five years from now.

Patient: A very funny incident comes to mind. It's about something that happened to me a long time ago. I think I was seventeen years old. That was during one of my first trips into the hospital. They had a conference of doctors to do an examination, and at seventeen I was kind of shy about any exposure, and the doctors were very matter-of-fact about it, exposing patients. They didn't care whether you were seventeen or seventy. They gave me two straight muslin binders, one across the bottom and one across the top.

Doctor: I'll remember that one. What do you feel now?

Patient: I still don't know why I told that story.

Doctor: Why not? Because it popped into your head. That's the kind that's interesting. It's just a fundamentally interesting story.

Patient: Yeah.

Doctor: Well you were pleased for a moment, you look delighted, but don't worry about it. You'll feel bad about it after a while.

Patient: Thanks a lot. Now you're putting me on.

Doctor: Yes, that's true. Well, you want to stop there?

Patient: Are we ready to stop?

Doctor: Well, I don't know whether we're ready to. It's time to. How do you feel about it?

Patient: I just felt we were getting started.

Doctor: That's right. Getting started, discovering if you can get started is half the struggle. To really work through to what it takes to get started, you know, we've been doing it for some time. It took us a number of exchanges to get started, and that's the way it is every place. So if you give up on getting started, because you haven't already got started, that's a severe handicap. It's a worse handicap than your physical handicap. But when you can discover what it takes to get started, then you really discovered something. I realize that I'm being a little bit sermonistic, but I mean it.

Patient: Yeah. I know you mean it. I really do know that.

Doctor: Let's do stop.

Discussion of Session—Conformance to Usual Style
Erving Polster

The similarities and differences of this session when compared with my "usual style" follow. It is *almost* unnecessary to say that my "usual style" has great range within it, and that often my work would have much common ground with this session and at other times I would be hardly recognizable as the same therapist. Nevertheless, here we go.

1. Similarities

a. I commonly answer questions when they seem simply human questions calling for simple human answer. There are times, of course, when questions feel tricky or avoidant, but I like to avoid the over-stylized form involved in turning everything back to the patient. Therefore, for me to have answered the question when she asked what I thought of her was in character and, in this instance, an event of great leverage.

b. I, as in this session, do foster the natural direction of specific feelings, statements, or bodily movements of the individual. For example, if the patient's "heaviness" makes her voiceless, it is common for me to encourage a dialogue between her and her heaviness, and thereby to move toward the relief she felt in this session and the accompanying perspective she felt about her own powers and her liveliness. Or, I commonly take certain key words or phrases quite seriously and follow them through. As, for example, when she expressed disbelief about anything she can't "anticipate," it seemed only natural for me to follow that up by extending her curiosity and facing her fear of surprise. For me to note her acceptance of my surprising her and to suggest she surprise me is also in character, because I commonly suggest people do what they might otherwise be inclined only to talk about. Do it is a common instruction, usually, though not always, through fantasy.

This patient seemed particularly distrustful of her excitement. Her felt heartbeat, flutteriness, and excitement all indicated a pent-up quality requiring release. The release took on several preparatory forms, as one might read in the transcript, finally resulting in an exchange of stories between us and a readiness to move further together. I try to stay with people step by step including small, as well as large, units of experience.

c. Sudden re-orientations are common for me. In this session I had one when I realized this woman was the ostracizing person rather than the ostracized. She probably had never thought of herself that way, and that kind of surprise adds dimension and power to a person's life.

d. I am characteristically gently brash and sarcastic, sometimes in humor, sometimes in irony, but I am almost always seen nevertheless as loving and patient. I felt much warmth for this woman and I think it was evident to her, and that is similar to many of my therapeutic experiences.

2. Differences

a. When I have more time to work with a person and where the experience is not as telescoped as in a public demonstration, I would be likely to give the person more space in which to unfold. I would be likely to listen longer, have more silent times, and be more oriented to her independently creating something through her struggle. I was more immediately active than I would usually be. Consequently, there were more themes left undeveloped than would be usual. There was enough undeveloped for several future sessions. The fabric of possibilities was very rich.

d. Usually in my work there would be more content to deal with. This content would then be relatable to the excitement levels in a fuller way. I like to evoke content and feel that sessions which deal only with process, feelings now, excitement, etc., are incomplete, though they may be valuable as a part of the greater whole. An example of content was her story about the doctors. There would have been more to say about that if not for the need to end.

c. Correspondingly, I like to deal with people's sense of unfinished business which in this session was only hinted at, once in referring to the fact that talking too much distanced her from people, another in alluding to being ostracized by her parents, and a third in her exposure at a doctors' conference when she was seventeen. Any one of these allusions could be a basis for at least a whole session.

d. I rarely have such abrupt endings. I am likely to be better tuned into the relationship of time to that which is happening, or to just run over, if necessary. In this instance I didn't want to take her more deeply into the memory of the doctors at this late point in our work. It seemed too important to allow us to get caught in the middle of it, and the point we did reach seemed valid for a public demonstration, not disturbing, and with some illuminating qualities for her.

Chapter 9

TRANSACTIONAL ANALYSIS:

SOME DEVELOPMENTS IN THE RELATIONSHIP BETWEEN TRANSACTIONAL ANALYSIS AND PSYCHOANALYSIS

Harris B. Peck, M.D.

Harris Peck, M.D.

Harris Peck is Professor of Psychiatry at Albert Einstein College of Medicine. A graduate of the William A. White Psychoanalytic Institute, he was one of the founders of the American Group Psychotherapy Association, and for ten years he served as Editor of the International Journal of Group Psychotherapy. He is a Provisional Teaching Member of the International Transactional Analysis Association.

Eric Berne, the founder of transactional analysis, was well acquainted with the principles and methods of psychoanalysis. Although denied certification as a psychoanalyst, Berne was in training at both the New York and San Francisco Psychoanalytic Institutes (with interruptions during the war years) from 1941 to 1956, when, according to him, he and the psychoanalytic movement "officially parted company on the friendliest of terms." Berne began his practice of group therapy while in the army in 1945 and 1946, and the first of his papers on the subject appeared in 1953. In 1957 he began work on a series of papers and books which have been characterized as reflecting his determination "to add something new to psychoanalysis" and to develop "a new approach to psychotherapy. . . ." (1) The "new approach" was ostensibly designed to meet the need for a conceptual framework which would lend itself to his group studies.

This presentation will draw on some of Berne's writings from the time when he was developing and setting down his first ideas about transactional analysis and will suggest that there are some indications that, despite his "official" departure from psychoanalysis, Berne continued to be substantially influenced by the psychoanalytic viewpoint and initially saw transactional analysis as a complementary body of knowledge and practice. However, some of the later developments in transactional analysis by both Berne and others influenced by him, suggest a progressive movement into areas which Berne had initially indicated were primarily the province of psychoanalysis, as well as some innovations in sectors of psychiatry in which orthodox psychoanalysis had few pretensions and little success. Some illustrative material drawn from the literature will be presented to demonstrate these developments in the field.

According to Berne, transactional analysis was intended as a theory of personality and social action as well as a clinical method of psychotherapy. Berne's involvement with group therapy may have contributed to his emphasis on the social and interpersonal, and, as with Adler and Sullivan, led to a focus on consciousness and on the ego. Berne was influenced by Federn in developing his concept of "ego states" and defined them as "coherent systems of thought and feelings manifested operationally by corresponding patterns of behavior." Transactional analysis is based on the analysis of all possible transactions between people on the basis of such specifically defined ego states. A transaction consists of a stimulus and a response which comprise a "unit of social action in which each party gains."

Berne's early papers (3, 4) on transactional analysis reflect a progression from the structural analysis of ego states to the analysis of transactions in a therapy group. By 1961 he had incorporated the major elements of his theory and therapeutic approach into a book, *Transactional Analysis and*

Psychotherapy. (2) In the preface to this volume, Berne says that ". . . structural analysis is a more general theory than orthodox analysis," and suggests that ". . . psychoanalysis easily finds its place methodologically as a highly specialized aspect of structural analysis." Structural analysis is concerned with the segregation and analysis of ego states and must, according to Berne, precede transactional analysis, which often involves several people and is designed to achieve "social control." Berne explains that such control is achieved through assisting the patient to bring his behavior under control of the Adult ego state, which then acts as the "executive" which decides when to release Child or Parent behavior.

Berne refers to the treatment of a particular patient in which, after the goal of structural analysis had been attained, three possible options were available to the patient: (1) to terminate treatment; (2) to go on in transactional analysis in a therapy group; or (3) to undertake psychoanalysis. He reports that the patient initially terminated, but "eventually returned for psychoanalytic treatment." He suggests that the "previous structural analysis stood him in good stead . . ." and "averted the impending ruin which might well have overtaken the patient during the preliminary phase of orthodox psychoanalysis, if that had been the initial procedure." At this stage in the development of TA, Berne seems to hold to the view that psychoanalysis methodologically is indeed only a "highly specialized aspect of structural analysis." In his therapeutic approach during this period he stresses the need to do a thorough structural analysis. Once this is achieved, he suggests that it is possible to proceed with either transactional analysis or psychoanalysis. In practice, as reflected in many of his procedural directions and case illustrations, he seemed to favor individual psychoanalytic treatment for the latter phases of therapy.

In discussing the therapy of the neuroses, Berne suggests that social control and symptomatic relief may be attained through structural analysis. He indicates that such relief and control resemble the "transference cure" of psychoanalysis, which "in structural terms means the substitution of the therapist for the original parent, and in transactional terms . . . the therapist permits the patient 'to play the game' in a more benign form than the original parent did or does." All of the above procedures are distinguished by Berne from "psychoanalytic cure," which means "deconfusion of the Child with a largely decontaminated Adult as a therapeutic ally." Such decontamination is the function of structural analysis, which is "to decontaminate the Adult as a preparation for psychoanalytic treatment. . . ." "Decontamination," or helping the patient develop boundaries between his ego states so that he can think clearly, is one of the prime functions of structural analysis.

In the chapter on group therapy in this 1961 volume, there is little to suggest that during this period Berne was making much use of the group for "psychoanalytic cure" or for deconfusion of the Child. There are, on the other hand, numerous references to the group's role in bringing about "social control and symptomatic improvement."

Finally, in a brief chapter in "regression analysis," Berne describes a technique "for the readjustment and the reintegration of the total personality," which is also presumably the goal of psychoanalysis. This procedure of deconfusing the Child in the presence of a fully commissioned Parent and Adult, he says, is achieved in psychoanalysis by the device of free association. Berne is concerned with the drawbacks of this technique, because "a great deal depends on the interpretive ability of the therapist." Instead, he suggests that "the logical development of transactional analysis is a direct appeal to the Child in the waking state." The approach involves "not the Adult talking about the Child, but the Child talking about itself." Berne compares the procedure to the abreaction of Freud and the "gut memories" of Kubie. The primary instruction Berne gives for employing the technique is that "the therapist plays the role of the Child of five, and the patient is instructed that he be whatever age they choose under the age of eight."

In most of the case illustrations in the chapter on regression analysis, the procedure is carried out within the context of individual treatment. In one instance reference is made to the use of the couch. A page or so is devoted to the use of the technique in group therapy, and this is described as yielding "equally interesting results." After a twenty-minute trial in one group, the entire group voted against repeating the procedure and it was not again attempted for several weeks, although Berne reports that it introduced "many new things to talk about in concurrent individual therapy." Understandably, Berne refers to regression analysis as being ". . . at present, the farthest frontier of transactional analysis. Everything known about it so far is tentative, and any further statements would be ill-advised." It would appear then that in 1961 Berne was not yet satisfied that he had found a way to carry out some of the goals and functions of psychoanalysis within the context of the group transactional approach. He seemed to be saying that theoretically it should be possible, but in the meantime he was using and encouraging the use of these new methods for more limited goals and to prepare patients for psychoanalytic procedures.*

As late as 1966, in his book the *Principles of Group Treatment,* (5) Berne outlines eight therapeutic operations which form the technique of transactional analysis. The first six operations have as their primary object "the cathexis and decontamination of the Adult." When this is achieved the

*In a personal communication Jacqui Schiff points out that for Berne the essence of structural analysis centered about changing the flow of psychological energy, and that he saw psychoanalysis as being more concerned with content.

therapist has several options. He may move on to "crystalization," offering the patient "immediate relief and social control, which is the terminal phase of pure transactional analysis." The therapist can, however, postpone crystalization until the Child has been deconfused through the process of "interpretation." Deconfusion of the Child was related by Berne to "psychoanalytic cure." He indicated that such cure could be more easily achieved by the therapist with the ally of the patient's Adult decontaminated through the methods of transactional analysis in the therapy group. This 1966 posture does not seem essentially different from his view in 1961 that the "symptomatic relief and social control" achieved through transactional analysis are valuable outcomes in their own right as well as serving to prepare the patient for psychoanalytic-type "interpretation" which consists of "decoding, detoxifying and rectifying the confusion residing in the Child."*

The achievement of "social control," which Berne, in his earlier writings, indicates may be the "terminal phase of transactional analysis," is quite different from the goals of an "autonomy contract," which according to Holloway, (6) means that the person is capable of the full use of options . . . and that specifically excluded is the option of a single fixed dependent relationship. The implication is that in achieving an autonomy contract, the patient will both resolve his maladaptive ties to parental figures from his past and move beyond a "transference cure" associated primarily with "permission" transactions with a therapist who is perceived as a more powerful parent.

In these terms a social control contract may be the end point for some patients. Others may employ it as a base on which to build or to bring about changes toward the fulfillment of an autonomy contract in which the patient will both free himself from his ongoing dependency and establish the conditions for achieving intimacy. Thus, the progression from social control to autonomy roughly parallels the Freudian ascent through the levels of psychosexual development and moves transactional analysis into a realm which Berne's earlier writings seem to reserve for psychoanalysis. The developments within the transactional analysis movement from the theoretical and technical level reflected in *Transactional Analysis and Psychotherapy* (1961) and *Principles of Group Treatment* (1966) rest on a number of significant later contributions by Berne, his disciples, and colleagues. Most relevant in this connection are the developments of the script matrix and the refinement of script analysis. Theoretical elaboration of

---

*Steiner, in a personal communication, notes that in Berne's actual practice he advanced beyond the time lag of his published writings, and that by 1966 he seldom used transactional analysis to prepare patients for psychoanalysis.

Berne's ideas about scripts as well as improvements and innovations in therapeutic work in this area are particularly notable in the works of Claude Steiner, Bob and Mary Goulding, and William Holloway.

Steiner, a psychologist who received the first of the Eric Berne Memorial Scientific Awards for his development of the script matrix, initially presented his idea to the San Francisco Transactional Analysis Seminar conducted by Berne, and published the material under the title of "Script and Counterscript" in 1966. (7) The script matrix as developed by Steiner is a relatively simple diagram showing the parental directives which form the basis of the script. Although Steiner followed the general idea originally proposed by Berne, (8) he specified what each ego state in the parent does and delineated the channels of communication to the offspring. In effect, he succeeded in formulating a plausible transactional diagram showing the parental Child as the source of behavior disturbances, which, as Berne implied, seemed to indicate how such behaviors might be changed through transactional rather than psychoanalytic methods.

In evaluating his own contribution, Steiner (9) states that ". . . the script matrix could not have been constructed without previous knowledge of the ego states, without which the diverse channels of attributions and injunctions in scripts could not be understood." Steiner's 1966 paper, according to Berne, (8) marked "the first appearance in print of the concepts of counterscript and injunction."* (The injunction concept refers to prohibitions or negative commands from a parent, generally covert and usually disavowed by the giver.) Steiner acknowledges the influence of learning-psychology, and in his original article refers to the injunction reaction as "negatively reinforcing." He goes on to state that, "Negative reinforcement is known to be most effective in shaping avoidant behavior extremely resistant to extinction."

As will be noted in the discussion which follows, the concepts of script, counterscript, and injunction embodied in Steiner's script matrix idea appear to have exerted a major influence on Berne himself, and also on both the theoretical orientation and therapeutic approach of workers like the Gouldings and Holloway. The Gouldings, both of whom participated in some of Berne's early seminars, acknowledged that they were also much influenced by Fritz Perls and gestalt therapy. Both influences are reflected in the development of their treatment approach which emphasizes the concepts of decision and redecision. (10, 11, 12) In these concepts, the Gouldings, although stressing the impact of the injunction on the patient's

---

*In Berne's final, posthumously published volume, *What Do You Say After You Say Hello?*, Berne says of the script matrix, "Its value cannot be overestimated, containing as it does the programming for a whole human life as well as indicating how to change it."

script, call attention to "another element . . . that we think Berne and his close followers missed." This element (the decision) pertains to the deceptively simple observation that the injunction's power to influence depends on the Child's agreement or "decision" to obey that injunction. It then follows, as stated by the Gouldings, ".. . that if the Child made a decision, he could, and often did, change it later . . . ," i.e., make a "redecision."

The techniques employed by the Gouldings in assisting patients to make a redecision involve hearing about the patient's initial ". . . early decision in some gestalt work when he is in his Child ego state in an early scene. . . ." This statement and other descriptions of the Goulding's technique are obviously very similar to Berne's (2) view of regression analysis, which involved ". . . not the Adult talking about the Child, but the Child talking about itself."

The Gouldings' effectiveness in utilizing Berne's idea of regression analysis appears to rest on several concepts and techniques in the field, some of which had not been developed when Berne wrote *Transactional Analysis and Psychotherapy* in 1961. Others were apparently either unknown to Berne or disregarded by him. We have already mentioned some of the significant theoretical and technical developments within the field of transactional analysis after Berne published his *Principles of Group Treatment* in 1966. We have noted Steiner's acknowledgement of the influence of learning theory on his contributions. Similarly the Gouldings freely allude to their indebtedness to Perls and gestalt therapy. It is beyond the scope of this presentation to review in detail the specific contributions and impact of the gestalt approach on the Gouldings and other contemporary transactional analysis practitioners, many of whom, like Holloway were trained and influenced by the Gouldings. However, a number of the elements derived largely from gestalt are clearly discernible.

The Gouldings link the making of a redecision to working with a patient who is in various degrees of "impasse."* In addition to a paper devoted solely to the subject of impasses, (13) Goulding in the most extensive presentation of his methods to date, in referring to the treatment of a patient, says, "Over weekends of intensive therapy we taught the patient the transactional analysis approach and worked with him concurrently in the gestalt approach, so that he could get through him impasse by making a redecision." Goulding does not specify which components of the "gestalt approach" he employs, but a review of his published discussions and case material reveals the use of several particular techniques closely identified

---

*Perls refers to an "impasse" in the following terms: (14) ". . . in life and especially in therapy we come to a sick point . . . to the point where we are stuck, to the impasse. The impasse occurs when we cannot produce our own support and when environmental support is not forthcoming."

with the work of Fritz Perls and his colleagues, although not necessarily unique to them.

A number of the techniques employed by gestalt therapists are outlined in a paper by Levitsky and Perls entitled "The Rules and Games of Gestalt Therapy." (15) Many of the techniques enumerated will be familiar to those who have had the opportunity of working with the Gouldings. Some of these are outlined below.

1. *The principle of the "now"*
2. *"It" versus "I" language*
3. *The awareness continuum*
4. *Changing questions into statements*
5. *Games of dialogue:* between the patient and some significant person from his past or current life, as in the so-called "double chair" or "empty chair" technique where the patient plays all the roles
6. *Making the rounds:* where the patient is asked to express a particular theme or feeling to every person in the group
7. *Unfinished business*
8. *"I take responsibility:"*
9. *Reversals*
10. *Rehearsal:* in preparation for actual social roles
11. *Exaggeration:* particularly of abortive, underdeveloped, or incomplete gestures
12. *May I feed you a sentence:* therapist proposes sentence to patient to "try it on for size"

It is evident that the development of the redecision component in transactional analysis could not have been introduced by the Gouldings in the seventies without the foundation laid down by Berne in the fifties and sixties. Steiner's script matrix and his formulation of the injunction and counterscript pointed the way to the emphasis on the decision, and Perls and gestalt therapy provided the final element needed to bring Berne's early efforts at script analysis to fruition. Gestalt approaches, such as those enumerated above, facilitated the work on regression analysis and encouraged interpretation in a group setting rather than in the analytically-oriented individual sessions which Berne apparently employed to carry some of his early patients beyond social control contracts and symptomatic relief.

Holloway (6) points out that "the autonomy contract . . . is the consequence of redecision;" that "with redecision the individual initiates a change and stops living a programmed life. . . . The individual begins to live a new life by kicking the old script and not adopting a new one."

The fulfillment of an autonomy contract thus appears to approximate some of the goals of treatment which Berne believed were sometimes attained by psychoanalysis. He apparently hoped to introduce a theory and method capable of achieving those goals in a more effective way through the introduction of a theoretical orientation which would be relevant to the practice of group therapy. This initial effort produced a very lucid teachable theory of personality and social action which did a great deal to illuminate and facilitate the work of the group therapist. A method of psychotherapy evolved which was capable of assisting the patient to fulfill a social control contract in a highly effective and impressive fashion. It also prepared some patients, but not all, for psychoanalysis.

Berne reminds the reader in *Principles of Group Treatment* (1966) that "psychoanalysis is the preferred treatment in those conditions it was designed for, namely, the transference neuroses, phobias, hysterias, and obsessional neuroses, together with the character abnormalities that have been developed instead of these diseases." Berne goes on to say that "Freud was right" and that psychoanalysis is not suitable for the treatment of other conditions. He then goes on to report that "transactional analysis, in qualified hands, has turned out to be a happy remedy for this defect in the treatment of conditions outside the 'classical triad.' " At this stage Berne was apparently sufficiently encouraged by his results to stake out a small claim to the "classical triad" as well, and he adds the note that, "Even in the transference neuroses, it may be the best treatment when circumstances do not favor the employment of the psychoanalytic procedure, as is the case in the majority of patients in psychotherapy."

In his introduction to the issue of the *Transactional Analysis Bulletin* devoted to reparenting in schizophrenia, (16) Berne again affirms "as a good Freudian" his agreement with Freud that psychoanalysis is unsuitable for other than the transference neuroses, and reminds us that Freud emphasized the unsuitability of psychoanalysis in the treatment of schizophrenia and its limited success in the cases of Anna O., the Rat Man, and the Wolf Man. Berns seems to imply that some of the latter day analysts may have made some useful contributions to the treatment of schizophrenia and specifically cites Federn, John Rosen, Fromm-Reichman, and Sullivan. Berne goes on to suggest that transactional analysis has shown some effectiveness in that merely having a "sorting system" (structural analysis) was of decisive benefit to schizophrenics. He also reports some results from game analysis in diminishing paranoia, and that script analysis revealed to some schizophrenics that they could become "completely self-sustaining."

Despite these encouraging results Berne says, "There was, however, one element still missing—so that medication in many cases was still necessary—this was the early (oral if you like) feeding, caressing, stroking, gurgling."

Berne then goes on to pay glowing tribute to the Schiffs who "took the final step, reparenting." He adds an even more definitive appraisal: "The contract was to cure schizophrenia, and it worked." Whether or not the Schiff approach represented in *The Cathexis Reader* (17) is indeed a cure for schizophrenia, other observers have confirmed Berne's enthusiastic statement that "it transformed schizophrenics from sick people doomed to lifetime hospitalization into well people with individual idiosyncrasies and personalities and perhaps even some residual disabilities, but well people."

If the initial reports of the Cathexis Institute over the past decade are supported by systematic research, it will be particularly significant in this day of the almost universal use of psychotrophic drugs for the schizophrenias. Schiff states in *The Cathexis Reader,* "It is significant to our philosophy that we use structure instead of medication. Moreover, we have found no justification for the utilization of medication related to the patient's welfare and social functioning." Although this posture is both unusual and generally viewed with some skepticism on the current psychiatric scene, a paper from the National Institute of Mental Health appearing in the January, 1977 issue of the *American Journal of Psychiatry* comes to conclusions which give some support to the Cathexis position. The paper is entitled "The Treatment of Acute Schizophrenia Without Drugs: An Investigation of Some Current Assumptions." (18) The authors examine the course of a group of acute schizophrenic patients at the National Institute of Health (NIH) for whom psychosocial treatment was emphasized and the use of medication sharply limited, and contrast it with that of similar patients receiving "usual treatment." Twenty-two patients receiving medication and twenty-seven drug-free patients had similar outcomes after one year. Patients receiving medication were significantly more likely to have a post-psychotic depression, and relapses during drug administration appeared to be of greater severity than in the drug-free group. The authors come to conclusions similar to that of Cathexis and of a growing number of workers in the field, that "our present day practice of immediate and massive pharmacological intervention may be exacting a price in terms of producing 'recovered' patients with great rigidity of character structure, who are less able to cope with subsequent life stresses." The "therapeutic environment" offered to drug-free patients in the above study was admittedly superior to that offered in most public institutions, but substantially below the level of protection, intensity, and specificity of the Cathexis Program.

The Cathexis approach to the treatment of schizophrenia, although based on T.A. theory and practice, introduces a number of creative elaborations of transactional analysis theory and a host of innovative therapeutic strategies. At Cathexis, schizophrenia is characterized as "a locked system of messages in the Parent, corresponding adaptations in the Child, and an

Adult which is misinformed." Passivity is seen as a major force in disrupting social functioning and is believed to result from unresolved symbiotic dependency. The treatment approach stresses reparenting and regressions. In reparenting the patient is helped to exclude or cut off old Parent programming and to incorporate a new Parent structure. Regression is supported and carried out by the patient on a contractual basis. The Schiffs originally provided such support within the context of a family in which some young adult schizophrenics were legally adopted. (19) In the current program regressive techniques are also employed on an outpatient basis which permits the patient to cathect Child for several hours daily three to five times a week, and seriously disturbed schizophrenics appear to be making it without hospitalization. The approach of Schiff and her co-workers at the Cathexis Institute incorporated much of the basic theory and treatment approaches already formulated by Berne, when they began their work with schizophrenics in 1965. The dimensions added by the Cathexis Institute grew out of their work with seriously disturbed psychotic individuals. As with Freud, the challenge of these difficult patients forced refinements in both theory and therapeutic technique, which have already enriched the entire field of transactional analysis and contributed significantly to the understanding and treatment of both psychotic and non-psychotic behavioral disturbances. The Cathexis Institute's approach to the treatment of schizophrenia outlined above draws heavily on concepts and techniques of regression. There are both differences and similarities to the "regression analysis" described by Berne in 1961. (2) Both Berne and Schiff are indebted to Freud's initial formulations on the subject.

As transactional analysis enters the third decade of its brief history, there would appear to be good reason to maintain the spirit of Berne's "friendly" departure from psychoanalysis. T.A. shares a common heritage both with Freud's more orthodox descendants and with such heretics as may be found among our gestalt colleagues, the Sullivanians, Adlerians, et al. The maintenance of neighborly relationships can only enrich the diverse branches of a family which traces its proud origins to the last decade of another century and may well enter the next one with continuing vigor and excitement.

References

1. Cheaney, W.D. Eric Berne: Biographical Sketch. *Transactional Analysis Journal,* 1:1, 1971.
2. Berne, E. *Transactional Analysis in Psychotherapy.* New York: Grove Press, 1971, 17.
3. Berne, E. Ego States in Psychotherapy. *American Journal of Psychotherapy,* 1957, 11:293–309.

4. Berne, E. Transactional Analysis: A New and Effective Method of Group Therapy. *American Journal of Psychotherapy,* 1958, 12: 735–309.
5. Berne, E., *Principles of Group Treatment.* New York: Oxford University Press, 1966.
6. Holloway, W.H. Beyond Permission. *TAJ,* 4:2, 15.
7. Steiner, C.M. Scripts and Counterscripts. *TA Bulletin,* 5:18, 133.
8. Berne, E. *What Do You Say After You Say Hello?* New York: Grove Press, 1972.
9. Steiner, C.M. Scripts Revisited. *TAJ,* 2:2, 62.
10. Goulding, R.L. Decisions in Script Formation. *TAJ,* 2:2, 62.
11. Goulding, R.L. New Directions in TA: Creating an Environment for Redecision and Change. *Progress in Group and Family Therapy.* Edited by Sager and Kaplan, Brunner Mazel. New York, 1972.
12. Goulding, R.L., and Goulding, M. Injunctions, Decisions and Redecisions. *TAJ,* 6:1, 7.
13. Goulding, R.L. Thinking and Feeling in TA: Three Impasses. *Voices,* 10:2.
14. Perls, F.S. Four Lectures. *Gestalt Therapy Now.* Edited by Fagan and Shepherd. Palo Alto, California: Science and Behavior Books, 1970.
15. Levitsky, A., and Perls, F.S. The Rules and Games of Gestalt Therapy. *Gestalt Therapy Now.* Edited by Fagan and Shepherd. Pala Alto, California: Science and Behavior Books, 1970.
16. Berne, E. Introduction to Reparenting in Schizophrenia. *TA Bulletin,* 8:31.
17. Schiff, J.L., et al. *The Cathexis Reader: Transactional Treatment of Psychosis.* New York: Harper & Row, 1975.
18. Carpenter, W.T., McClashon, T.H., and Strauss, J.S. The Treatment of Acute Schizophrenia Without Drugs: ANN Investigation and Some Current Assumptions, *American Journal of Psychiatry,* 134:1.
19. Schiff, J.L. *All My Children,* New York: M. Evans Publishing Co., 1970.

Chapter 10

PATIENT INTERVIEW

Case History: "Jean"

The patient defines her problems in life as centered about the behavior of others. She says, "I want to feel like a couple again. I don't want to grow old by myself." Similarly, in reference to her former marriage, she defines the difficulty as, "He was running around with someone else . . . he was not interested." Consequently, even though the patient experiences intense anxiety at times (she has made three suicidal gestures), it is often difficult for her to talk in terms of her own feelings and inner experience.

Although the patient has been coming out of her depression, the question remains as to what would help to decrease the possibility of further suicidal efforts.

The patient often presents her life as being overburdened and meaningless, especially when she is depressed, e.g., "I don't see any future for myself." Human relationships appear to be fraught with mistrust and emptiness. What therapeutic alternatives are available in response to the patient's feelings of desperation at such times?

A. The patient entered treatment complaining of depression, a feeling of emptiness and hopelessness about her life. In particular, she was fearful of loneliness and isolation after having broken up with her boyfriend in March. She had made two suicidal gestures in March and April following the breakup before entering treatment.

B. Jean is a 45-year-old divorced woman. From her marriage of 21 years she has three children: a son, 23, living with her and about to graduate from college; a daughter, 22, who lives on her own; and a son, 17, living at home and going to high school. She works as a teacher's aide and receives alimony from her ex-husband. Her depression started about three years ago when she separated from her husband who was interested in another woman. At that time she made a suicide attempt with sleeping pills. Following a period of psychiatric consultation in 1974 she decided to divorce her husband. Her current relationship with a boyfriend who lived with her for a year is unstable. In March, 1976, they broke up and she made two suicidal gestures in the weeks that followed prior to starting treatment.

Her mother died at age 39 when the patient was 20. She describes her mother as someone she fought with a lot. Her mother burdened her with cleaning chores and left the responsibility for caring for a 17-year-old younger sister in her hands. She says her sister "was often thought to be my child." There was also another sister, five years younger than the patient. She states that, while her mother was an active joiner of organizations and

141

"a kind person to everybody," she sees her as an unhappy woman, standing alone, burdened by the pressures of a dominating mother-in-law who lived with them. Her father, age 66, lives in another state. She describes him as loving, kind, and affectionate, but never home too much because of his work and activity in social organizations. Her earliest memory is that when she was about nine years old "in school I was a crossing guard . . . wearing a white stripe."

C. During the eight sessions held during May, focus was placed on helping the patient to see herself as a person with feelings of her own. She recognized certain strengths within herself as, for example, her exploring, experimenting, rather venturesome qualities. She was able to question her readiness to conform to the presumed feelings and expectations of others. She became somewhat more self-assertive in her relations with family. She reestablished her relationship with her boyfriend. While recognizing the elements of mistrust and submissiveness inherent in it, she felt she "belonged" again, stating, "I belong in the world as a couple." She expressed an interest in the question of interpersonal trust, asking, "How do you learn to trust someone?" Her depressed feelings decreased significantly.

D. In the transference there is a strong element of over-estimating the power of the psychologist to provide her with answers as she presents herself as weak and resourceless.

E. In my counter-transference there are feelings of anxiety in response to the pressure to produce helpful, constructive answers for the patient, especially when she presents herself as helpless and directionless or responds with a sense of emptiness and silence.

This case history presented by Irwin Bosgang, Ph.D.

Patient Interview

Harris Peck, M.D.

Doctor: I have talked briefly with Jean and with her therapist, Dr. R., and I explained what I'd like to say again, and that is that I'm here conducting myself as I might if Dr. R. asked me, as a colleague, to look at the patient to see if there was anything I could contribute to the course of treatment. I have explained to Jean that my chief question is: do I have anything to contribute and what information do I need to do so. So Jean and I already had about two minutes of discussion in the hallway before we came in. I recall telling you that one of the reasons I was really pleased to be able to meet you and review your case was that it seems to be literally a life and death matter. I don't think any precaution we can take to preserve a patient's life is a luxury. One of the things I'm really concerned about is that I recall your telling me that you had some treatment from a psychiatrist which was just after your divorce, or right after your separation . . .

Patient: No, it was right after my separation.

Doctor: After separation from your husband and at the time you were feeling quite depressed . . .

Patient: Extremely so . . .

Doctor: I'd like to ask you something about that because you told me in our brief exchange that the treatment for awhile led you to feel pretty good, and then after some recent problems you were feeling suicidal and as if life wasn't worthwhile. If I misstate anything I trust you'll correct me, because I will sometimes say things not because I'm sure they're right, but because I want to test them out and see if they are. I could be way off and I expect you to tell me so. That will allow me to try out ideas on you to see if they're so. Your recent difficulty was with a man whom I understood you broke off with and whom you're now seeing again?

Patient: Right.

Doctor: At what point was it that the relationship broke off? How did it break off?

Patient: It broke up because he started to see someone else very innocently at work—from work—and I found out about it, and it was almost like the same thing all over again—the divorce.

Doctor: Okay. Almost like the same thing all over again as in the divorce. And in the divorce, what was the same thing that was very similar to that?

Patient: He was also running around.

Doctor: Your husband was running around?

Patient: At the time of the divorce it wasn't the first time.

Doctor: Jean, I wonder if you're in touch with the fact that in describing both incidents you talk about them as if the difficulty was really caused by the other person.

Patient: I realize that. I talk that way, but I know that there is more to it than just one side.

Doctor: Will you tell me what the other side is?

Patient: I guess if I could do that I wouldn't need therapy.

Doctor: Well, let's get more specific. In either of the instances when you think about it to yourself, not just for purposes of telling me or anybody else, do you think of yourself as having some part in bringing about what occurred?

Patient: Sure.

Doctor: What do you think your part in it was?

Patient: First, I think it was the way I acted with my husband and the way I reacted to the person I'm seeing now.

Doctor: Tell me about that.

Patient: Well, we lived together for a while . . . the one I'm seeing now . . . for about a year with my seventeen-year-old, and then my 23-year-old moved in, and I don't know why, but I just sort of got tired of him . . . He annoyed me. He would come home from work and I would ignore him . . . wouldn't sit down and talk to him. He said he felt like a boarder in the house, and these feelings of rejection toward him. . . .

Doctor: Okay. . . . So as you review it you think that you came to engage in some rejecting behavior.

Patient: I know I did.

Doctor: And that rejecting behavior came about because you felt yourself being bored or turned off.

Patient: I also felt my older son interfered a lot. . . .

Doctor: Okay, and what behavior of yours, or feeling or thinking, do you attribute to starting these sequences which ended in divorce from your husband?

Patient: I just didn't like him running around like that. That was all.

Doctor: You'd been married how many years?

Patient: Twenty-one.

Doctor: At what point did he begin running around?

Patient: The first time was '63.

Doctor: Which made it how long before you took some action?

Patient: Seven years.

Doctor: What led you to finally take action after seven years?

Patient: I began seeing a psychiatrist.

Doctor: I see. What led you to go to a psychiatrist?

Patient: They insisted on it when they put me in the hospital. I was under treatment in the hospital.

Doctor: Okay. What I'm really trying to see is how it began. You knew about it seven years . . . and then it was some years after that before you really became depressed and made a suicidal attempt. At what point did these things begin to happen? You'd been married like 13 years before he started running around. Was there anything you were doing that contributed to his running around?

Patient: No.

Doctor: You think it had nothing to do with you?

Patient: The fact is that he was never the pursuer . . . he was the pursuee.

Doctor: Yeah, guys get pursued and they may or may not respond.

Patient: Yes, but he was very easily led.

Doctor: He was easily led. I want to let you hear yourself again. At the beginning of it, it wasn't you, it wasn't even him . . . it was those women out there. I want you to be aware that you're putting the blame way out there. Okay. When it comes to the act of actually taking your life or making a gesture . . . you were trying to take your life?

Patient: Uh-huh.

Doctor: Who is responsible for that?

Patient: Me.

Doctor: And how do you explain that?

Patient: I don't like being alone. I just saw no point to living anymore if I had to live by myself.

Doctor: Okay. Let's take that up. Right now you're not living alone. Right?

Patient: Well, I have my two children.

Doctor: Didn't you have your two children then?

Patient: I had three then.

Doctor: Three. So you weren't living alone in that sense.

Patient: No.

Doctor: Are you talking about not living with another person with whom you have an intimate relationship?

Patient: Right.

Doctor: Okay. What do you think is the probable outcome of your present relationship?

Patient: I have no idea.

Doctor: If you had to make a bet and you were standing up there looking down at Jean, what would you say are the odds against this relationship really staying together and continuing as a really intimate relationship? Do you think it is more likely or less likely that you will stay together?

Patient: From my point of view, less likely. From his point of view, more likely.

Doctor: He seems to be interested, but you're not so sure. Okay.

Patient: He's been married four times. And that's a four-time loser.

Doctor: Okay, so even just looking at his batting average. . . .

Patient: I stand to lose a lot financially if this happens.

Doctor: How is that?

Patient: Well, I'm very well provided for from the divorce, and I would lose my alimony.

Doctor: But not getting married does not mean you could not continue to have an intimate relationship with each other.

Patient: No.

Doctor: I'm saying that, but I'm not you.

Patient: I realize that, but it is not the same type of thing.

Doctor: Yeah, in other words, for you real intimacy would mean getting married.

Patient: Yes, right.

Doctor: Okay.

Patient: Yes, but at the same time I don't know if I would remarry.

Doctor: Now let me ask you, and if I misstate you, correct me. You said that you made your suicide attempt because you couldn't stand the idea of being alone. Right?

Patient: Ummm.

Doctor: You've just said that it's possible, even given all the chances, that you may be alone again. What happens then?

Patient: I imagine the same thing would happen all over again.

Doctor: Okay, please notice what you said. The same thing "would happen" all over again. Do you hear how you put that what "would happen" outside yourself?

Patient: Ummm.

Doctor: Okay, I want to tell you something about that. You saw me drawing some of those diagrams. . . .

Patient: I couldn't see them to well.

Doctor: Okay, but whether you saw them or not, when a person is a small child what happens to him is largely not in their control. Whether he survive or not depends on the parents. Right?

Patient: Ummm.

Doctor: If you don't take care of a little kid, what happens to him?

Patient: He goes to pot.

Doctor: Not only goes to pot . . . he literally dies. You know that. Okay. And if you don't give a kid the kind of love and support and interest he needs, although he might not literally die, what happens?

Patient: He falls apart.

Doctor: And as I read your history. . . .

Patient: I had one like that. . . .

Doctor: Yeah, but I'm going back now to your own parents. The kind of care you got wasn't always that great as I read it. So back in those days your parents really had your life in their hands, right?

Patient: Ummm.

Doctor: I want to put you in touch as I go back, not to your current situation, but to the past situation, that maybe the way you keep yourself thinking that maybe a third party caused your life to go down the drain is because some of these situations remind you of a time when indeed you didn't have any choice about what would happen to you. I'd like to talk about that time a little bit. What is the worst thing that ever happened to you when you were a really young child?

Patient: I remember very little about my childhood. The very worst thing. . . .

Doctor: Let's put it this way, and I'm going to give you several choices so you'll see what I'm trying to get at, as you look back at your childhood and you think about what wasn't good about it . . . what is the thing you think about when you were really a little kid?

Patient: I remember my parents arguing . . . my mother threatening to leave a few times. That sort of thing.

Doctor: What was her big complaint about your father?

Patient: She didn't trust him.

Doctor: She didn't trust your father. Do you think that, even though she didn't trust him, she loved him?

Patient: Uh-huh.

Doctor: Did they have a good sex life, do you know?

Patient: Oh, I don't know. No one ever talked about that kind of thing.

Doctor: By the way, when you were married did you have a good sex life?

Patient: Yes.

Doctor: Do you have orgasms?

Patient: Uh-huh.

Doctor: Good. When you became a little older, like in adolescence, how was life then for you?

Patient: My father used to be after me a lot, although he was a very warm, affectionate man. This is the way I pictured him, and he still is to this day.

He wasn't around that much. He was a joiner, and my mother was a joiner. She died very young.

Doctor: What age were you when she died?

Patient: I was 21. She was 39.

Doctor: So, prior to the time of her death, your father wasn't around very much, so you didn't think he was intensely interested in you.

Patient: No, he was always in his workshop.

Doctor: You didn't get to feel that you were an important person to him?

Patient: No, one thing I remember overhearing one time when I was very small was the fact that when I was born he was hoping that I was a boy. He never did get a boy, he had three girls.

Doctor: So between that and the fighting, and when parents are fighting I don't suppose they have much energy to really take care of kids, so. . . .

Patient: Well, I never felt neglected.

Doctor: Did you feel safe and loved and good and happy?

Patient: I can't remember.

Doctor: But that isn't the way you ordinarily think of your childhood, because people who have experienced that usually are able to say, "Hey, I had some great times!" I didn't see a smile on your face. . . .

Patient: No, I can't say that, because I really can't remember.

Doctor: Maybe there are some things you would just as soon not remember. Most of us do forget. When things get too painful we shove it away, but you do remember what happened after your mother died. That's pretty clear to you, right?

Patient: Uh-huh.

Doctor: What was your role in the family after she died?

Patient: It didn't change much. I was married then, and she died a month before my eldest was born. My grandmother, my father's mother, took over the family. I had a four-year-old sister. She sort of took over.

Doctor: And you also had a sister that was just a little bit younger than you.

Patient: Five years younger than I am.

Doctor: There are three in all, yeah. Was your mother ill at all?

Patient: No, she just dropped dead one day.

Doctor: When she was alive did she do all the taking care, or did you help her take care. . . .

Patient: No, I did a lot.

Doctor: Okay. You did a lot . . . for both kids or. . . .

Patient: The youngest.

Doctor: The very youngest one who. . . .

Patient: My mother always said when she was pregnant that she would never be tied down at her age with a baby. She wasn't, but it tied me down. If she had someplace to go and I had someplace to go, I had to stay home.

Doctor: Again, Jean, I want to call to your attention that you said "it" tied me down. When did you start taking care of this little kid?

Patient: I was sixteen.

Doctor: Sixteen. Okay, I have a 16- and a 17-year-old, and I know what a 16- and a 17-year-old can do and, of course, maybe those days were a little bit different. . . . If they don't want to do something they might not say outright they don't want to do it. You did it . . . you did the taking care of. How come? Were you wildly enthusiastic about it?

Patient: No.

Doctor: Well, how come you did it?

Patient: I guess I just didn't want to hurt my parents. I wouldn't talk to my parents the way kids do today to begin with. I would have gotten knocked across the room.

Doctor: You would have gotten knocked across the room if you had. Literally?

Patient: Uh-huh.

Doctor: Who was the one. . . .

Patient: My father. But he never really raised a hand to me, but I had the feeling. . . .

Doctor: The threat of violence was there. What would your mother do if you didn't do what was expected of you?

Patient: Just fight with me.

Doctor: Argue. Did you actually fight?

Patient: No, argue.

Doctor: When she argued did she get unhappy herself, was she an unhappy person?

Patient: Uh-huh.

Doctor: In addition to fighting with you, would she be unhappy or sad or angry?

Patient: She would be unhappy. Sometimes she would cry.

Doctor: She would cry. Can you hear her crying still?

Patient: Uh-huh.

Doctor: Do you ever cry that way?

Patient: From what?

Doctor: Whenever you cry. . . . The reason I'm asking is that sometimes when I think of my parents . . . my father, for instance . . . things I didn't like about him, and I suddenly catch myself, and I look in the mirror and say, "Oh my God! Here I am doing some of the same things he did. . . ."

Patient: No.

Doctor: Do you cry?

Patient: Sure.

Doctor: How do you cry when you cry?

Patient: It all depends on what is happening.

Doctor: When you really feel depressed about your lost husband or boyfriend, how do you cry?

Patient: Not only inwardly but outwardly, too.

Doctor: And what are you feeling at that particular moment?

Patient: Despair . . . complete despair.

Doctor: Give me some other words.

Patient: Downhearted.

Doctor: Downhearted. Sad?

Patient: Yeah.

Doctor: Yeah. Okay. Do you get angry?

Patient: I get angry, sure.

Doctor: But the sadness is usually the more dominant feeling?

Patient: Yes.

Doctor: Do you ever get angry at your mother or father?

Patient: Not really. I don't think I ever really did.

Doctor: In effect, what I hear you saying is, given the situation you're in, you are still like that little kid with the kind of parents you essentially went along with and made an adaptation as you had to, to get along in the family.

Patient: Right.

Doctor: And really being Mrs. Goodguy, huh?

Patient: I guess you could say that.

Doctor: Do you sometimes feel that that is the kind of role you have in life? And that people take advantage of you?

Patient: No, I don't ever really feel people are taking advantage of me.

Doctor: No?

Patient: Maybe sometimes my kids, yes.

Doctor: How about when your husband or boyfriend starts running around with somebody else?

Patient: I think it is a putdown on me, but I don't know if it is taking advantage of me. . . .

Doctor: As if putting you down . . . finish that sentence.

Patient: There is something wrong with me.

Doctor: Something wrong with you. Is there?

Patient: I don't know.

Doctor: If there was anything wrong with you, what would it be?

Patient: I really don't know.

Doctor: Okay, let me ask you something else. Tell me what's good about you. Tell me, when you're really liking yourself what things do you really feel good about?

Patient: I don't think I ever really thought about it . . . myself in that way.

Doctor: I don't know you very well, but whatever difficulties your kids have had, considering how stormy things have been, they haven't done that badly. Sounds as if they have accomplished some things. Who's responsible for that?

Patient: I guess they are . . . aren't they really?

Doctor: Did you contribute anything?

Patient: I guess I must have, if you want to look at it that way.

Doctor: Boy, you don't like to give yourself strokes at all. You're really not accustomed to letting yourself feel good about stuff you have done.

Patient: I think things I've done are things any normal parent would do.

Doctor: You know, that is a way of discounting and not letting the stroke nourish you. And I want to tell you one of the things I think. I want you to really get with this. You're here and in treatment because you had some problems. You've done a lot of things in life besides have problems, and right now you're doing some things. I understand you're working right now, what are you doing?

Patient: I'm a teacher's assistant.

Doctor: Feel good about that?

Patient: Oh, I like my job. I like working with kids.

Doctor: I want you to hear how you answered my question . . . it was an interesting discount of the question. I asked you if you felt good about your job and you said, "I like my job." Are you doing anything you feel proud of, or confident about, or good about in that job?

Patient: Yes, I feel a lot of accomplishment when I can sit down with a youngster with grammar or English or something like that and really teach him something. I feel that he is learning something, and that makes me feel good.

Doctor: Great! One of the things I suggest is that you get into the habit of accepting from yourself and from other people positive strokes when you're entitled to them. I'm not talking about phony strokes. I think it is enormously important to you. I think that in the family situation you've told me about you received a lot of negative strokes. . . . I'm not saying there were no positive strokes there, but to get along you had to take some negative strokes. Right?

Patient: But isn't the thing today to blame everything on the parents?

Doctor: As a matter of fact, I'm not blaming everything on the parents. I want to talk about the present, and like I said before when you were a little kid, then your life was in their hands. Even when you were 16—I don't blame them, because you made a decision to go along and take care of that little sister. And right now, if when you tell me that if you were alone life would be meaningless and you get ideas of taking your life, I would not blame that on your parents. I would not blame that on your boyfriend. I would not blame that on your husband. I would not use the word blame at all. I would say there is one person responsible right now for whether you live or die. Who's that?

Patient: Huh, me.

Doctor: You bet it's you. And because of that, I'd like you to consider something, and I'd be glad to talk to your therapist about it. It seems important to me. When I told you I was . pleased to have the opportunity to work with you I reminded you that you had worked with a psychiatrist— you felt fairly good for a while and then something else happened, and you thought of taking your own life again. You hope that the things you are working on will turn out differently and that things work out well, but there is nothing in life to guarantee it.

Patient: There are no guarantees, I know that.

Doctor: You're in charge of whether you live or die, and in your old family you said your dad could not have cared less especially since you weren't a boy. In effect, he sort of gave you the message by not being around, "Hey, get lost."

Patient: It wasn't just directed at me, it was to the three of us.

Doctor: I understand, but when you are a little kid you don't care who else is being talked to, you want to be seen and welcomed for you. And you weren't. That's why you don't remember much—it's painful. Okay. I'm not a mind reader and if stuff I say doesn't sound right, tell me.

Patient: Okay.

Doctor: So you're in charge now as you weren't then. Then they could control the strokes. And you're doing some stuff right now that makes life better. You're going for therapy. And that has improved your life . . . the way you feel. . . .

Patient: It has.

Doctor: You got yourself a job, and that's important to you, right?

Patient: Uh-huh.

Doctor: Don't say yes unless it is true.

Patient: Yes, it's true, but I've been working for five years.

Doctor: I know . . . and you're doing stuff you feel good about which is really important. Your whole life doesn't only revolve around . . . an intimate relationship. It is very important, but you have other things. . . . Your kids are important. That means you have set up a situation, unlike the one in your childhood, where you don't have to let life become empty. You can fill it. At least you have a part in whether it is full or gratifying, right?

Patient: Well, I don't feel it is full.

Doctor: Remember when you first talked about what happened with your husband, your boyfriend. You said that third party did it. What I'm saying is that you have a part in whether that relationship goes well. You have a part in it if it is not going well. Now I want you to hear this. You could not change your parents, but if you were persuaded that this relationship was not good for you, what options do you have?

Patient: I guess to get out of it.

Doctor: Right. I heard you say that with a lot of hesitation. It might not be that easy, because remember when you were a kid you had no options—you were stuck with your parents. You have a lot of things you can determine, not only whether you live or die. And therefore, because of that, I want you to consider something. You know that if you take your own life—I don't know what your religion is—that is irreversible. You can't change that. Right?

Patient: That's why you take your own life, right?

Doctor: That's right. I want you to be aware that people take their lives more often than not when things get up to here, and then they come to and things look better and they say, "Wow, I'm glad it didn't work." I hear by the things you're doing that, regardless what your father or mother communicated to you, you're doing some things that say you want to live and make your life as good as you can make it. Is that right, and don't say yes if it isn't true.

Patient: I think it's true, yes.

Doctor: Okay. It is not possible to do that as well as you might as long as you keep thinking—and I hear you thinking—things are too bad, so I'll do what they expected me to do when I was a little kid and take my own life. That will rob you of the energy for the very thing you're doing. Can you see how that might be? If I'm starting to go to California—then decide to go to Florida—and I'm packing for a trip to Canada, it is not a very good way to start a journey. In this journey you're deciding whether to live and still considering the possibility that if things are too bad you'll just die. That's not likely to get you where you want to go.

Patient: But it's a way out.

Doctor: It is a way out. It seemed that the only way out was to not be too important, not be who you wanted to be in the family. Let's imagine the most awful thing happens. What's the worst thing that could happen to you?

Patient: Right now, that my boyfriend and I will break up.

Doctor: Notice what you said, "my boyfriend and I will break up." How would that happen? I know you can't foresee the future, but try. . . .

Patient: If either one of us caught the other cheating.

Doctor: Who would catch who cheating?

Patient: Either one of us.

Doctor: Who might? If you had to bet on it, who would catch who?

Patient: Me.

Doctor: Are you fooling around?

Patient: I was.

Doctor: So it's a nice way to maybe screw up the relationship, huh?

Patient: Uh-huh.

Doctor: This would be a nice plan. One of the reasons you're in therapy now is so you don't do things that are not in keeping with where you want to go. I'm not going to get into that. Are you working with Dr. R. on it?

Patient: Uh-huh.

Doctor: Okay, but let's assume for one reason or another there's a slip and that does happen. Okay? And the relationship breaks up as a result of something you did, and you might not handle it well.

Patient: But I've covered myself this time.

Doctor: How did you do that?

Patient: Because I have someone sort of waiting in the wings.

Doctor: Hey, you're sneaky. You were holding that one behind your back! I'm really pleased. I'm not trying to tell you how to run your life. I really liked the little smile you had when you said that. Because you admitted you're not a helpless person. You are saying, "I've got ways of managing if I have to." Isn't that true?

Patient: Yes.

Doctor: I love that. I really love that! And that's exactly what I meant. You're not going to be in a spot again like way back when you were a little kid. You are saying, "I don't have to kill myself. I can do some other things." And you know what? I was trying to get you to agree to something, and I have a hunch you have already begun to agree to it yourself. You know what I think you've agreed to do?

Patient: What?

Doctor: Live! I'm not sure you know that, and some days you may not feel that way, but I think you're beginning to decide to live.

Patient: I don't know. You probably have talked me into it.

Doctor: All right, I am doing that, and I'll tell you why. You're right on. I'm working hard at this. I'm selling. You know why? Because you were sold such a crumby message when you were a kid. Your parents may have had their own problems, so I'm not putting them down. I'm talking about how it appeared to you as a little kid. That message was "get lost." Somewhere that came across.

Patient: I really can't look at it that way.

Doctor: Okay, tell me how you look at it.

Patient: Well, I really don't remember all of it. My father, I know, drinks too much, but he's still a very kind, gentle, and loving man. He lives in Virginia. He's far away, but. . . .

Doctor: Jean, I want you to hear your voice now, so I'm going to turn back my tape recorder. Remember what you told me you overheard at the age of . . . how old? Take a guess.

Patient: Around 8 or 9.

Doctor: 8 or 9. . . . Will you tell me again the words you heard?

Patient: He said he wished I had been a boy when I was born.

Doctor: You know what that means to a little kid at that age?

Patient: Oh, I remember that it hurt. They were having a party downstairs and didn't know I was on the stairs. I just happened to hear my father say that, and it hurt.

Doctor: It hurt. And do you know why?

Patient: A form of rejection, I guess.

Doctor: They were saying, "We really don't want her. We wish she had been somebody else." And now you see your father as a fairly kind man. And that's from your vantage point looking back. Most kids don't have that kind of perspective. What is a little kid supposed to feel? I want you to really experience the hurt of that little 8-year-old kid. I'd like you to do something—a small experiment. Where were you?

Patient: I was on the stairs.

Doctor: For about the next three minutes I'd like you to be that little eight-year-old kid. Where was your father?

Patient: Downstairs.

Doctor: And at that time you would not have dreamed of telling him?

Patient: No.

Doctor: You never have told him?

Patient: No, I never have.

Doctor: I don't want you to see him as he is now. You're eight years old and he's in his what, thirties? You've just heard this conversation. It's a way I have of getting in touch. Really say to him, "Hey, I heard what you said!" And instead of seeing me here, I want you to imagine him and his face, and just say to him whatever you might be feeling. I want you to be 8-year-old Jean, in other words, a little girl. No little girl might really do this, but you're a very spunky kid. Go ahead. I'll stand behind you and I might add a few lines, but if they don't sound true don't say them.

Patient: Daddy, I just heard you tell the people that you wished I had been a boy.

Doctor: Tell him what you think about that.

Patient: I don't think it was very nice to say.

Doctor: Tell him what you're feeling about it.

Patient: It hurts.

Doctor: Tell him how it hurts.

Patient: It hurts very much.

Doctor: Okay. I want you to go over to that chair over there and sit down. I want you now to be your father, and a little girl has just told you, "I heard what you said." Be the father. What would you say?

Patient: I know what he would say. I didn't mean it.

Doctor: Yeah, I didn't mean it. Tell her what you did mean. Tell her.

Patient: I don't know what he would say.

Doctor: Make it up. What might he say? I didn't mean it . . . go on. . . .

Patient: I didn't mean it in the way you thought I meant it. I'm happy that I have you and that you are a girl.

Doctor: I'm happy that you are a girl, okay. Come over here. Tell him if you believe him.

Patient: It's hard to believe. I don't believe you.

Doctor: I don't believe you. Tell him, "Daddy, you're lying."

Patient: Daddy you're lying.

Doctor: Say it stronger.

Patient: Daddy, you're lying.

Doctor: I want you to say it three times each time stronger.

Patient: Daddy, you're lying. Daddy, you're lying! Daddy, you're lying!!

Doctor: What do you feel now?

Patient: Resentment.

Doctor: How long are you going to wait for Daddy to be glad you're alive and that you're a girl?

Patient: I don't know.

Doctor: How long would it take for him to go back to that time and say, "Wow! I'm glad I had a girl?" When is that going to happen? Never?

Patient: I don't think so.

Doctor: Are you going to continue to play out that little piece of history?

Patient: I didn't know that I was.

Doctor: You are doing it because Daddy said to you, "Get lost, I want a boy." You know what you've been doing? Not all of you, because some of you is strong. Remember the strokes you gave yourself? That part of you is good and confident and wants to live. But there's a little piece of you that comes out when you feel just as abandoned and lost and left alone as you sometimes did in your family. Right? And then Daddy's message, "get lost," takes over, doesn't it? See what I'm saying?

Patient: Is that why I don't particularly like women?

Doctor: Tell me about that.

Patient: I don't know. I just don't particularly like women. I don't like joining women's organizations. I think they're terrible. I don't like to be with a group of women for any length of time.

Doctor: Who was the woman you first didn't care for in some way? Anybody?

Patient: My grandmother, I guess.

Doctor: Your grandmother. I'm looking at my watch and we've done a lot today. Just one more thing. The piece of work you just did was neat. That was a real important scene. I want you to be aware that you have a lot of strength and a lot of stuff going for you. That was only one scene, and there must be dozens you don't remember. When that scene begins to take over, you want to follow those old messages. I want you to give a chance to the good messages you're building now. And I'd like you to consider with your therapist making a contract not to take your own life. Not to follow the old messages. I want you to consider that and talk with your therapist about it, because those are old, crazy messages as seen by an eight-year-old kid. Now you're an older woman with a lot of ways of filling that emptiness, even if the worst happened. Will you consider what I have asked of you?

Patient: I'll think about it.

Doctor: Thank you.

Discussion of Interview

Harris B. Peck, M.D.

This interview embodies many of the elements which are characteristic of my own therapeutic style and that of other transactional analysis (TA) therapists. I am pleased with the interview, and that is the case most of the time these days. Both patients and I generally leave sessions feeling okay about ourselves and each other. I like the interview's clearly defined sense of direction and relevant application of TA concepts to the patient's presenting concerns. I was prepared to respond to where she was and was not prepared to go. The session largely rests on a *contractual* understanding between the patient and myself, whether we are dealing with the goals of the interview, the implications of any given transaction, or the steps the patient is prepared to take in therapy or in life. At the end of the session this contractual mode is utilized in establishing the basis for a "no suicide" contract with her therapist.

Considerable therapeutic work is devoted early in the session to establishing the patient's role in determining the outcome of events in her own life and encouraging her to "own" her feelings, thoughts, and actions. She is introduced to the assumption that if she was in charge of events she regrets, she can be in charge of changes she desires. This emphasis on the *decisional* process is characteristic of TA therapy and is crucial to this patient, who seems only too ready to assign to others the "blame" for taking her own life.

Although I invite the patient to modify certain aspects of her behavior in the session, there is a growing recognition that certain of her behaviors have become crystallized into patterns which I begin to delineate with her, utilizing several familiar TA concepts. I call particular attention to *injunctions,* or prohibitions, from her father who would have preferred her to be a boy, and explore the possibility that Jean perceived this as his not wanting her to exist. I relate this to her readiness to be whatever her parents seemed to need her to be, as a way of justifying her existence.

In the interview these beginnings are related to her overall sense that she was not okay, but that everyone else was, the marked deficiency and discounting of positive strokes, and her readiness to adapt to the needs and demands of others. I suggest to her that these behaviors may have seemed essential to survival as a youngster when few other choices were available, but remind her that she has already given evidence of her readiness to improvise more gratifying alternatives. I make a particular point of acknowledging and warmly stroking the steps she has taken to meet her own needs.

Following this positive stroking, Jean seems more receptive to recognizing the ways in which she *may* foul up the life she presumably wants to build herself by continuing to follow the *script* patterns initiated in her own family. I let her know that I think she can alter these early decisions and redecide to conduct her life differently. I convey to her that I have an interest in a redecision to allow herself to live and achieve fulfillment. This *permission* will, of course, need to be implemented by actual changes in the way she conducts her life and her relationships.

In the final phase of the session I recognize the need to complete unfinished business from her early family life as represented by the unresolved feelings of anger toward her father. Rather than continue to talk about these feelings, I utilize the gestalt technique of the "double chair," enabling her to deal directly with persisting messages from her father. In the course of continuing therapy such redecision work might well need to be repeated a number of times and related to messages from other significant figures, such as the grandmother who is introduced by the patient in the closing minutes of the session.

In terminating the session I re-emphasize the importance of establishing a "no suicide" contract with her therapist. The suggestion is linked with a reminder of her demonstrated ability to gain control of her own life and make autonomous decisions for meeting her own needs. Thus, a link is made between the work she has done in the interview and her continuing work with her own therapist.

Chapter 11

AN INTRODUCTION TO MULTIMODAL BEHAVIOR THERAPY

Arnold A. Lazarus

Arnold A. Lazarus, Ph.D.

Arnold A. Lazarus is a Fellow of the American Psychological Association and a clinical Diplomate of the American Board of Professional Psychology. He has had faculty appointments at Stanford University, Temple University Medical School, and Yale University (Director of Clinical Training, 1970–72). He is author of more than 100 scientific papers on methods of therapy. He has served as president of the Association for Advancement of Behavior Therapy (1968–69). He is presently Professor of Psychology at Rutgers University, and has a part-time private practice in Princeton, New Jersey.

Descriptively, we are beings who move, feel, sense, image, think, and relate to one another. These functions, in turn, rest upon an elaborate substrate of biochemical and neurophysiological processes. In other words, every day of our lives we experience or engage in Behavior, Affect, Sensation, Imagery, Cognition, and (unless in social isolation) Interpersonal relationships. If we subsume the bedrock of biochemical/neurophysiological factors under the term "Drugs," this, together with the foregoing modalities, yields the convenient acronym BASIC ID (the first letters of each modality).

Human "personality" may be said to comprise the BASIC ID. When referring to a person's significant and characteristic behaviors, affective responses, sensory reactions, images, cognitive processes, interpersonal styles, and somatic effects under a variety of circumstances, we are making far-reaching statements about that individual's "personality." However, the essence of "multimodal personality theory" is the assumption that each modality of the BASIC ID is separate yet interactive. It is hypothesized that through a "ripple effect," a change in one modality will influence all modalities. Nevertheless, since each modality is held to have discrete boundaries and functions, comprehensive therapeutic change requires *specific* interventions across each modality. It is usually insufficient to rely on the "ripple effect" or on presumed generalization to ensure thorough therapeutic results.

Another fundamental assumption is that most events have an influence across the entire BASIC ID. Almost any significant occurrence—"I got divorced," "My father died," "We moved to Boston," "I argued with my sister," etc.,—will generally have specific behavioral, affective, sensory, imaginal, cognitive, interpersonal, and physiological repercussions. Comprehensive assessment of any event requires a clear elucidation of the precise impact it has upon each modality, plus an appreciation of the various interactive effects (Lazarus, 1976, Pp. 30–43).

The overall content and style of multimodal therapy may readily be inferred from the previous paragraphs. Information derived from life history materials, interviews, tests, and anamnestic inquiries will carefully be placed in a "Modality Profile" so that maladaptive excesses and deficits will span each area of the BASIC ID. Therapy will then consist of specific and systematic attempts to remedy each problem area. Multimodal therapists eschew general diagnostic labels and descriptive personality traits. For example, one of my clients whom a traditional psychiatrist had diagnosed as "a manic-depressive psychotic with obsessive-compulsive tendencies" was shown to have the following *Modality Profile:*

Behavior

Excessive smoking (two packs a day); frequent bruxism; bathroom rituals (spends up to two hours each morning showering, shaving, cleaning, etc.); nail-picking (frequently causes cuticles to bleed and become infected); sedentary habits (watches a lot of T.V., does not exercise); insominia.

Affect

Over-anxious about germs, cleanliness, catastrophic illness; moody, frequently depressed; angry and resentful toward father who allegedly deserted family when client was eight years of age; undefined areas of guilt; primitive rage toward mother.

Sensation

Frequent stomach aches; food is often tasteless; often has pain in jaws; occasional attacks of paroxsysmal tachycardia (seems to be associated with hyperventilation); very sensitive to heat (perspires excessively in hot weather).

Imagery

Nightmares about combat experiences in Vietnam (at least twice a week); occasional homosexual fantasies during masturbation; vivid and troublesome recollections of mother's violent outbursts, especially when he was 12–15 years of age.

Cognition

Perfectionistic ideals; dichotomous reasoning; overgeneralization; statements of self-hate; faulty ideas about germs and contamination.

Interpersonal

Usually submissive or aggressive rather than "assertive," no close friendships, no deep attachments, sexually promiscuous.

Drugs

Overweight—5 ′10 ″, 195 lbs; on lithium (1200 mg. per day) and on amitriptyline (Elavil) (200 mg. per day). Takes clorzapate (Tranxene) intermittently.

Each entry on a Modality Profile requires further elucidation in terms of specific antecedents and consequences. Therapy is aimed at each and every component. Depending on the exigencies of each case, the most pressing problems are carefully established, and one commences therapy by devising particular strategies for overcoming each specific problem. In the foregoing case, while continuing with the medication, we added a graduated exercise regimen, a contingency contract to reduce smoking, and daily practice of a progressive relaxation training cassette (Lazarus, 1976a). Our twice-weekly sessions were devoted to assertion training and cognitive restructuring. It seemed that these interventions would remedy certain major problems, and that other strategies (e.g., desensitization, response prevention, sex education, various imagery techniques, etc.) might be introduced after initial gains had accrued. An "implosive imagery" technique subsequently proved especially effective. He was asked to picture himself at age eight (when father left the home). This image provoked a high degree of rage. He was then instructed to see himself murdering both parents. He selected knives and a hatchet, and an extremely gory and violent scene was enacted in fantasy. The therapist then introduced various authorities, a juvenile court, a reformatory, and other reality-based consequences. In short, the rationale was that by condoning feelings of primitive rage (to assuage guilt) one drew a clear distinction between the subjective acceptance and recognition of violent feelings, as opposed to the forbidden expression of violent overt emotions. This led smoothly into further training in assertive (as opposed to aggressive) responses (Lange and Jakubowski, 1976). Employing the well-known "empty chair technique" several assertive dialogues were enacted between the client and his parents. The final objective—a direct, assertive, interpersonal confrontation with his parents—called for additional behavior rehearsal.

The practice of multimodal behavior therapy is predicated on the assumption that therapy is a teaching enterprise, and that the more a client learns during the course of therapy, the less likely he/she is to relapse. The approach is "eclectic," in that effective techniques drawn from any discipline will be incorporated into the clinical armamentarium. But there are important differences between multimodal therapy and the usual multifaceted eclectic treatment approaches. In the first place, multimodal behavior therapy does not borrow theoretical notions from divergent schools; general systems theory, social learning, and cognitive behavior theory provide its conceptual underpinnings. Logical positivism is endorsed without succumbing to unnecessary reductionistic reasoning. Most significantly, while many eclectic practitioners claim to cover the BASIC ID in their daily practices, close scrutiny of their work and their writings reveals that they tend to gloss over or ignore at least one or two modalities. Multimodal therapists employ the BASIC ID format not only for initial diagnosis and assessment, but also throughout the course of therapy to ensure systematic and thorough intervention. For example, in the case already alluded to, the first entry on the Modality Profile under Interpersonal is the problem of "perfectionistic ideals." Tracking the impact of "perfectionism" across the BASIC ID, the following patterns emerged:

Multimodal Impact of Perfectionism

Behavior:

Attempts to cover up all skin blemishes; painstakingly thorough when shaving, washing, dressing, and grooming; avoids many activities (especially sports) because he cannot excel or perform perfectly; too slow at work because he keeps checking for shortcomings or imperfections.

Affect:

Often feels disgruntled, frustrated, and angry at failing to meet his perfect standards; is easily embarrassed when errors are brought to his attention; seldom feels any sustained degree of personal satisfaction.

Sensation:

Chronic tension; always on guard; especially sensitive to visual and auditory imperfections ("A wrong note in music or an error in print almost drives me up the wall!").

Imagery:

Pictures perfect people having perfect friendships, perfect marriages, looking perfect, being perfect. His self-image falls far short of his personal expectations.

Cognition:

Definite and rigid ideas of "right" and "wrong," and about what "should" and "shouldn't" be.

Interpersonal:

Over-critical; looks for real and imagined shortcomings in self and in others; sex becomes an athletic performance; very impatient with others.

Drugs:

It would appear that his perfectionism creates unnecessary tension for which he resorts to clorzapate from time to time.

The preceding discussion has attempted to underscore the fact that multimodal assessment is both thorough and systematic. Furthermore, in this approach, there is no discontinuity between assessment and therapy. As specific difficulties are identified across and within each modality, a series of discrete interventions will be tailored to deal with every problem. An obvious question that may be anticipated is whether this meticulous attention to detail is really warranted. It can readily be appreciated that multimodal therapy calls for the therapist to expend consistent effort and concentration. There is little room for the pleasures and comforts of protracted empathy, warmth, and therapeutic genuineness without a deliberate and systematic transfer into *action* designed to overcome each response deficit and particular "hangup." It needs to be emphasized that the multimodal orientation was developed when follow-up studies revealed the relative impermanence of other broad-spectrum treatment interventions (Lazarus, 1971). Follow-ups now point to the durability of outcomes following multimodal behavior therapy (Lazarus, 1976).

A simple analogy might help to underscore an essential point. Consider an orthopedic surgeon who would far rather converse with his patients than attend to the routine and systematic aspects of x-raying for broken bones, operating, making plaster casts, etc. A patient with a broken arm consults him and they lunge into lengthy conversations about love, life, and poetry. The doctor plies the patient with painkilling drugs to remove the nagging and persistent discomfort, and week after week, doctor and patient meet and talk about sex, religion, philosophy, dreams, and forgotten memories. Soon, the broken bone is healed, and if not badly fractured to begin with, the arm may require no further medical attention. But to give credit for the "cure" to the doctor-patient relationship and/or to the various conversational areas that had been traversed, is to rob "nature" of the credit to which she is entitled.

While the analogy falls short in certain respects, it nevertheless captures the essence of what probably occurs when psychotherapists, who offer little more than drugs and a supportive relationship (plus perhaps some insightful interpretations) find that certain patients recover from "neurotic problems" after months or years of "treatment." This is not to gainsay the significance, and the crucial importance of the client-therapist relationship, however. Within the interpersonal modality, one of the most critical considerations revolves around various tactics and qualities that can enhance client-therapist attractiveness, and that can permit the therapist to remain a potent source of positive reinforcement.

Referring again to the aforementioned case, the client's over-critical penchant soon spilled over into the therapeutic relationship. In his zeal for perfection he was, quite logically, in search of the "perfect therapist." The following dialogue (reconstructed from memory) ensued after the third or fourth session:

Client: I think I spotted two contradictions during our last meeting.

Therapist: (*He seems to be setting me up. Last time when I tried to deal with his criticisms in a factual manner we merely became embroiled in his obsessive and passive-aggressive intellectualizations. Let's see what happens if I approach him paradoxically.*) Only two? I must be getting better. One day I may even be perfect. This morning someone else managed to spot three contradictions. Are you sure there were only two?

Client: I'm serious. First you said that medication is a crutch, and then you said that I might have to take lithium for years. Don't you see the contradiction?

Therapist: (*I don't recall talking about medication as a crutch, but he may be genuinely confused.*) Think about a diabetic who takes daily insulin but who uses Valium or alcohol or other drugs as a crutch.

Client: So lithium is my psychic insulin.

Therapist: Well put! I hope that's not too much of a contradiction.

Client: No, I see the point now.

Therapist: (*Now I might be able to use a paradoxical approach to drive home the anti-perfectionistic ethos.*) Gee! I'd sure hate to be perfect. You mentioned two contradictions. What was the other one?

Client: No, it was nothing important.

Therapist: How can an imperfection in me be unimportant? You can't be in therapy with a fallible human being. A subhuman creature like you needs a superhuman god.

Client: (Laughing) Okay. I get the message.

Therapist: Do you really get the message? I'm sure that you can find some therapists who will fall into your trap and play the godlike or perfect role— until you really spot their inevitable flaws. I'm trying to get you to give up your perfectionistic ideas. Even if I did make a mistake or contradict myself, why would that be so terrible?

Multimodal behavior therapy is not a series of mechanical procedures. The twelve practitioners who contributed chapters to the first book on *Multimodal Behavior Therapy* (Lazarus, 1976) consider themselves well-versed in general clinical processes to which they have added the multimodal format to ensure greater thoroughness and technical precision. They are well aware of the fact that certain cases call for a suspension of all specific techniques until the attainment of genuine trust has been achieved. In other instances, it is necessary to step outside the BASIC ID and reorganize or manipulate the client's environment so that positive "personality" changes will not be reversed by inimical life circumstances. There are two basic principles that are constantly kept in mind: (1) The need for continual *flexibility* in the face of personalistic differences from case to case; and (2) The eventual assessment and (when and where necessary) systematic treatment across the BASIC ID. The latter calls for a certain degree of discipline on the part of the therapist. Whether treating an individual, a couple, a family, or a group, the multimodal therapist constructs a Modality Profile, and adds or removes items from the profile as therapy progresses. This literally takes no more than five to ten minutes at the end of each session, but appears to add tremendous therapeutic momentum and introduces a degree of precision that can save months of otherwise fruitless effort.

It is understandable why so many theorists still seek for a "master key," some unitary method or procedure that can enduringly assuage if not eliminate emotional suffering. The ardent followers of primal therapy, transcendental meditation, est, orthomolecular psychiatry, and so forth are completely at variance with the multimodal approach and philosophy. If the BASIC ID theory is correct, no unitary cure can exist. Significant change then requires multimodal not unimodal intervention. If durable results are desired, the degree of attention devoted to each modality needs to be quite extensive and intensive. For example, a well-known authority on transcendental meditation commented that TM covers the BASIC ID. While meditating, he pointed out, one is engaged in a behavior that has direct affective, sensory, imagery, and cognitive effects. Furthermore, he added, studies have shown that TM yields positive psychophysiological effects and facilitates calm and peaceful interpersonal dealings. Thus, TM covers the entire BASIC ID (cf. Bloomfield, Cain and Jaffe, 1975). Of course, multimodal behavior therapy calls for direct and specific attention to each modality, rather than incidental coverage or consideration. It can be argued that every method of therapy touches on the BASIC ID. However, it cannot be overstated that multimodal behavior therapy holds that to treat or deal with a modality *en passant* is simply insufficient and inadequate.

By using the BASIC ID as a constant compass to ensure therapeutic thoroughness and goal-directed interventions, even novice clinicians have reported gains in subjective confidence and objective outcomes. The multimodal approach is not yet another orientation to add further chaos or confusion to the plethora of psychotherapeutic schools. It is perhaps a step toward the dissolution of all schools of psychotherapeutic thought into a congruent body of knowledge that pays due credence to data, and to constant scientific verification and disproof.

Multimodal Values: A Brief Outline

A multimodal orientation does not tell a practitioner what specific techniques to withhold or to administer in any given situation. The multimodal approach says: Assess clients' salient behavioral repertoires, affective reactions, sensory input, imagery content, cognitive inclinations, interpersonal relationships, and biochemical/neurophysiological deficits and excesses; thereafter, apply the best available methods to overcome the problem areas that emerge. The diagnostic phase, or problem identification sequence, can draw upon all assessment tools and diagnostic batteries that have some validity—life history questionnaires, anamnesis, interviews with significant others, direct observation, standardized psychometric instruments, various psychophysiological measurements, and psychodiagnostic tests. All the material is then organized into a BASIC ID format, and decisions are made concerning when, where, and how best to intervene.

Well-trained clinicians will have more than "intuition" to guide them. They will be able to gauge when to offer no more than a sympathetic ear, when to display empathy, reflect emotionality, clarify misconceptions, challenge faulty cognitions, prescribe homework assignments, call in family members, issue ultimatums, apply hypnosis, recommend drugs, and so forth. A basic assumption of the multimodal orientation is that therapists must be taught to adopt a wide range of facilitative styles, while also being trained to apply a broad repertoire of effective techniques. The end result of therapy is to increase the client's overall favorable consequences and to augment the person's self-efficacy in general. We employ a technology of social influence, but nobody can specify exactly how this approach should be applied. We are provided with no ultimate values. Of course, all therapists must be on guard against any system that calls for unquestioning conformity. Self-management and self-reinforcement are to be encouraged, and whenever possible, an explicit therapeutic contract is advisable. The effects of therapy must be under constant surveillance so that accountability is never overlooked.

Basically, multimodal therapy belongs in a broad humanistic framework. We have no room for models that account for human behavior on the basis of animal experimentation or mechanical analogues. Our interactive conceptualization of human functioning stresses feelings, ideas, ideals, personal fulfillment, and interpersonal development. The focus is upon distinctively human interests, chief among them being *humanitarianism,* viz., a far-reaching concern about humankind, and a deep committment to solving problems and relieving suffering. However, unlike some humanistic therapists, multimodal practitioners do not concentrate almost exclusively on internal, subjective and experiential processes. Overt behavior is considered no less important than covert processes.

In multimodal therapy emphasis is placed upon the uniqueness of persons, which, in turn, calls for great versatility and flexibility on the part of therapists. In addition to the alleviation of suffering, the multimodal approach is interested in discovering how each person might attain the highest levels of functioning. Our findings suggest that instead of pursuing an ill-defined path toward "self-actualization," the systematic elimination of response deficits and excesses across the BASIC ID is a clear way to attain "personality growth," and to pursue one's potential for optimum development.

It is widely noted and generally agreed that all therapists control and manipulate the behavior of their clients. All behaviors, no matter how nondirective or client-centered, are a communication of one's own view of the ongoing relationship with a given individual. How can any behavior fail to exert influence on a person? The very act of "merely" listening to a client exerts a tremendous amount of influence and serves as a potent reinforcer of the ongoing events. The question is not how we can avoid influence, control, and manipulation, but how we can best use them to enhance the welfare of the people who seek our assistance. We must try to exert our authority and control in a manner that is in the best interests of the patient. The type of control one wishes to avoid is the deliberate use of methods and tactics designed to have certain effects upon people without their knowledge or consent. Thus, in multimodal therapy we attempt to foster a therapeutic climate in which a situation of openness and awareness exists between client and therapist.

While we are opposed to extremes—we are critical of any compulsive confessions, compulsive honesty, or compulsive self-disclosures—the multimodal therapist readily shares the set of values he or she espouses. We are for assertion and against aggression, and in the conduct of all interpersonal interactions, we value reciprocity (positive reinforcement) and deplore coercion (negative reinforcement). Consequently, whenever our clients display any destructive interpersonal behaviors (power-plays, negative games, control tactics, aggression, duplicity, etc.,) we intervene at the first judicious moment and encourage the elimination of these interactions in favor of prosocial, authentic, and genuinely empathic responses.

I am convinced that people who value extrinsic achievements and possessions excessively, and who downplay intrinsic virtues, follow a path toward greed, over-competitiveness, suspicion, and violence. I cannot speak for all multimodal practitioners, but my own values center very heavily on the pleasures of personal sharing and the joys of close human togetherness. Consequently, I tend to influence people away from what Erich Fromm calls *having* (i.e., an exclusive emphasis on property, profit, and power) toward the mode of *being* (i.e., a striving for personal freedom, a willingness to share emotional experiences, the abandonment of one's egocentricity, a search for genuine awareness). But it is by no means necessary to starve in a garret in order to prove one's authenticity. The intrinsic mode does not negate the comforts of life or an appreciation of its luxuries, but it opposes the notion that self-respect is predicated on the attainment of these external accoutrements.

During the course of multimodal therapy, the various values alluded to in this brief overview are amplified and exemplified, especially when dealing with the Cognitive and Interpersonal modalities. Many of these values have been derived from outcome research which demonstrated that when people maintained their therapeutic improvements in the face of inimical circumstances, referral to their case notes "revealed that their improvements were often contingent upon the apparent adoption of a different outlook and philosophy of life and increased self-esteem, in addition to an increased range of interpersonal and behavioral skills," (Lazarus, 1971 p.18).

References

Bloomfield, H., Cain, M., and Jaffe, D. *TM: Discovering Inner Energy and Overcoming Stress.* New York: Dalacorte, 1975.

Lange, A.J., and Jakubowski, P. *Responsible Assertive Behavior.* Champaign, Illinois: Research Press, 1976.

Lazarus, A.A. Notes of Behavior Therapy, the Problem of Relapse, and Some Tentative Solutions, *Psychotherapy: Theory, Research and Practice,* 1971, 8, 192–194.

―――. *Multimodal Behavior Therapy.* New York: Springer, 1976.

―――. *Learning to Relax* (Cassette) New York: Institute for Rational Living, 1976 (a).

―――. *Behavior Therapy and Beyond.* New York: McGraw-Hill, 1971.

Chapter 12

PATIENT INTERVIEW

Case History: "Irene"

Is there help you can give in aiding this patient to blame herself less, to act more constructively, to function the way she wants to function, and to enjoy her life more in all respects? The impasse, in more specific terms, is that the patient reports that she is outwardly behaving in a way she does not really feel. She cries, but apparently doesn't feel the sadness. On the other end of the continuum, she smiles at her boyfriend and apparently acts as if she feels warmly toward him, yet she doesn't and has no awareness of any feelings of closeness toward him either. The patient has a knack for undoing any joy she might feel, and deprecates herself in her description of her life circumstances, whether it be about her job or her social life. This leaves her feeling that she has nothing in life. She says, for example, "I don't feel close to people. They are there, but I don't feel them." At work she makes invidious comparisons between others and herself. She says she does her work sloppily, that she doesn't plan or execute or organize her job well. She imposes artificial external deadlines and limits in order to keep herself functioning. And yet, she has been functioning for six years as an account executive in a large New York City advertising agency, a position which has not been known as being non-competitive or non-demanding. She says she is sliding backward, can't get things done, and has lost her "distancing defenses" which previously enabled her to work.

A. Her presenting problems in our initial psychotherapy sessions were, "I am not making contact, and I have no feelings in my sessions." She reported one year of treatment with each of two well-trained medical psychoanalysts. The reasons these courses of treatment did not work was that, as she explained it, one of the therapists couldn't take her aggression and personalized her anger. She said of him, "I don't know if he was trying to fuck-up my head or if it was personal." The other couldn't establish contact. "I know more about him than he does about me." Her inner discontents were

1. *"I feel no joy."*
2. *"I do not have much confidence in myself."*
3. *"I have no friends, although they would deny it if asked."*

B. The patient is 34 years old and is the oldest of three children, all girls, born to her Boston social register, upper class, withdrawn, unrelating parents. Her younger sister, Ruth, is 31 and married with two children.

Joan, her youngest sister, is 24 and has been married two years. The patient is closer to Joan. About her parents, she said, "I had two parents who died in 1969." She then casually explained that her father shot and killed her mother and then himself. She said he did the latter "poorly, as usual, however, as he didn't die immediately. My father was an alcoholic and a loser as a father. I had no patience with him. He made money once, then was taken advantage of." About her mother, she told me little if anything spontaneously, although it was she who had the money and the house they lived in and whose parents the patient now sees in terms of contact with the family.

Life, as she grew up, was stark, empty, and unrelated. She was sent to boarding school, a finishing school type of high school, and one year of junior college. She describes her sister Ruth as "always having all the answers. That was her way of life." She and her husband Harry had had difficulties. Now Ruth is going back to school, since she had never been to college before and wants to be more unique. Although Ruth calls her the dumb little sister, Joan is now in Harvard Graduate School. She is married to Bob one of Harry's friends, and is very successful. Ruth is very jealous of Joan. Irene says, "I grew up always feeling very mediocre. It was only in camp that I saw myself as good. I wasn't. I am a mediocre tennis player and am mediocre on the job. With people I am even less than mediocre." She characterized her background as follows: "I thought of my social register type of background as something I had tried to reject, yet I tried to see some good there also. There are a lot of similar people with a lot of similar backgrounds. You do whatever is expected of you, you do what your family did, you wear identical clothes because it wouldn't occur to one to be different. The women do not work, the husbands are probably stock-brokers, they are probably going to divorce and remarry their best friend's husband. They drive a BMW, wear Gucci shoes, they go to Bermuda for one month in the summer. Life is what they do, not how they think." I think the following dream high-lights the isolation and emptiness of her life:

> *"Two kids are out on the ice, freezing, yet somehow they are stuck out on the ice. Their parents couldn't save them, so they tried to freeze them quicker so they could die quicker."*

After this dream she wanted to cry, but didn't quite know why and associated it with her distance from people and the coldness that she experienced from people.

There has been a series of men with whom she has lived. The latest is Dave who she describes as follows: "He has his own public relations firm and had been married ten years. His wife kicked him out and she's now screwing other people. He's rougher and cruder than the people I know. He's very much more lower class than anyone I have ever met. He is open and can communicate. He does pull things out of me. He had a lot of negative associations with women. We spend many nice times together. Sex is terrific.''

C. *A great deal of the time has been spent talking about Dave, her boyfriend, and their relationship. The minute details of their interactions were discussed in an effort to find out more about her vulnerability and self-defeating behavior. One little vignette is as follows:*

> *"Everything gets to me. I wanted to do my thing and read last night. Dave wanted to sit in the dark and just be with me. I made a big thing out of it, insisting on doing my thing and I went into the next room to read, but it left us more apart than anything. I don't really have my own thing. Dave likes music, dancing, and dope. I can't really share these things with him. I don't know what I really can share with him, yet I don't have what I want for me, either.''*

The other big area covered was her job, where she feels that she is not functioning well. There is a great deal of exploration of dreams, and these are given, even the most detailed ones, with little or no association. They are given to the therapist only as presents, as though he uniquely understands the image they are giving.

D. *She describes little or no feeling toward her therapist, saying that it's just someone who she pays to listen and try to help her. On the other hand, she says that in the past with "shrinks" she has had nothing to say and "with you, this is not so.'' In terms of this presentation at Adelphi, she says that she doesn't know if she's doing it for herself or for me, her therapist. She frequently makes angry and critical remarks at the therapist, all as a matter of course and all without apparently changing the general flow of the hour.*

E. *I try hard to respond to her—perhaps too hard—and on some level wonder if I force interaction by responding to her feelings as I hear them. It is in the model that Dave relates to her, although she says he pounds at her and she considers me to be gentle. Perhaps both of us together are undermining her defenses at too rapid a pace by our demanding contact and a lessening of her defensiveness.*

This case presented by George D. Goldman, Ph.D.

Patient Interview

Arnold Lazarus, Ph.D.

Doctor: We were just discussing the fact that this is a somewhat artificial situation. We hope it won't contaminate too many of the brilliant clinical interventions which are about to follow. Do you want to say something so the audience can hear you? See if the microphone is switched on.

Patient: Sure.

Doctor: That sounds fine. Okay. What I've done is glance through a brief history that was given to me, and I've got some vague idea of some of the things which have been troubling you. If you were given one word in the whole English language to describe the essence of your difficulties, what would that word be? Just think about it.

Patient: Detachment.

Doctor: Detachment, Okay. Now I'm writing down detachment. That is the main problem, which means you want to find a way of becoming less detached. Is that correct?

Patient: Yes.

Doctor: Fine. So the one word is detachment. Now you're allowed one sentence. It's like saying, "Tell me the major problem in your life in one sentence." What would that sentence be?

Patient: I think I am detached from everything I get involved with, and I would like to be involved instead of detached.

Doctor: Okay, now let's just focus in on this word, the basic idea of detachment. I'm just wondering what detachment means to you. So often we use a word and we think everyone knows what it means. In other words, I think I know what you are talking about, but I may not. Could you elaborate and explain to me what it feels like to be detached?

Patient: It doesn't feel.

Doctor: It doesn't feel?

Patient: It is standing back and watching everything, rather than feeling involved or feeling anything about the situation.

Doctor: Okay, so there's a feeling of being outside of it. Now here you and I are in this crazy situation. What are you feeling?

Patient: Detached.

Doctor: Yeah, so am I. Now, I'm just wondering how we each feel. What the difference is in the basic quote detachment. You say you feel detached. Do you have an idea what it would be like if you were not detached? What would the different feelings be? Let's just use this to start with. Let's say you are not detached, then you would feel something right now that you are not feeling. What would it be, what would that something be?

Patient: I don't know, nervous maybe.

Doctor: You might feel nervous, yeah, what else?

Patient: Feeling a part of it, maybe.

Doctor: I'm wondering what "a part of it" means, feeling a part of it.

Patient: That I was a part of it, really involved in it.

Doctor: Again I am wondering what these words really mean. How would you be behaving differently if you were not detached? How would your behavior differ?

Patient: I don't know.

Doctor: What would the people be seeing that would be different? Ah, look how she is when she's detached, look how she behaves when she's not detached. Any difference?

Patient: Sometimes, there's a difference. I can't think of what it would be right now. Sometimes it is more animation or more enthusiasm.

Doctor: You said that if you were not detached right now you might be feeling nervous. Did I understand you right?

Patient: Yes.

Doctor: Well, one of the thoughts I had was that being detached at least has one benefit, it saves you from nervousness. Would that be correct?

Patient: Yes.

Doctor: Let's do an about-face. We are talking about something you say you don't like—detachment. Something you want *not* to be. You want to be involved and not detached. But nothing, they say, is 100% bad, and if you would cooperate with me I would like to do an experiment. The experiment will consist of the following things . . . I will give you a sentence and I want you to just keep on saying whatever comes into your mind. But use the beginning of the sentence. For example, if the sentence I give you is "When I went to town," you might say, "When I went to town, I ate bananas," "When I went to town I looked at the shops," "When I went to town I looked through a window." YOU say the whole sentence . . . Okay? Let's take the following: "When I feel detached . . . ."

Patient: When I feel detached, I don't get hurt.

Doctor: Just keep going.

Patient: When I feel detached I seem to operate better, when I get detached, I . . .

Doctor: You can say anything as an experiment. Let's shift to this one, "Being involved."

Patient: Being involved gives more satisfaction. Being involved would let me make a commitment. Being involved, I keep coming back to satisfaction in my head.

Doctor: Okay. The good thing about detachment is, fast, what comes?

Patient: The good thing about detachment is I don't get hurt. The good thing about detachment is I don't get afraid. The good thing about detachment is that I can be assertive. The good thing about detachment is I don't have to worry what people think.

Doctor: Now tell me. What you've given me are four endings. Are these endings true of you? As you think about them now, is it in fact true that the good thing about detachment is that it is an antidote to hurt, to being afraid? It enables you to be more assertive, and it doesn't make you so bothered about what people say? Thus, if you give up the detachment, you might be hurt, afraid, less assertive, and really bothered about public opinion?

Patient: Right.

Doctor: So now what that leads me to feel is that, first and foremost, we have to show you how not to be hurt, whether you are detached or involved. How to remain assertive whether you are detached or involved. Does it make sense? Does it ring any bells? How does it feel? Are you detached as I'm saying this, or what happens?

Patient: I guess I'm detached.

Doctor: But it registers, it rings bells, it makes sense.

Patient: Yes.

Doctor: So now we have four objectives. Number one is: Let's try to show you how not to be hurt. You don't have to remain detached in order to prevent fear. Let's convince you that you can actually be involved. I wonder if you could try some imagery. Can you get a picture, some kind of image of yourself involved, whatever that means to you, and not being hurt? Can you get some sort of picture in your mind? There you are, Irene is involved and she's not being hurt, and she's not afraid. What happens? What comes to mind?

Patient: Something hits me inside saying that's impossible.

Doctor: Okay, so in your mind there's a kind of synonym. Involvement means danger, hurt, something of that kind. By the way, if this was a genuine therapy session and I had a feeling that I could spend much more time with you over a series of weeks, I might be looking into these things in greater detail. But what I want to do now is cover a kind of smorgasbord, get much more of an overview. So I'm going to be flitting around much more than I would in actual therapy. Okay, let me then switch to another dimension. Could you think of something that would make you afraid, a fear as if you were involved? What would produce the afraid feeling you were referring to, something that could do it to you?

Patient: Being abandoned, or not succeeding, not doing something right.

Doctor: Okay, that again seems to tie very much into public opinion, because those two examples seem to be what I would call interpersonal.

They all involve other people. So now I have a hypothesis; I'm asking myself, is it really that Irene cares too much about public opinion, although she says, "I'm detached and I don't care?" I'm saying, is it really that she *does* care, and that one of the things she would need to learn is not to give a darn about public opinion, to be her own person?

Patient: I would answer yes.

Doctor: Answer yes to what, that you do care about. . . .

Patient: That I must care and it is important not to care.

Doctor: But that doesn't feel right. It doesn't connect, that's just an intellectual statement. I guess you would rather not feel it.

Patient: Yes.

Doctor: Okay, I'm going to jump to another scene which is as follows. And this, by the way, is to give me a little bit of a three-dimensional understanding of some of the things we're talking about. I want you to picture your childhood home. Most people can think of one place, that was their childhood home. Can you think of a place?

Patient: Thinking of the outside of it?

Doctor: The outside of it, okay.

Patient: Looking at it, I have a picture of the home.

Doctor: Can you look at it and tell me where your mother is? Now look at it and see where's your mother. Don't think as much as see. Where is she?

Patient: Sitting on the porch.

Doctor: Sitting on the porch. What is she doing?

Patient: She has a drink in her hand and she's sitting on a kind of chaise lounge kind of thing.

Doctor: And where is your father?

Patient: Standing at the bar with a drink in his hand.

Doctor: So both of them are there on the porch with a drink.

Patient: Yes.

Doctor: Is anyone else in the house as you look at it?

Patient: A cat came in. We never had a cat, so I don't know why a cat came.

Doctor: Okay. Let's switch right to this question. As you were doing this, can you recall any feelings it produced? Meaning, was there just deadness of feeling or was there some other feeling?

Patient: Well, I was kind of wondering who might be there?

Doctor: So there was more of a thinking than a feeling. Can you take a tour of that house from room to room, and when you take the tour really look carefully at the house and almost sniff the air so that you can smell any odors, whatever is in the air. Can you just for a moment take a tour from room to room.

Patient: And talk about it as I do it?

Doctor: Sure, why don't you talk about it as you do it. Ordinarily, I would just ask you to think about it, but since we have an audience . . . If it interferes with just thinking then don't talk. But let's take the tour.

Patient: Then I would rather not talk.

Doctor: Then just think about it. (one-minute pause) Now, I'm especially interested in whether you are having a feeling as you are doing this, or a sensation.

Patient: No, I'm watching myself do it.

Doctor: You are watching yourself do it. Okay. So the one thing that seems rather clear to me is that there is a very strong protection, that you are protecting yourself from certain feelings. Am I right?

Patient: Yes.

Doctor: Yes, intellectually, I think so. You see, what I'm looking for is to see whether some of these things temporarily produce a feeling or involvement, a sensation. When I say something you have a feeling. And the feeling could be you want to bash me in the face, or the feeling could be you want to say "gee thanks," a warm feeling, or any other kind of feeling.

Patient: When you first started talking about going through the house, it was a kind of clutching thing, but not that I could associate with anything. A mild clutching.

Doctor: A mild clutching. What does that mean?

Patient: A little tightening inside. Here (Points to her chest).

Doctor: Tightening, where, in the chest?

Patient: Yes.

Doctor: What else?

Patient: That's all.

Doctor: Just a slight tightening in the chest? Unpleasant, not pleasant?

Patient: I guess, more unpleasant than not.

Doctor: But it went? It didn't stay as you were going through the exercise?

Patient: No.

Doctor: Now I want to jump again to another element and ask you the following question. How can people hurt you? You see, what I'm asking is something like this. Let's say that somebody had said to you, "If you can hurt Arnold Lazarus this morning there will be a million dollars for you and a million dollars for him and a million dollars for all these good people out there.'' Well, the quickest way for us all to become millionaires is for you to kick me in the shin. I say, ''Ouch! That hurts!'' and we each get a million dollars, and you've accomplished your mission. But they say to you, ''Sorry Irene, you may not touch him physically.'' Okay, in other words now, you are left to hurt me with some kind of words or actions. How are we going to become millionaires is my question. Can you tell me what you would do? And I'm saying, please do something to hurt me, because I would like a million bucks. How are you going to do it?

Patient: I suppose I would walk out and leave you there.

Doctor: You have prearranged with everybody in here that at certain signals you all say, ''He's really crummy,'' and out you go?

Patient: Right.

Doctor: Would you believe me if I told you that I would be incredibly curious. I would be saying, ''What the hell is going on here with these people? Is this a bunch of kooks I have here? What is going on?'' Do you believe that, or do you think I'm kidding you? What do you feel?

Patient: I think that is probably what you would do.

Doctor: What I'm saying here is that I have been thinking through rather carefully what we all say as kids, ''Sticks and stones may break my bones, but words will never hurt me.'' We seem to forget this as adults. I will decide when I'm hurt, rather than let someone else tell me. Now what happens if you try that on for size as a thought? Say to yourself, ''I will decide when I am hurt.'' How does that feel? Does it fit, does it not fit? What happens? Think it aloud in your head. Think, I will decide when I'm hurt.

Patient: It feels I wouldn't be free to make the decision.

Doctor: You wouldn't be free to make the decision?

Patient: Yeah, I'd be hurt anyway.

Doctor: Can you tell me something that could hurt you? Will you give an example?

Patient: My man leaving me. Being left alone. I just don't like being left alone.

Doctor: By whom? By anybody?

Patient: By anybody, but particularly the man in my life.

Doctor: Let's take that sort of a picture. You are very involved and you've taken this big risk. You've allowed yourself to become involved with this man. And your biggest dread occurs, he up and leaves you. Now there you are. What would you be feeling? I guess hurt, right? What else?

Patient: Probably, just as well, he was going anyway. I'm not really worthy.

Doctor: Okay, there lies a very interesting concept. One has to decide rather clearly whether or not one is a piece of turd. Are you some kind of a crap heap taking up space? Do you have to apologize for breathing the fresh air on this contaminated planet? Or like any other human being, do you have the right to be just as shitty as the rest of us, no more, no less? For me that seems to be rather fundamental. What is your reaction to that?

Patient: Yeah, it would be nice to feel that I was just as shitty as everybody else.

Doctor: But you think you are much more shitty?

Patient: Yes.

Doctor: You are, in fact, the greatest shit in the world, is what you seem to be saying.

Patient: Well actually, no, because being the greatest shit in the world would be too positive.

Doctor: I see. So what are you? The second greatest . . . or

Patient: Oh, no, probably not that good, not even being worth the greatest shit in the world.

Doctor: Are you in touch with the opposite, because a lot of times when people feel quite irrationally how full of crap they are, they sometimes swing and feel a lot better than anybody else. Do you get both feelings, and sometimes you really feel a heck of a lot better than anybody?

Patient: Not really, no. Maybe in some situation it was better. I can't think of a situation right now, normally not, normally I feel inferior.

Doctor: So most of the time you feel you are just not as good as others.

Patient: Right.

Doctor: Whomever it is you are with?

Patient: Yes. I guess it is as much as not as good as, as even good. It's not necessarily comparative, but that's the word. . . .

Doctor: You are made of inferior material, is that the feeling?

Patient: Yes. And it's not the most inferior.

Doctor: And if you had been the most inferior, at least it would have been something, is what you're saying. It's just a run of the mill inferior?

Patient: A mediocre inferior.

Doctor: A mediocre inferior, okay. What does this amount to, this mediocre inferior? I'm just wondering what it is about you that is so mediocre and inferior. I mean, here we are surrounded by many, many people and you are quite clear in your own mind that in this room you are the most mediocre inferior of everybody. You have no doubt about that?

Patient: Well, maybe a little bit, but basically yes.

Doctor: I'm wondering what that is all about. Which is to say, can you just convince me, prove your case?

Patient: I can only, I guess, I put it in terms of what to do. I can only do things mediocre. I don't guess I can do anything well. I guess, I think I am what I do or what I don't do.

Doctor: That's what I think is very, very crucial. Let me share with you a very, very important view that I hold, and have you react to it. My belief is that most people are essentially equal, but different. Which is to say that if you ask the question, "Who is the most superior person in this entire assembly," I think it has no answer. Let us say that you and I have to appear now in a competition and these people are the judges, and the question is, "Who's superior, Irene or Arnold?" That's the question. Now some people in the audience might view musical knowledge or ability as the be all and end all. For them, the one who knows most about music is superior. Others might have different standards. Others might be athletically-minded and would say that the one who could run faster or throw stones further is superior. Others might have different standards. What I'm saying is that, by the time they got through their assessment, people would have to say there are things that Irene knows that he doesn't know, because she is a different human being. She's been places he's never been. She's seen things he hasn't seen. She's done things he hasn't done. She's thought things he hasn't. And vice versa. In the end the audience would have to come to the conclusion that they cannot say whether you or I am superior. But there are things I do better than you, and things you do better than I. Reaction?

Patient: It's rationally logical. It would be good to react that way. But I can say that to myself and I still feel inferior, and I know I am.

Doctor: How do you know that with such certainty? What is the evidence you base that on?

Patient: Because I'm not doing whatever I'm doing well.

Doctor: What would it be like if we get a Hottentot, you know, from one of the primitive African communities. And this Hottentot is a delightful person. We get to know this Hottentot, and we speak his language, and he's really a warm and decent guy, an honest and fine person. But he thinks of himself as shit. Why? Because he's cross-eyed and he's never been a good hunter, and his definition of worth is to be a good hunter. But he's not a good hunter, therefore, he's shit. Now we've got a helluva job convincing him "No, you're not a shit, you're just not a good hunter." This is how I feel about you. You've got some kind of definition of excellence, of performance, of achievement or something, and if you don't reach that, you are nothing. As long as you stick with that definition you're going to keep on proving it over and over again. We've got to get you to change that definition, like we have to get the Hottentot to change his definition. Do you see what I'm saying?

Patient: Yeah, and I haven't been able to find out how to change the definition. I can't say I'm mediocre in what I do, and I can't (tape cut)

Doctor: I sense that you can be warm, intelligently responsive, understanding, a good companion, etc. There are very important interpersonal things that not too many people who are brilliant and computer-like but not very warm and responsive are, and I don't regard them as quote superior. However, at the moment you have so much invested in your detachment, that these other components are not even known to you. And so you feel blah, and that's perfectly consistent. Do you see what I'm saying?

Patient: Yes, but when I am those things, and I can be, that's like, so what.

Doctor: It will remain "so what" unless you forget accomplishment, overt achievement, performance, and brilliance. If there are qualities in you which are submerged because of the detachment, let's see them come out and have you recognize them as positive. How do you feel when I say that? What is the feeling?

Patient: It's clenched inside again. Like that's not enough. You just can't survive on being warm and whatever the other things were. That doesn't give me enough satisfaction, maybe because of my definitions.

Doctor: Do you think part of your problem is a perfectionism, which is to say that when you do something well, you still think it is mediocre?

Patient: No, I think I do it mediocre. I think I know the difference between perfect and mediocre. I was going to be better. I don't expect to be perfect.

Doctor: What you do, do you do it adequately or really not even adequately?

Patient: It seems to be adequate. It's adequate.

Doctor: I'll tell you why I ask that. I feel that people who aim for perfection cannot achieve it, because it doesn't exist, and that what we need to aim for in life is adequacy. Take the situation I'm in now. Here I sit in front of my colleagues. They are critically watching me trying to be helpful to you. They are seeing where I'm missing the boat, where I'm scoring, and where I'm totally screwing up, whatever their views may be. I would be totally overwhelmed by anxiety if I felt the need to give a perfect performance, or even an excellent performance. From my viewpoint, as long as it is adequate, that's all one could ask for.

Patient: And now I'm thinking it is just under adequate.

Doctor: My performance at this moment, or yours in general?

Patient: My performance. What I do is under adequate.

Doctor: What is it that you do that is under adequate? For example?

Patient: I'd say my job. I just leave one thing undone with every detail. That is not adequate. I get a lot of it done, but not all of it done. There are lots of levels. How much should I do? I try to do everything adequate, but on top of that there's lots more that can be done.

Doctor: Again, I'm going to shift right to a different direction to see if we can answer some of this. How much time do you spend getting pleasure in life?

Patient: Not very much. It's every once in a while

Doctor: And what are the things that give you pleasure?

Patient: I get pleasure from feeling part of a group and, or feeling good with a person. Looking at certain (inaudible). It's doing things. Except for the people, it's doing things rather than (inaudible).

Doctor: Is there anything wrong with that?

Patient: I don't think so. I want to get pleasure out of participating.

Doctor: So you want to get pleasure from ballet, looking at arts and crafts, etc. And that's fine. But then as you are looking at the ballet you say, "I should be the ballerina."

Patient: Not really, there's some kind of frustration, more with the crafts than the ballet. Now I know I can watch it more and enjoy it, with the ballet.

Doctor: And with the crafts?

Patient: With the crafts, I think I should be doing it, and that something is stopping me from trying that. Like it is so far in between starting it and getting through something you're looking at and admire, that it is not worth it.

Doctor: You cannot enjoy the process then. Just the very fumbling act of trying and doing, even though you turned out a mediocre thing, and it's been fun.

Patient: No, because I try it and give it up, I never complete it.

Doctor: Because it is not superb or excellent?

Patient: Maybe, I don't know. I just never finish it.

Doctor: I'm just wondering to what extent there is some kind of hidden perfectionism tucked in there. It is either great or it is nothing. I just wonder about that. Can you give me a lead? Is it possible as you see it?

Patient: Well, with the everyday stuff I think I'm not just seeking perfection. I really think I know the difference. When it comes to craft-type things, I'm seeking good, or better than adequate.

Doctor: In the everyday things, however, you could easily do better than you do. And it's not difficult.

Patient: Yes. And I don't get involved enough to do it. Sometimes I say, "Okay, today I'm going to do it," and I find a way *not* to do it.

Doctor: Okay, this brings me right back again to this question of hurt. Because my thinking once more goes something like this. I'm jumping the gun and I'm giving my impression right now. Here is a young woman who is very sensitive to criticism, rejection, disapproval, failure. These four things seem to be very, very crucial. And because you are so sensitive, you have a life style that keeps you detached. Because it makes you less vulnerable. It takes the criticism away from you; the sting is out of it. But what if you really put everything into it, and you thought it was pretty good, and someone said to you, "Irene, you did a lousy job." So what I have abstracted from this is that therapy might get the most mileage and movement if a lot of work was done on this hypersensitivity. You started out by saying to me, "I'm detached." And I'm saying, "Uh-uh, she's hypersensitive. That's why she's detached." So I'm saying, basic to the detachment is hypersensitivity to criticism, rejection, disapproval, failure.

Patient: Sure, I am. I can't tell you if that is the most important area.

Doctor: But you recognize that sort of (inaudible) for that is true. Okay, I'm just wondering about one thing. We talked earlier about being hurt. Let's assume that I started getting very critical of you. Here I'm a stranger, I don't mean a damn thing in your life, and I suddenly start up and I'm very critical. I say, "How can you give me this creepy dame to work with in front of all these people?" How would you react? What would you feel?

Patient: Probably that you would be able to handle the creepy dame, and that they can learn from that, too.

Doctor: The feeling. You see what you now have done is just defended nicely from a criticism. You have thrown it back in that way.

Patient: I know when I get criticized in the real world and that I take it very badly.

Doctor: You take it badly, it hurts.

Patient: Yeah.

Doctor: What would be some of the worst criticisms? I'm wondering what would be some of the things that would be most hurtful?

Patient: That I was empty and had nothing to offer.

Doctor: I see. Someone turning to you and saying, "You are really an empty shell of a person. You have nothing to offer." That is the most hurtful?

Patient: I think so.

Doctor: I wonder whether you really believe that? You say you do, but I wonder whether you really believe that?

Patient: Well, I haven't been able to fill it with a positive. I mean, I think I believe that.

Doctor: Well, you're still entitled to happiness, fulfillment, and contentment, even though you are an empty shell. Even an empty shell is entitled to his or her place under the sun, and perhaps it is my job to prove that you are not an empty shell. But either way, you are entitled to happiness. It's a birthright. Can you accept that?

Patient: No, I can't somehow. I can say, "Sure an empty shell, there's always happiness." But I can't believe the empty shell can have happiness.

Doctor: Okay, what is it about you, then, that is so special that makes you not deserve it?

Patient: I don't know.

Doctor: You're a very special empty shell. All the other ones deserve happiness, but here is one very special one that doesn't deserve it. What is so special about this one? All the others deserve happiness, but this one doesn't.

Patient: I don't know. Being special makes it too good.

Doctor: Okay, and one of the terrible things about good is that it can get bad. One of the thoughts I had in a large part of this is, "I musn't admit to anything good, because then it could be taken away from me. If I am just bland crap who can hurt me?" So we get back again to hypersensitivity. Tell me one thing now which is a tough assignment, but try it if you will. What do you think about this situation thus far? Imagine that you are telling someone else. It's not me. But somebody says to you, "Irene, you went through that interview, what was it like?" What would you say to him?

Patient: I guess that is was interesting, and I would have to think about what's been said. But I can't think of anything else to say about it.

Doctor: It is interesting that you'd have to think about the things he said. Is that what you said?

Patient: Yes. I don't know whether it is information or not.

Doctor: I think it is familiar information that might be packaged somewhat differently or grouped somewhat differently. I would hope it can produce some kind of a direction. Let's talk about any feelings you might have had throughout this discussion.

Patient: Certain times I felt doubtful, but not associated with anything. I can't say I felt total anxiety associated with being afraid to go through my house or whatever. I could say I felt tight inside when you were talking (inaudible) it was before when I was into being mediocre or not crap, I had total anxiety, because I was agreeing or because I felt it was helpless.

Doctor: I see, okay. You struck me as an intelligent, honest, attractive person whom I thought of as being tremendously hypersensitive and needing to overcome that so that you will become involved and not be detached. What can you say on that level? Talking about the way I came across to you.

Patient: He seemed to be trying, and he had good perspective, and I liked the way he followed. I liked his tracking and his thinking.

Doctor: What we're still getting here is an interesting sort of detached intellectual statement. Not that you felt very comfortable, uncomfortable, or something of that kind. How did you feel in terms of comfort, discomfort?

Patient: I felt comfortable, occasionally aware that we should (inaudible).

Doctor: Now I'm wondering what you do from here (addressing Drs. Goldman and Milman). Do you allow audience participation before we have a discussion, or how would you like to proceed?

Patient: I'll leave.

Dr. Milman: We'll have a discussion without Irene.

Discussion

Arnold A. Lazarus

I give myself an "A" for *effort* but an "F" for *impact*. Most readers will probably agree with the latter, although some might be less impressed with my ardent attempts to break through this woman's defenses. While my usual clinical style is pedagogical and my therapeutic tactics are often didactic, the interview with Irene is somewhat atypical. I am not usually that verbose and so willing to "let the client off the hook." But the presence of a large audience in a situation where I was literally "on stage" produced certain demand characteristics that sometimes allowed a performance to take precedence over a session.

Irene seemed to frustrate every one of my efforts to undermine her self-deprecatory reactions. While she was quick to deny her feelings, she would admit to them when caught off guard, and then cover up. She is like an organ transplant patient who has fallen victim to the rejection processes of her own immunological defenses. I did not emerge from this meeting with any sense of accomplishment.

In a private session I would probably have been more confrontative and less prone to fall victim to some of Irene's passive-aggressive maneuvers.

Without the need to demonstrate my methods or to entertain the crowd, I would have focused in much greater detail on some of the leads that emerged. I wonder how much of Irene's misleading acquiescence was a function of the stage, the microphones, the tape recorders, and the audience.

The brief case outline I was given before the session suggested a much more aggressive, uncooperative, disturbed, and schizoid personality than I experienced Irene to be. Despite her resolute resistances, she was far more cooperative and agreeable than I had been led to expect. I think I correctly identified some of the main ingredients behind her detachment and self-abnegation. The sentence completion strategy (which I learned from Dr. Nathaniel Branden) was especially revealing. Exactly how to proceed from there remains an open question.

The need for a thorough BASIC ID assessment stands out in my mind. Because Irene uses intellectualization and passive agreeability as smoke-screens, I would be inclined to dwell more heavily on affective, sensory, and imagery modalities while avoiding the cognitive quicksands that our initial interview so clearly identified.

Some people, familiar with my previous writings, may wonder why I did not conduct a focused BASIC ID analysis during our first meeting. An obvious but elusive point is that a multimodal therapist, like any other sensitive clinician, does not plunge in with specific or preset tactics before first making preliminary assessments of presenting complaints and creating a positive cadence of patient-therapist interaction. In Irene's case, I felt that a greater level of general rapport was necessary before applying more structured interventions.

INDEX

Adjustment neurosis, 3
Adult ego state, 131
Affect mode, in multimodal behavior therapy, 162, 163, 165
Aggressive impulses, 62–63
AMERICAN JOURNAL OF PSYCHIATRY, 138–139
American Psychiatric Association: borderline diagnosis, 4; classifications, 4; DSM II, 4
Analysis: didactic, 6; therapeutic, 6
Analytical ideal: as attainment of happiness, 3; as normal behavior, 3
Analytical therapy, 6
Anno O., case of, 5, 61
Assertion, in multimodal behavior therapy, 162, 163, 164, 165
Autonomy contract, 133, 136, 137

Basescu, Sabert, 31
BASIC ID, 162, 164, 167, 168, 169; components of, 162
Behavior mode, in multimodal behavior therapy, 162, 163, 165
Berne, Eric: case studies in regression analysis, 132; Federn's influence on, 130; involvement with group therapy, 130; theory of regression analysis, 132; theory of structural analysis, 131; theory of transactional analysis, 130
Binswanger, L.: as a Freudian, 32; as an existential analyst, 32; definition of philosophic anthropology, 32
Borderline diagnosis, 4
Boss, M.: as an existential analyst, 32; partitions of Freud's work, 3

Cathexis Institute: AMERICAN JOURNAL OF PSYCHIATRY support of, 138–139; treatment of schizophrenia, 138–139
CATHEXIS READER, 138
Child ego state, 131
Closure, 96
Cognition, in multimodal behavior therapy, 162, 163, 164, 165
Conformity, as cause of adjustment neurosis, 3
Contact functions, sharpening of, 104
Counterscript, 134
Countertransference, 112
Creative focus, in existential psychoanalysis, 37
Creativity phenomenon, in gestalt therapy, 100–101
Crystalization, 133

Decision, 135
Decontamination, as function of structural analysis, 131
Dewey, John, 106
Didactic analysis, 6
Discovery phenomenon, in gestalt therapy, 100
Drugs: for treatment in multimodal behavior therapy, 163, 165; for treatment of schizophrenia, 138
DSM II, 4
Dynamic inactivity, 29

Eclectic approach, in multimodal behavior therapy, 164
Ego states, 130–131, 134
Emphasis of here and now, in existential psychoanalysis, 36
Empty chair technique, 164
Existential approach of understanding, 33
Existential knowledge, 34
Existential psychoanalysis: 31–41; case history of, 43–58; creative focus of therapy, 37; experiential mode of knowing, 33, 34; emphasis on will and choice, 37; explanatory mode, 33; phenomenlogical mode, 33; understanding mode, 33
Existential truth, 34
Experiments, development of, 106

Experiential mode of knowing, in existential psychoanalysis, 33, 34
Explanatory mode, in existential psychoanalysis, 33
Eysenck, thesis against psychoanalysis, 5

Failure, example of in therapy, 34–35
Federn, influence on Eric Berne, 130
Fine, Rueben, 1
Flexibility, in multimodal behavior therapy, 167
Freud, Sigmon: abreaction of, 132; commitment to psychic determinism, 38; levels of psychosexual development, 133; metapsychological analysis, 32; therapeutic analysis, 32
Freudian psychoanalysis: 1–13; case history of, 15–29
Free will: existentialist's belief in, 38; humanistic, 38; reference to present and future, 38; Will James' definition of, 38
Fromm, Erich, 170

Gestalt experiment: directed behavior in, 107; enactment in, 107
Gestalt therapy: 95–108; case history of, 109–127; five elements of contact, 102; principles of 96–97; recognition of, 96; resistance in, 98
Glover, study of psychoanalysis, 6
Goulding, Bob: concept of decision in transactional analysis, 134–135
Goulding, Mary: concept of decision in transactional analysis, 134–135

Happiness, as pursuit of analytical ideal, 3
Hegel, 102
Holloway, William, 133, 134
Hooker, Evelyn, theory on homosexuality, 5
Humanitarianism, in multimodal behavior therapy, 169

I-Boundary, expansion of, 104
Imagery mode, in multimodal behavior therapy, 162, 163, 165
Improvisation, 106–107
Injunction concept, 134–135
Interactive climate, in gestalt therapy, 102
Interpersonal mode, in multimodal behavior therapy, 162, 163, 164, 165, 170
Interpretations, 68–69
Intrinsic mode, in multimodal behavior therapy, 170

Joining approaches, in patterns of resistance, 68–69

Kubie, memories of, 132
Kuhn, T.L., theory of scientific revolutions, 8

Lazarus, Arnold, 161
Libidinal impulses, 62–63

Maladjustment neurosis, 3, 10
Maturation, 61–62
Medication, for treatment of schizophrenia, 138
Modality Profile, 162
Multimodal behavior therapy: 161–173; affect mode, 162, 163, 165; assertion in, 162, 163, 164, 165; behavior mode, 162, 163, 165; case history of, 173–189; cognition in, 162, 163, 164, 165; diagnostic phases, 168; drugs, for treatment, 163, 165; eclectic approach in, 164; flexibility in, 167; humanitarianism in, 169; imagery mode, 162, 163, 165; interpersonal mode, 162, 163, 164, 165, 170; intrinsic mode, 170; sensation mode, 162, 163, 165
MULTIMODAL BEHAVIOR THERAPY, 167
Multimodal personality theory, 162

191

Narcissistic countertransference, 65
Narcissistic transference, 63; as prevention of frustration/aggression, 64
Negative reinforcement, use in transactional analysis, 134
Negative transference, with preoedipal patient, 63
Neurosis, 3
Nonanalytical therapy, 6

Object transference, 63; increased by narcissistic transference, 64
Oedipal period, 61
Oedipal transference, 63

Peck, Harris, 129
Perls, Fritz: influence on transactional analysis, 134, 135, 136; "The Rules and Games of Gestalt Therapy," 136
Personhood of the therapist, 103
Phenomenological mode, in existential psychoanalysis, 33
Polster, Erving, 95
Polster, Miriam, 95
Positive transference, 30, 63
Preoedipal period, 61
PRINCIPLES OF GROUP TREATMENT, 132, 133, 135, 137
Psychiatric illness, concept of, 2
Psychic determinism, of Freud: reference to infancy, childhood, past, 38; scientific, 38
Psychoanalysis: 59–69; as preferred treatment, 137; case history, 71–93; classical, 60; contractual arrangements, 61; ego defenses, 60; Freudian behaviorism, 2; Freudian behavior therapy, 2; Freudian case history, 15–30; Freud's definition, 60; theory of, 2; verbalization in, 61
Psychohistory, 2
Psychological space, 102
Psychosexual development, Freud's levels of, 133
Psychotherapy: as cure of emotional disturbance, 2; focus on knowledge and truth, 34; goal of, 34; limitations, 10; task of, 33; third force in, 96; value of, 9; when it begins, 9; who does it, 8; who goes, 8

Questions, on intrapsychic problems, 68

Redecision, 135
Regression analysis, 132, 135
Repetition, 105
Resistance: 66, 111; as symbolic communication, 66; patterns of, 68

Ripple effect, 162
"Rules and Games of Gestalt Therapy," 136

Safe emergency, 106
Scientific revolutions, 8
Schiff, J.L., structural analysis of Berne, 132
Script analysis in transactional analysis, 133–134
Script matrix in transactional analysis, 133–134
Schizophrenia: cure rate, 7; treatment of, 138
Self-disclosure of therapist, 40
Sensation mode, in multimodal behavior therapy, 162, 163, 165
Social control, 133
Spotnitz, Hyman, 59
Steiner, C.M., work on injunction concept, 134; work on script matrix, 134
Structural analysis: 131; advantage of transactional analysis, 137
Subjective countertransference, 64
Superego, 3

Therapeutic analysis, 6
Therapeutic relationship, 39
Third force in psychotherapy, 96
Toxoid responses, 69
Transaction, 130
Transactional analysis: 129–140; case history, 141–159; crystalization in, 131; decontamination in, 131, 133; defined, 130; interpretation in, 131
TRANSACTIONAL ANALYSIS AND PSYCHOTHERAPY, 130, 131, 133, 135
TRANSACTIONAL ANALYSIS BULLETIN, 137
Transcendental meditation, 168
Transference, in transactional analysis, 131, 133
Transformation, in therapeutic relationship, 40

Unconscious: as function of self, 37; as influence of conscious, 38; as result of choice, 37
Understanding mode, in multimodal behavior therapy, 33

Verbal contact, 67
Verbalization in psychoanalysis, 61

Will and choice, in existential psychoanalysis, 37